WEIRD IS WONDERFUL

By Sally Chamberlain

Disclaimer

The contents of this book are based upon personal opinion and experiences of the author and are not intended to be acted upon as advice in a professional capacity. If readers of this book are concerned about any aspect of their health, they should consult a medical professional.

ISBN 9781973325598

Sally Chamberlain
Visit my website at www.karmapaws.co.uk

Dedication

This book is dedicated to my Dad, Richard Victor Taylor.

A wonderful, funny, warm-hearted man who inspired me to write the words of this book and help others on their journey through life.

He may have been taken too soon but will always be in our hearts.

We miss you, Dad.

Table of Contents

INTRODUCTION

This book is an exploration of everything it means to be highly sensitive, intuitive and empathic, especially when it comes to animals. 'Weird Is Wonderful' ventures into intuitive development, spiritual awareness, emotions, human nature, animal communication and Reiki, encouraging others to find strength in who they truly are. I invite you to share in my journey so that you can better understand your own and discover how to embrace the wonderful world of weird.

We are all our own brand of 'weird' and many aspects of being an Empath and Highly Sensitive and Intuitive Person could easily be construed as beyond the 'norm' - whatever that may be! There only exists what is 'normal' for each person in any given moment. If it doesn't do any harm, we can all be as weird as we like!

In this book, I delve into every facet of what it means to be intuitive and live life with an open mind and sense of spiritual awareness. 'Weird Is Wonderful' is a complete work with a unique energy. Being highly sensitive and intuitive brings with it many advantages, such as enabling us to experience some fascinating phenomena. This is why my book covers such a breadth of subjects including aspects of the paranormal, dreams, psychic phenomena, our connection with animals and the world of Spirit; all of which I approach in terms of my own experience in order to reassure others that these should be celebrated and seen as a gift, rather than something to be afraid of.

My childhood was filled with animal companions and time spent in the great outdoors. I grew up with a fine layer of pet hair on my clothes and the scent of fresh air in my lungs. Animals and nature have always called to me through my five physical senses and beyond. They have been an intrinsic part of my life since I was born. It took me forty years to discover a name for what I have been experiencing all my life: I am an Intuitive Animal Empath. I experience life through my intuition and feel the emotions of people and animals as if they were my own. This has some wonderful advantages but it can seem a little overwhelming at times. I have to take good care of myself in order to maintain my energy levels and remain positive.

I have spent my whole life with animals and have so much love and gratitude for them. I set up my own pet sitting business in 2011 and have since become a Reiki Master Teacher, Animal Communicator and studied courses in animal behaviour. Animals have taught me so much. In this book, I refer to non-human animals as simply 'animals' for ease of reference. There are several chapters about the spiritual and healing side of working with animals and how to set up an animal communication and healing business.

I work from a non-religious perspective and encourage others to empower themselves from within by developing their intuition and spiritual awareness. This gives us greater clarity and a sense of peacefulness and calm, enabling us to perceive life as it truly is and connect more deeply with all living beings through the Universal energy that flows through and connects us all.

Much of what I have written has come from a higher source. Once I started writing, I was absolutely compelled to continue and had free flowing 'downloads' of information rushing through me on a daily basis. I was writing notes left, right and centre, trying to keep up with all of the inspiration and ideas that kept coming from out of nowhere! I would like to say a big 'thank you' to Spirit, my higher self, the animals and my intuition for imparting all of these wonderful words upon me to share with the world. This book is an expression of my soul. Each and every word is infused with the energy of who I truly am. I have included some of my most interesting and intriguing journal entries to add to the energy flow.

I speak my own truth and express how I see, think and feel about the world. Some people may not like some of my truths but they cannot be denied; I can only perceive life through my own eyes. I know what it is to feel pain and to suffer but I also know what it's like to feel pure joy and experience things beyond our wildest imagination. It is by acknowledging our own deep truth that we can begin to grow and inspire others.

Everyone has different opinions, views and stories to tell. None of them are 'wrong' but the best teachings are the ones that leave it open for you to make up your own mind. It's good to have some guidance but it's not good to feel that you are being told what to do, especially when you may feel uncomfortable about it. It is my intention for this book to reach out to people who need guidance, encouragement and wish to learn more about how we are all connected through Universal energy; humans and animals alike.

'Weird is Wonderful' is intended to offer support and reassurance to those us who feel that they are intuitive, psychic, highly-sensitive, clairvoyant or an Empath. These abilities are perfectly natural and simply mean that we are more sensitive to subtle energy than others and are able to receive information from higher energetic sources.

We were not put on this Earth to become perfect spiritual beings, floating around in iridescent clouds of dust in a saintly manner; we are spiritual beings having a human experience, including all of the dirt and drama that goes with it. Human beings are complex and powerful creatures yet so often become lost and unable to find ourselves. When we seek out the truth within ourselves and the wider world, our own story starts to unfold. Being who we truly are is a voyage of discovery with many twists, turns and tidal waves along the way but only by being honest can we being to grow and flourish. Life is not about being perfect, it is about being the best version of ourselves that we can aspire to be. Strengthening ourselves from within gives us greater confidence in our abilities and becoming spiritually aware helps us to see the truth in the world.

Throughout my book, I use capital letters when referring to the world of Spirit, the Universe and Reiki as a mark of how much respect I have for these amazing forms of energy. They are powerful entities and very much alive, just like you and me. In my journal entries and other parts of my book, I have not used people's names unless I have permission to do so in order to protect the privacy of my family and others I know.

My urge to write this book has gathered in strength since the sudden and unexpected loss of my father in July 2016. I am dedicating this book to him and the wonderful upbringing and inspiration that he gave to my brother and I, and the love and unfaltering dedication that he showed towards his whole family, especially my Mum and my own two children. He will be terribly missed but his love and amazing spirit will always be with us.

'Weird Is Wonderful' gradually took shape over a long period of time. This is what I wrote about the early stages of its development in my journals:

Journal 27.03.15

'I'm putting together all of my intuitive and paranormal experiences in writing so I can eventually write an inspiring book to help others.'

Journal 04.11.16

'Completely out of the blue, I have started preparing notes for my spiritual teachings to help others such as myself. It's basic things such as not comparing yourself to others; feeling your own truth; being honest with yourself and learning how it feels to be calm and centred from deep within. It feels fabulous and luxurious doing this...not from a point of ego but from a deeply nurturing spiritual place within me and the energy all around me, wonderful! Like an elixir.'

And now my book is complete. Enjoy!

I have also written two books promoting kindness for animals. 'Power Of The Purr' and 'Being Kind To Dogs' are available on Amazon as paperback and ebooks. I hope you enjoy those too!

CELEBRATING WEIRD

What Makes Weird So Wonderful?

Weird is out of the ordinary; it sticks two fingers up at conformity, refuses to be dull and will never compromise.

Weird is an expression of the uniqueness of our soul. It will never follow the masses or fall into the trap of normality.

Weird is wonderful, colourful and vibrant – it is who we truly are and no-one can ever take that away from us.

Be weird, be proud and, most of all, always listen to your intuition. The next time someone dares to call you weird, you may already find yourself one step ahead. At the heart of 'weird' is the incredible power of our intuition, which should never be underestimated...

The Spark of Intuition

Human beings have one very powerful tool at our disposal to help us better understand the processes of the Universe – our intuition.

Unlocking the power of our intuition makes daily life as a human being much easier to navigate and gives us a greater depth of understanding of our connection with each other and the world around us.

We all have the spark of intuition, it's just a matter of whether or not we choose to ignite it and allow its flames to rise up and burn brightly.

We were all put here on this planet to live our lives in the best way we know how. Given the vast array of personality types and influence of nature and nurture, we can expect to encounter many extremes and sets of circumstance that affect our lives and everything around us, including the activity of the planet itself and the rest of the Universe beyond.

Each person's intuition is uniquely adapted to suit them and once they learn to recognise and harness it, it can become one of their greatest assets. Intuitive development does not have to be a full-blown spiritual experience if that is not comfortable for a particular person. Intuition is a sense in addition to our five physical senses which has the potential to become just as familiar and functional as being able to see or hear. Connecting with our intuition can enrich our lives in many ways.

Intuition is our internal barometer and guide; it shows us the truth. Intuition points us in the right direction, guides us towards our soul purpose and keeps us safe, whenever it can. It helps us to discern truth and make decisions. Intuition can come through to our conscious awareness in many forms. It may be a voice, images, feelings, sensations or communicate with us in our dreams. Sometimes, our intuition screams at us but we often ignore it! Our logical mind has a habit of attempting to override it by saying 'oh, it'll be all right' and, when we listen to that instead, we often discover that our intuition was right all along and we should never have doubted it. Fortunately, once we learn to recognise our intuition speaking to us, we can get a better feel for things and make wiser decisions.

Intuitive development is no big secret. It is open to everyone because it is one of the most natural things in the world. There are no hard and fast rules. It is very simple. For those of us who wish to develop our intuition, the best place to start is to become as healthy as possible and keep our hearts and minds open. Reducing our stress levels and prioritising our self-care routine are vital. There are so many possibilities when it comes to intuition, it is important to learn to trust what is being received and relax. It's difficult for our intuition to communicate with us when we are a stressed out mess!

Everyone has the potential to be intuitive, spiritual and sensitive and some people are born this way. For others, it is a matter of increasing awareness of their intuition and enhancing their abilities through various practices, such as meditation. Making our intuition something tangible that we can recognise is the first step. We all use our intuition every day in our decision making processes. From something as simple as choosing a new colour for our lounge walls or whether or not we should call a friend, intuition is always there guiding us. It's simply a matter of becoming aware of the form it takes for us as an individual.

My intuition is rarely quiet and I wouldn't want it to be! It is the guiding force in my life and has not only helped me out on many different occasions but becoming more aware of my intuition has enhanced every aspect of my world. My physical senses are sharper, I'm more keenly aware of subtle energy and I have learned to take better care of myself by getting to know the subtle energies that are at work and affect us on every level. Being intuitive isn't just about making psychic predictions or impressing people with your abilities; it's about improving your own life and increasing your spiritual awareness so that you can gain a greater sense of well-being, stability and not become depleted when you offer help and healing to others.

Intuition is a powerful source of energy and information that works on higher vibrational frequencies of which so many people are unaware. Intuition is limitless and abundant; it offers us infinite learning opportunities and incredible insight into so many aspects of our lives that seem mysterious and elusive yet there is still a stigma attached to those with heightened sensitivity and enhanced intuitive abilities. I shall always be intuitive and feel a deep sense of gratitude and humility for the abilities with which I am blessed. Intuition opens our eyes to the truth. Once you experience things in life beyond the realms of logic and reason, there really is no turning back. Intuition is always there for us; we simply have to remember to listen.

We all have awareness of our physical senses, bodies and what is going on around us in the physical world but not all of us are aware of the intuitive feelings, sensations and information available beyond this. All of us receive information from higher vibrational sources, often on a subconscious level before it is processed and brought to the attention of our consciousness. Some of us have a greatly enhanced awareness of these processes but others are unaware of the source of this information and only respond to it on a subconscious level. Some people with a higher level of conscious awareness thrive on it and embrace it whereas others find it overwhelming and scary, wishing it would go away and leave them alone. Knowing certain things that you feel you could not possibly know on a logical level can cause fear and unease, especially when it is a prediction about future events that turn out to be unpleasant. It's not all bad news though and there are many joys to being intuitive and sensitive. It can be a true blessing once we understand how to welcome and utilise our abilities in everyday life to help ourselves and others.

Animals are naturally in touch with their intuition. Developing our intuition deepens our connection with animals. In this book, when I refer to animals, I am really referring to non-human variety. We too are animals but our modern lives tend to reduce our awareness of our intuition, which needs to be re-awakened. Changing our lives for the better is possible, and this starts from within.

Some people believe that intuition is our 'higher self' or spirit guides communicating with us. Our higher self is a level of consciousness that is higher in vibration than the usual chatter that we hear in our mind. Our higher self is closer to spiritual energy and wisdom. It helps us to better understand ourselves and work from our hearts in a place of peace and compassion. It is our soul speaking to us.

Our spirit guides are those in the energetic realm who step forward when we need guidance or we can ask them for help to take us in the right direction when we need to make important decisions. Both our higher self and spirit guides are part of our intuition but to keep it simple, intuition is a natural ability that we all have and, just like our five physical senses and bodily systems, it guides us through our lives and becomes part of our natural flow once we learn to acknowledge and nurture it. We are all made of and connected through Universal energy and this is another way that intuitive information can come through to us.

The source of intuition is at a higher energetic vibration than our physical bodies but it does not come from just one place. It is pure energy and, just like our thoughts, feelings and emotions, there is not one singular origin from which our intuition derives, it is part of who we are and its mystery and magical qualities are what make it all the more exciting and fascinating to work with. Intuition helps us to feel our way through life and gain a greater sense of satisfaction and fulfilment.

Spiritual Awareness

Intuitive development increases our sense of spiritual awareness, opening our hearts and minds to become wiser as we perceive the world through fresh eyes. Some people are born with a high level of spiritual awareness but for others, their sense of spiritual awareness may develop slowly over their lifetime. It is also possible for a sudden 'spiritual awakening' to be triggered by a particular life event or trauma.

A spiritual awakening is exactly that. It is our spirit waking up, opening its eyes and seeing the world for what it really is. This includes our third eye, which enables us to see things beyond the physical dimension. The third eye is an energy centre in the middle of the forehead that allows us to receive and perceive spiritual information. The awakening process usually happens slowly and is different for everyone. Some people may never awaken in this way; it depends on their path in life. If a spiritual awakening happened all at once, it would overwhelm us and probably blow our minds! This is the reason why it is often a gradual unfoldment, filled with mystery, wonder, sometimes a little fear of the unknown and days when it all may seem too much but overall, it can change us for the better.

For some people, their spiritual awakening happens organically as a natural process. For others, a highly emotive event seems to be a catalyst for their spiritual awakening. This may be the passing of a loved one, a car accident or serious illness. It is usually a situation in which a person is forced to face their own mortality or the vulnerability of their loved ones and they are left feeling the need to seek answers to find some comfort or positivity to enable them to understand why this occurred. It may also be that around this time, they might have started to become highly intuitive in order to cope and may receive messages and support from the world of Spirit, which can either seem very scary or a great comfort. Either way, strong emotions can intensify a spiritual awakening. This process should not be forced as it may become too much, too soon.

A person who realises that they are going through a spiritual awakening should be kind to themselves and take their time. There are many things that can support a spiritual awakening, such as meditation, spending time in nature, exercise, healthy eating and reading inspirational books. A spiritual awakening needs to happen at a pace that is right for each person and is not something that should be hurried along.

As we go through this process, layers of emotional baggage start to peel away, revealing parts of us that require healing. We may have days when we are forced to give these areas attention and let go of past hurt that seems to be holding us back. We learn that we have to forgive ourselves and others so that we can reach the core essence of our being and feel lighter and less burdened. Major changes can occur in a spiritual awakening. It may not always be sweetness and light but just like our journey through life, it is a continual process with many ups and downs.

When we go through our daily routine of self-care and spiritual practices, we can heal these parts of ourselves that come to the surface. Sometimes we may require additional support from our friends, family, practitioners, spiritual teachers and healers. Reaching out to others for help is not a sign of weakness; it is part of growing stronger and becoming wise enough to know that we don't always have to go through everything alone.

Seeking out spiritual teachings to expand our knowledge and develop our intuition can be highly beneficial but a little caution should be applied. There are so many resources and spiritual teachers, it is truly mind-boggling. Choosing wisely and not over-analysing the plethora of information available is vital. Listen to your own truth by sitting back and feeling what resonates beautifully with you deep inside. If it feels right, you will experience pangs of excitement, a desire to know more, exhilaration and curiosity. Take in and absorb what you need then move on. You do not have to take everything on board as if it is absolute truth; it just has to feel as if it resonates with your own truth.

Achieving enlightenment is considered to be the highest form of spiritual awareness. Some spiritual teachers speak of enlightenment as if it is unattainable to the 'average' human being but I believe that enlightenment is achievable for everyone. It is our intrinsic nature; the very essence of our soul. We are already enlightened beings who have simply forgotten this because of our upbringing, social conditioning and often Westernised mind-set that we must all compete with one another in order to be successful. Competing only diminishes our success. True success is when we all pull forward in the same direction for the good of everyone.

Enlightenment is not some far away fantasy that is only possible for the chosen few. It is the most simplistic thing of all. Enlightenment is becoming our true self so that we are able to see the Universe through fresh eyes and reconnect with the spiritual being of light within ourselves.

Learning about spiritual matters can greatly enhance intuitive development. Spiritual teachers come in all shapes and sizes. Some may completely capture your attention and leave you wanting more, whereas others may make you feel irritated and disinterested. It is very easy for some spiritual teachers to become seduced by feelings of power that their abilities give them, especially when they start to attract adoring followers. Do what feels comfortable for you and avoid anything that involves obeying a 'leader', takes you away from friends and family or requires you to part with large sums of money. Trust your instincts, they are very rarely wrong.

Self-care

Be kind to yourself! This may sound simple enough but so many of us are always giving to others but not nurturing ourselves or being honest about how mentally, physically and emotionally drained we are truly feeling for fear of 'letting everyone down' by asking for some time and space to take care of our own needs to replenish and recharge ourselves on every level. Self-care is important for everyone, especially those who wish to develop their intuition. Looking after yourself should go without saying but some people go through their lives being so busy working and looking after others, forgetting to care for themselves becomes a habit. It is vital to ensure that you look after yourself well and nurture your body, mind and spirit.

Self-care and self-love are not self-ISH, they are necessary for good health and well-being. We must listen to our bodies and nurture ourselves with good nutrition, exercise and quiet time alone to reflect and recharge. Doing the things we love nurtures us on a deep soul level, which will in turn nurture our whole being from the spiritual to the physical. This raises our energy and makes us feel relaxed and content. Go out and have fun with friends and family! Enjoy holidays and long weekends. Make the best of times and have a good laugh. Keep life happy and buoyant. Do what makes your heart sing! Don't ever feel guilty for looking after your own needs. When you are happy, it will rub off on those around you.

Whole, nutritious and locally produced foods are best for us, especially organic unprocessed food with as few air miles as possible. Vegan and vegetarian diets can be highly beneficial as they raise our vibrations but care should be taken to ensure that the correct nutritional balance is achieved. Each person has their own set of unique nutritional needs.

Setting healthy boundaries to protect our energy levels and well-being should also be included in our self-care routine. We must learn to say 'no' to some people who seem to take us for granted and ask us to do things that may compromise our health, integrity or family commitments. If someone that we know always wants us to give them a lift somewhere at short notice or keeps coming round to our house when we need a break or some alone-time, we can kindly but firmly start putting boundaries in place so that our good nature is not taken advantage of.

Boundaries are about respecting ourselves as individuals and may include other situations such as not allowing our partner or spouse to be controlling or expect us take on all of the household chores. When we show respect to ourselves, other people will notice and be inclined to show more respect. These are just simple examples but this is where setting healthy boundaries starts. It is not selfish to look after yourself. Over time, you will become aware of what you need to stay fit and well on every level and not allow your well-being to be compromised.

Spending time in nature without the confines of modern living, pollution and technology is so good for us. We are animals after all and were never created to live our lives in an unnatural environment. Sunlight and fresh air nourish and revitalise us.

Practising daily self-care is vital for our well-being and getting into a routine helps us to remember to care for ourselves, even when our lives are very busy. Simple things such as a nice, hot bath, reading a good book or meditating can become part of this routine. If you enjoy doing something and find it relaxing and energising, there is no reason for you not to do it. Do not feel guilty. The happier and more energised you are, the better you can care for everyone else and do all the things you need to do every day.

We must care for our own physical, mental, emotional and spiritual well-being in order to be a complete human being. We are not automatons and cannot run on empty. Listen to your body, mind and spirit. If you need time to recharge, take it. Set aside time every day for it.

Self-care is vitally important, especially to avoid tiredness and exhaustion, which can distort our thinking and result in feelings of fear, depression, anxiety and negativity. Tiredness can consume you if you do not listen to your body, mind and spirit and take care of your own needs first. Balance out your days and keep some energy in reserve.

De-cluttering, refreshing and organising all elements of your life such as your home, clothes, car and paperwork can also take a great weight of your shoulders and help you to feel rejuvenated and energised. Dealing with any jobs or tasks that you've been putting off for a long time can also be a source of relief once they are done.

Life is about balance and pacing yourself so that you do not become burnt out, stressed or anxious. You are your own priority. When you feel happy and well, it will have a ripple effect into every aspect of your life and spread through the entire Universe. Not every day will be perfect but you will be better placed to deal with any challenges or upsets that may come along. Life is not a smooth ride but you can make it more comfortable!

Universal Energy

Universal energy is exactly that. It is throughout the Universe, all around us, within us, flowing through us and connecting us all. This interconnectedness is the reason we must look after ourselves. Do you ever feel down when those around you are depressed or feeling tired? Can you imagine what the world would feel like if everyone was miserable? Our thoughts, feelings and physical actions are all made of Universal energy, as is the wind, the pull of the moon and absolutely everything else. Universal energy is the essence of life. It is existence itself.

It is true that we can choose how we feel to a certain degree but low energy can drag us down so we should make sure that we spend time with people and in places that raise our vibration and make us feel happy and relaxed. It is difficult to think straight and piece together our emotions when we feel exhausted and low. Higher vibrations uplift us and allow us to feel energised and filled with joy! The healthier and happier we are, the higher our vibration.

Universal energy is visible to our physical eyes. When you look up to the sky on a clear day, you can see tiny, shimmering particles swimming before your eyes. If you relax your eyes and gently focus on them, you can see that they are not high up in the sky, they are all around you and right in front of your face. You can even see it on a dull day once you are used to noticing it. It's amazing!

Reiki is a Japanese word that is pronounced as 'Ray-key' and can be translated as 'Universal' for 'Rei' and 'Energy' for 'ki'. 'Rei' can also be interpreted as 'Spirit'. This life-force energy is also referred to as 'orgone', 'chi' and 'prana', depending on the culture or belief. Reiki is a form of energy healing that allows Universal energy to flow into the recipient to promote healing and restore balance. There is more detail about this in 'What is Reiki?' in the 'Reiki for Animals' chapter.

Sometimes, people can become fearful when we talk about spirits or spiritual energy but there is no need to be afraid. Universal energy works for the greatest and highest good and comes from a place of pure love and healing. Everything around us is an expression of Universal energy, vibrating at its own unique frequency. When we work with this pure, white light energy, it protects and guides us, keeping negative energy at bay. Negative energy comes from a place of fear and we can choose not to interact with it. There is more about this in the 'Emotions' chapter.

Our spirit is made of Universal energy and is an expression of our soul in this lifetime. It is the energetic essence of our being that gives life and vitality to our physical body. It is who we are as a person and is the spiritual energy that leaves us when it is time to move on from our physical body into the higher vibration of the world of Spirit. Our soul is vast and timeless and we may return to Earth again in another lifetime as different spiritual expression of our soul. The world of Spirit is not limited by time and space so there are endless possibilities.

Reincarnation and karmic debt are very mysterious. I believe that we do come to Earth with a purpose or a set of goals to achieve but these are not set in stone down to the finest detail. Our purpose seems to be more of a guideline with the finer points to be added by the eclectic mix of people we meet and situations in which we find ourselves. There are so many different possibilities and decisions to make. Life as a human being would be made even more difficult if we had to try to stick to one rigid path on and learn to deflect any shrapnel and distractions along the way. Some things are inevitable yet others are flexible and remain open to outside influences such as the law of attraction and being in the right place at the right time. It is the unexpected things in life that can make it all the more interesting. This is why intuition is important as a guide in our lives. It helps us to make decisions that are right for us.

As for karmic debt, the fact that we are supposed to keep incarnating on Earth until we 'get it right' seems more like a punishment than a pleasure. It seems to be a disconcerting thought that the loving world of Spirit and Universal energy could be responsible for creating such a concept. Every human being makes mistakes and hurts others, even if they do not intend to. It seems much more likely that our soul chooses to return to Earth to learn lessons rather than being forced into some kind of punishment regime by superior spiritual beings. Our soul is wise and eternal and may voluntarily wish to right its wrongs or simply have another interesting life experience on our amazing planet. Of course, reincarnation does not necessarily mean that we choose to return as a human being. We can incarnate as any species that we wish. I would like to come back as a cat but there is a strong possibility I have already been one at some stage as I have a very strong feline connection. We all seem to have a certain path to follow which leads us to discovering who we truly are at soul level, whichever form that may take.

Auras and Chakras

Our physical body is surrounded by our aura. This is the electromagnetic energy field that permeates, extends outwards and all around our physical body. It has many layers from the dense vibration of physical matter to the higher vibration of spiritual energy. Auras can be seen by some people and animals. Some people see them as a pale grey and others see vibrant colours. Kirlian photography was developed in order to photograph the aura. Everything and everyone has their own energy signature and, therefore, an aura. When we are well, our aura can extend to around

25 feet, with the largest portion at the front. We subconsciously shrink and extend our aura, depending on our surroundings.

Everything has its own electromagnetic field so this is not some kind of fantastical concept. Our body would not function without billions of electrical signals firing throughout our systems every second of the day and night. There is a vast array of different types of cells in our bodies, each with their own specific function. They are tiny power units in their own right and energetic imprints can be left on them when they suffer trauma or experience optimum functionality. Cells have their own memories and the old adage is true; our body is a temple and we should treat it as the sacred place that it is by showing ourselves love and respect. When all of our cells are working in harmony, our energy flows beautifully and our aura and chakras are balanced and we feel very well and happy.

The chakras are energy centres that receive and transmit Universal energy in and out of our energetic field and physical body. In Sanskrit, 'chakra' can be translated as 'wheel'. There are seven main ones. They are shaped liked cones that spin at a certain frequency, with the widest part of the funnel on the outside of our body, at the front and back, with the narrowest part feeding in through our spine. Each chakra has a colour and certain qualities associated with it. There are also several minor chakras and bud chakras on the body but I shall just mention the main ones here:

The root or base chakra is at the base of our spine and is associated with red or black, which are grounding colours. It is associated with a sense of security, instinct and survival and its funnel points downward towards the Earth.

The next chakra up is the sacral chakra in the abdomen. Orange is the colour associated with this chakra. Creativity, energy and emotion are related to the sacral chakra, especially those related to sensuality, sexual issues and orientation.

The solar plexus is located just below the stomach in the abdomen and represents the expression of ourselves, power, control, mental functioning and the colour yellow. It radiates our power into the world and assists with decision making and gives us clarity in our judgements. The area in which it is situated contains a large cluster of nerves that serves many organs in the body including those associated with the digestive system. It is literally a nerve-centre, especially for people who are very sensitive to emotions. Raw emotions are dealt with here and a healthy solar plexus gives us greater emotional stability.

Above this is the heart chakra in the centre of the chest, associated with pink and green. Balance, love and compassion are connected with this chakra.

The thymus chakra, or higher heart chakra, is located half way between the heart and throat chakra behind the breast bone. This is considered to be a minor chakra but some people do not believe that it exists. The physical thymus gland is between the heart and the sternum. The thymus is part of the immune system and the thymus chakra is the centre of spiritual development that connects us to our dreams and helps us to express what we feel in our hearts by ensuring that we speak the right words before they reach the throat chakra.

The throat chakra is above this and is represented by the colour blue. It symbolises self-expression and speech.

The third eye chakra is just above our eyes in the centre of our forehead. Psychic abilities and imagination are connected with this chakra, along with the colour indigo. The pineal gland is in this location, which forms part of the endocrine system and secretes the hormone, melatonin. We need to keep it healthy and uncalcified by eating a healthy diet, drinking plenty of mineral water and avoiding toxins such as excessive fluoride.

The chakra on the top of the head is the crown chakra, which connects us to Spirit, unity and knowledge. Its colour is violet and pure, brilliant white light. Its funnel points upwards toward the skies.

Grounding and Protection

In order for us to function well and work with energy at a higher vibration, we must remain grounded, centred and well-balanced. Grounding connects us strongly with the Earth and the flow of energy through our physical and energetic bodies, literally keeping our feet on the ground! A simple grounding exercise, which is best done in bare feet in direct contact with grass or other natural ground but can be done indoors if necessary, is to sit or stand straight with both feet flat on the ground. Imagine roots extending from the soles of your feet and into the Earth below, right to the core. Visualise the gentle healing energy of the Earth coming back up through your roots and into your heart chakra.

Stay with this pleasant feeling and imagine the pure white light of spiritual energy gently pouring in through your crown chakra. Allow it to flow down into your solar plexus to intermingle with the

Earth energy in this chakra, giving you a feeling of balance, cleansing and stability. Remain in this peaceful state for as long as you wish. When you are ready, gently pull your roots back up to the soles of your feet, visualise your crown chakra closing up slightly so it is open enough to remain connected to spirit then slowly come out of the visualisation. This will help you to stay grounded for the rest of the day and filled with protective, healing spiritual and grounding energy. It is good to do this every morning before you start your day.

Balance can be achieved when we embrace the wonder of being in our physical bodies and become grounded with the energy of the Earth in our root chakra and also connected with the higher vibration of Universal through our crown chakra, giving us harmonious balance and stability. Our physical bodies allow us the freedom to experience the incredible journey that it is to be human.

If you feel that you are sometimes drained by negative energies or people around you, it is good to put up a filter that will only allow pleasant, loving energy to enter your aura and keep negative energy away. You can do this by visualising a bubble, protective angel wings or anything that seems to work for you. This can form part of your daily grounding exercise.

Once you become used to working with energy and feel stronger from within, a filter will no longer be necessary as you are able to stand in your own power. We are energetic beings and the energy of the Universe keeps negative energy away when we learn to attract positivity into our lives. There is more the Law of Attraction and Manifestation in 'Emotions' chapter.

Protection and shielding are sometimes recommended by spiritual teachers but these can block our sensitivities and hinder our learning process. When we feel peace and calm within, we can transmute negative energy by infusing it with loving, nurturing energy, often without even being conscious of this. You will learn more about this as the book progresses.

Non-Religious Approach

When working with spiritual matters, it is important to understand that we should respect the beliefs of others and not try to force our own opinions and beliefs onto others. We are all different and what suits one person can bring great discomfort to another.

Some people turn to religion for comfort or may have been brought up within a particular religious setting. Religious beliefs and practices can be a source of stability for some but may also feel restrictive to others. Most religions are based on love and compassion. Sadly, there are certain individuals and groups of people who twist religion out of all proportion in order to gain power and control over others, carrying out terrible acts of harm in the process.

I believe that there are lots of beings of light but not just one God that needs to be worshipped and obeyed. Religion helps some people. It's very much an individual thing. I have been christened, got married in a Christian church and celebrate Christmas but I do not 'follow' Christianity. I go with the traditions of my family. I find attending church uncomfortable.

I work from a non-religious perspective because being spiritual is not a religion. Religion tends to place restrictions on our spiritual freedom because of the constructs and structure that is in place. The majority of religious practices encourage worship of a god or deity and have guidelines that must be followed. If this suits someone, that is their choice. I simply choose to go my own way with a sense of freedom and infinite possibilities.

For me, the best way to approach life is to work from a place of love and gratitude for the greatest and highest good without restrictions or being influenced by the will or ego of others. I have never been one to follow the masses. I like to make up my own mind and keep my options open.

I believe that the Universe is made up of subtle energy and that we are all part of this. There are beings that are made up of this energy vibrating at an incredibly high frequency who emanate love, compassion and wisdom into the Universe and that, when we transition out of our physical bodies, we return to this higher vibration as the spiritual energy that once gave life to the more dense energy of our physical body.

The Universe does not place requirements upon us to worship or sacrifice our true selves in order to live a healthy and happy life. That power is within us all when we work from a place of love, humility and gratitude. It is a simple process once we are able to feel peace and calm within. If we were to all achieve this state of being and embrace our differences, our world would be a very different and tranquil place but life is not perfect and the rest of this book explores this in greater depth. We all have an equal right to live our lives in the way that we choose.

Equality

Inequality is rife, even in spiritual communities, mainly because people of the same gender, religion, creed, colour or any other kind of inclination are often perceived as being the same. Human beings have the annoying habit of trying to put groups of people into the same box and placing labels on their heads, never taking their individual characteristics, background, thoughts and feelings into account.

Intuition and spiritual awareness are all too often perceived as purely female qualities. Men are held up as tough-nuts who should not dabble in such matters because they are immune to feeling emotions and being sensitive is perceived as a sign of weakness. This kind of attitude fills me with despair. Not because it sets out to portray females as being the 'weaker' sex but because it disempowers the male gender. There are a great deal of spiritually aware and sensitive males who are incredibly strong and wise. In all aspects of life, there are many different attitudes towards gender issues and to make generalised assumptions and place expectations on the qualities and capabilities of either sex is shockingly ignorant. Once again, it is about extremes and how extreme views create closed minds and rigid streams of thought.

There should be equality for both men and women. I cannot stand it when people try to place emphasis on one gender over the other. Men and women are different; there is no getting away from that fact. If they were not, the human race would not exist because we would be unable to reproduce! We should not place stereotypes on males and females because there are extremes in both sexes. Some men have strong feminine qualities and some women are quite masculine. I don't like wearing dresses and skirts but I do so when I have to look 'posh'. I don't force either of my children to view themselves in the light of their gender; I encourage them to be themselves in every way and not adhere to stereotypes. Men and women should have equal rights and opportunities but there will always be differences in these, especially regarding pregnancy and childbirth but one set of rights should not diminish the other. There is plenty of room for everyone, whichever way you choose to lean!

There seems to be a trend at the moment where it seems to be acceptable to promote the empowerment of women to the extreme that it becomes insulting to men. Even in adverts, it seems acceptable to suggest that men are dozy and a bit useless or that it's ok for women to drool over topless male models. There would be outrage if it were the other way around. It's all been blown out of proportion and become hypocritical.

Not all men are sexist pigs who are out to exert control over women. Some men are deeply kind and sensitive. Feminism goes too far and seeks to disempower men, tarring them all with the same brush. I love being a woman but I hate it when extreme feminists give the female population a bad name by being overtly sexist towards men! There are plenty of vile women out there who are far worse than some men would ever be. Women should be empowered and encouraged to be confident and independent but that doesn't mean that we should forget that men have feelings too.

Journal 12.11.16

'I've also found myself feeling a bit annoyed about books about empowering women and only focussing on spiritual development for women. I can understand why this would be the case but empowerment and spiritual development are for EVERYONE and focussing only on

women is disempowering to men. They need support and guidance too because, traditionally, and especially in the Western world, men have been conditioned to be 'macho' and 'tough' and expressing their emotions has been considered a sign of weakness. Empowerment for all I say! Males and females are different, of course, but to varying degrees. There has to be a balance in the Universe of masculine and feminine qualities. Both have their own strengths but some contain greater or lesser degrees of the other. It's all very fascinating!'

There is a balance of male and female energies in everything, just like yin and yang. We are all human beings with the same needs on every level and imbalances often occur in many forms. We should all look out for each other and extend a warm hand of kindness and support whenever we feel that it is right to do so. Whether we are male or female, we all experience problems from time to time and never deserve to feel that we are alone without any support.

Of course, equality does not just relate to sexism. Everyone of any race, religion, colour or creed has a right to be who they truly are, especially when it comes to navigating their way along their spiritual path. It is the ultimate freedom of choice. Intuitive development is for everyone.

INTUITIVE DEVELOPMENT

Where to Begin

So, where do we start with developing our intuition? We start with you. Intuitive development follows a path unique for everyone. No two journeys are the same.

Intuition comes in many forms, which may include a sense of 'knowing', gut feelings, images, sensations, words, thoughts, dreams or a natural flow of events which seem to effortlessly unfold as if you knew they were going to happen.

Some people may already have a highly developed sense of intuition and maybe some other abilities as well, such as being psychic, clairvoyant or having a connection with passed loved ones in Spirit. Others may be at the very start of their journey and are just becoming aware of their intuition.

Intuitive Abilities

Intuition is often given many different names and labels. There are so many abilities associated with intuiting information it can become confusing. As intuition develops, some people may find themselves having experiences that are known as psychic, clairvoyant or are associated with mediumship. These abilities do have their own distinct qualities and definitions but for the sake of clarity, they are all about rising up to a state of heightened awareness. The main types of 'clair' abilities and their interpretations are:

- Clairvoyance – clear seeing;
- Clairaudience – clear hearing;
- Clairsentience – clear feeling or sensing;
- Clairgustance – clear tasting;
- Claircognizance – clear knowing;
- Clairolfaction – clear smelling;
- Clairtangency – clear touching; also known as psychometry when we receive intuitive information from objects;
- Clairempathy – clear emotion, as experienced by Empaths.

These are all sensations that seem to tap into the part of our brain that processes information from our physical senses so that we become consciously aware of them and receive sights, sounds, smells, tastes and sensations as if they were being received through our physical senses but they are actually coming from higher vibrational frequencies through our third eye, other chakras and energy field. They are processed in the same place as those received on the physical plane to keep things familiar and enable us to understand the information that we are receiving and articulate it to others.

Everyone is different and some people may receive intuitive information through just one of their senses or they may experience a combination of them all, depending on the situation. Some intuitive people have a natural talent for something in particular, such as being a medical intuitive. They may be able to look at someone and immediately know what is wrong with them. They may feel the physical sensation of their symptoms or 'see' into them as if they have x-ray vision but this is through their third eye, rather than their physical eyes. Many intuitives do this kind of work as a profession because they become so accurate. Such an ability can help to save lives or provide answers if someone seems to be suffering from a mystery illness or disease that orthodox medical professionals have been unable to diagnose.

I often see and sense medical issues with people and animals in this way, both in-person and when looking at photographs of the living or those in Spirit. Sometimes it is spontaneous and other times it is during a Reiki or animal communication session. I always trust my first impressions because they are usually right but I never say anything that would shock or upset my clients. Tact and discretion are always required.

When we are more aware of higher vibrational energies, we can connect more easily with spiritual energy and become aware of how the Universe is not limited by time and space. We may receive glimpses of future events, sense or communicate with loved ones in the world of Spirit or be able to receive intuitive information about other people and animals, both living and passed. Our third eye chakra, where the pineal gland is located, plays a key part in receiving and 'seeing' intuitive information.

Some people may find that they are able to predict certain events or situations, either on a global scale or things closer to home. This can be in the form of dreams, visions or feelings etc. Sometimes, these may not always be pleasant but a lot of intuitives may experience this, especially when they are starting out on their intuitive journey. This does not mean that they are only able to tune in to negative occurrences or will only ever get to know about unpleasant things. The reason negative predictions come through so readily is because their energy is usually much more intense than gentle, happy and lighter positive experiences. Most of these are often spontaneous and occur without us having to try.

The intensity and magnitude of something such as a natural disaster or plane crash has a strong, low negative vibration which is so potent due to the impact of the sudden energetic shift and highly charged emotions. It is not a reflection on the person receiving such a premonition; it is because they are more likely to receive the stronger energetic vibrations when they are first starting to become aware of their intuitive abilities due to their intensity.

This doesn't mean that everything is all doom and gloom. This simply means that when we seem to be going through a phase of only picking up on the 'bad stuff', it is because we are more likely to receive these stronger energies during the early stages. As our development progresses and we learn to recognise the subtleties of intuition, we become more open to receiving higher, less intense vibrations as our abilities become more varied and expansive. We become stronger and wiser as we work on strengthening our spiritual awareness so this starts to flow naturally. We do not have to take every emotion on as our own. Our inner knowing and wisdom guides us to understanding what we receive and how to process it appropriately.

Developing our intuition naturally heightens our awareness and is a different journey for every single person. As long as we practice grounding and infusing ourselves with protective light and standing in our own power, we will be working with the higher energetic vibrations that give us natural protection. We are in control of our intuitive abilities and can develop them as we so choose in a way that benefits us and those around us. Each person should do what feels right for them.

There are so many old wives' tales, myths and legends about intuitive and psychic abilities but they are nothing to be scared of. Fearing these abilities is why some people are put off and choose not to take them any further, but to those people who intuitively know that they come from a place of love, they can be a true blessing. They are something we have from before we are even born into this world. It really does depend on our upbringing and life choices as to whether or not we are aware of them and at what point we feel a deep desire to reconnect with that magical and mysterious part of ourselves to enrich and enhance our lives. Life is what you make it, as are intuitive abilities. We all have them. It's simply about allowing them to flourish and having the discipline and focus to work on their development.

The Reputation of 'Psychics'

The vast majority of intuitive and psychic people remain quiet and out of the limelight but there are some very talented and highly developed psychics and mediums who do choose to work very publicly and get up onto podiums to give readings to audiences packed with people desperate to hear messages from loved ones.

Sadly, some of these people are not genuine, just as is the case with those who prey on vulnerable people with psychic phone lines and demand high fees for personal readings.

It is these people who give the rest of us a bad reputation. For many decades, there had been an offer a 'psychic challenge' in which people who claim to have such abilities are tested in rigid conditions. The prize was revoked in 2015 because nobody ever passed. They were required to perform certain tasks to prove that they are psychic. If they were able to do this, within the parameters set by those organising the tests, they could potentially win a large sum of money. This makes my heart sink and I feel so let down by this view of intuitive abilities. These kinds of tests set participants up for failure. Intuition is a subtle, gentle energy but can also be powerful in its effects when it is allowed to flow naturally, without constraints or added pressures. Of course, many of the people undertaking the tests were likely to only be doing it for the money as they did not have genuine psychic abilities but others may have been left feeling let down and confused as to why they 'failed'.

When developing intuition, we should remain humble and grateful and not allow sceptics to challenge our abilities. It is best to allow them to go on their way without rising to their challenge. Encourage them to do their own research and read widely on the subject, should they wish to know more. A true sceptic will never be convinced and a true intuitive will never thrive in test conditions where the pressure is on and they are made to feel like a failure.

How do we know that such tests are not rigged? I would very happily go without the money and steer clear of such publicity stunts. They achieve nothing other than to discredit an intrinsic part of our nature that a certain group of sceptics set out to deny the existence of. They seem to be on some kind of power trip to suggest that they have the authority as to how we should try to prove that such abilities exist. They were never intended to be treated with such disrespect. Our sense of inner knowing should not be compared to a circus act or blatant trickery. It is very real and is a key part of the everyday life for those who have embraced these subtle qualities.

A true and natural psychic or intuitive reading starts with the feeling of being drawn to someone or them feeling drawn to you as a reader. This is the place from which the energy of the reading derives and escalates into receiving intuitive information through a strong energetic connection. It would be very difficult to feel the same way if a psychic was asked to go out into the street and 'cold read' every person that they meet. They may get snippets of information but a full, accurate reading would be doubtful. I know that I would not be comfortable doing readings in this way.

Giving a reading is a spiritual and sacred process that would not feel right if presented with random subjects to read in order to win a prize. It doesn't even seem ethical to take on such a challenge that goes against everything an intuitive person holds dear. In test conditions, that important initial energetic connection is absent, which completely takes away the whole point of offering a reading. Readings should come from a place of love, not the need to set out to prove something that intuitive people already know to be true. When working intuitively from the heart, I usually get a warm-headed, delightful, nourishing feeling like wrapping my arms around all of those who need it, reaffirming that we are all one.

That being said, many incredible things have been achieved through scientific experimentation and discovery. The branch of science known as Metaphysics has demonstrated that we are all connected through energy by the phenomenon of quantum entanglement and that we all have our own energy field, plus many more amazing discoveries that can easily be researched on the internet. Science and spirituality can work together harmoniously. There is a huge cross-over point but just as we are unlikely to ever fully understand how the Universe was created, some things will forever remain a mystery and that is what it is exciting about intuition; most intuitive experiences defy explanation!

Try not to allow yourself to be drawn into the stereotypical hype surrounding psychics, the spirit world and ghost hunts. A lot of things get blown out of all proportion by the media and those trying to make a fast buck. You will get a feel for what is authentic and what is not. Walk away from things that do not sit comfortably with you, especially if they only focus on the macabre, sinister or negative aspects of spirituality.

It saddens me when spiritual matters are taken to the opposite extreme and disrespect is shown in haunted locations and to spirits who are often in distress. Instead of goading them to provoke a reaction, it would be much kinder and appropriate to remember they were once just like us; a human being living a physical life. In those situations, they should be encouraged to find peace and go to the light to enter the spirit world. If there is any uncertainty about this, a medium or other experienced person should be called in to help. It can be great fun to feel spooked on a ghost hunt but it is all too easy to forget that we will one day be in spirit and would not appreciate being treated as a source of entertainment.

As for predicting the future, the best person to consult when looking for guidance about what your future may hold is yourself.

Looking to external sources for answers about your life is likely to lead to a never-ending quest that seems out of reach. This is because there are so many endless possibilities; nobody can predict the far-off distant future. Tools such as tarot cards and scrying with crystal balls may work for some people but they will only take things so far. Just look at how many times it's been predicted the world is going to end but we're still here! The answers that you seek are within you and can be accessed through your intuition and higher sense of awareness.

Spending time with yourself in a quiet, restful place can allow you space to breathe on the deepest level, especially during meditation. We make our own life and are the only ones who are truly responsible for making our own future. There are infinite timelines and we can only receive signs that we are on the right track. Predicting the future is like trying to pin the tail on the donkey when it keeps moving. Trust in the Universe and send out good vibes. What you are hoping for will come your way if it is right for you. We all have many lessons to learn and a little uncertainty can be refreshing. Some timelines are already set in motion by current events so potential outcomes can be predicted but may be subject to change.

We only receive the information that we are destined to receive to help ourselves and others. It is not something to be harshly judged or tested. Yes, validation is important to reassure ourselves and others that we are on the right track but there is always a margin for error, whether it's through our own misinterpretation or that the information is intended for someone else. Not trusting ourselves or our intuition sets us up for failure and unnecessary disappointment. Practice builds confidence.

There is no 'failure' with intuition. It is always a work in progress and we were not given these abilities to show off or brag about them. Once we are comfortable and confident with our intuitive abilities, it is up to us how far we take it. For me personally, I lay low and the people who need me tend to find me. I am not the one who does the healing or gives the guidance; it's my intuition and Reiki. That is why there are so many of us all around the world. Each intuitively developed person is placed perfectly and intentionally so that the right people find them in the right place at the right time. If developing our intuition was easy, everyone would do it! There have to be enough of us to go around to help others and encourage them to develop their own abilities.

Just like the web of Universal energy, there is a perfect web of intuitive people placed all around the world. Its strength and intensity is growing every day as it becomes illuminated with little pinpoints of light as more people become aware of their abilities. If you choose develop your intuition and increase your spiritual awareness, you add another glowing dot to the web and really can help to light up the world. That's just how amazing intuition really is!

Being sceptical isn't all bad though. A healthy dose of scepticism is wise with regard to assessing information received from others. People love to tell stories and may often exaggerate or miss-tell a story passed on through friends and family members. Photographs and videos can so easily be faked these days and only discerning truth-seekers will be able to sort the wheat from the chaff. We can all be mistaken and sometimes fall for optical illusions or hoaxes but we must remember that there are some very real, genuinely unexplained phenomena out there; we just have to learn to recognise truth when we see it. It is often the simplest video or experience that is real. Don't fall for drama or something that is too good to be true. Trust your intuition. After all, that is what it is all about. Look for an Earthly explanation first. Be your own investigator.

Journal 10.08.16

'I'm watching a video that someone has posted on the internet that is clearly a ship on the horizon on the ocean in a heat haze but they are insisting it's a UFO. No, it isn't! Get a grip!'

The best way to discover the truth behind intuitive and psychic abilities is to try them out for yourself!

Intuitive Experiences

Intuition is like a muscle. The more you use it, the stronger and more active it becomes. The first step in developing our intuition is noticing when it is 'speaking' to us and the form this takes. We may receive intuitive insight in many different ways such as hearing a voice in our head that is more noticeable than the usual mind chatter or seeing images flash into our minds. Dreams are also another source of intuition, as is noticing things that seem to keep repeatedly turning up that we don't normally pay attention to. Intuition guides us to feel our own truth and we should learn to trust it. We would not be given intuitive abilities if they were not there for a purpose.

One of the main ways in which intuition manifests itself for many people is a 'gut feeling' or 'hunch'. If something doesn't feel right or sit well with us, we should probably choose a different option.

Intuition can be quite persistent and if we keep feeling that we just 'know' something, we should pay attention to it. If we have a strong urge to call a family member or old friend, it may be for a very good reason and we should follow it up.

For instance, if we are on our way to work and something keeps telling us not to take the usual route and go the long way round, we should listen to it. We might later find out there has been a road accident on the usual route or that there's a long traffic jam. This is just a simple example but there are many situations in which intuition can be helpful and also sometimes life-saving.

Keeping a journal is a great way to keep track of our intuitive experiences and give ourselves validation. It is an amazing feeling when we write down some of our intuitive insights, only to find that they come true a day or two later. This kind of validation builds our confidence and helps our intuition to flourish. You will probably find that, over time, you write more and more each day and thoroughly enjoy keeping your journal. I'd be lost without mine. I write down even the smallest thing that gives me a glimmer of my intuition communicating with me. It nourishes my soul and raises my vibration. It is good to monitor your progress to keep yourself motivated.

Developing our intuition is a life-long process and it is never something to take for granted. Most of my intuitive experiences occur spontaneously. Intuition is not always available on demand. I am grateful for every experience that I have, no matter how small. It doesn't feel small to me when I know a minute detail about something that I couldn't have known any other way other than through my intuition. Some of the most common intuitive experiences that I have are when I 'just know' something, such as:

- When I am going to receive a text or phone call a few seconds beforehand;
- Hearing my mobile phone bleep or ring a few seconds before it actually does;
- When I need to ring someone and I know if it's going to be engaged or not. On a recent attempt to ring my doctors' surgery, the phone was engaged several times. Suddenly a voice said 'If you call right now, you'll get through' so I did and I got through immediately;
- Best before dates on food; I often know it before I pick the item up;
- Whether or not a delivery is going to be on time or not arrive at all;
- Thinking of someone I haven't heard from in years then they contact me;
- The exact price of something on TV, such as a house or antique;
- The location of a place on TV. The soap box races were on telly when I once walked into the lounge. A voice said to me 'Mumbai, Mumbai, Mumbai' over and over, 'they're in Mumbai'. My logical mind argued with the voice because the city had signs written in English everywhere so I asked my husband if it was Mumbai and the voice in my head was right; the races were in Mumbai;
- I often know the time without looking, to the exact minute and also often precisely how much time is left on a recorded TV show. I am told such things by the voice of my intuition, which is usually male, or shown the image of a number;
- When my husband is going to be late home from work even before his usual arrival time;

- Being on high alert when driving and receiving lots of helpful intuitive information whenever I am out and about;
- When someone is going to cancel an appointment or night out;
- What the weather is going to do, despite it being different from the forecast;
- Whether or not someone will reply to a text or email and what their response will be;
- 'Looking ahead' to see what vehicles are coming towards me, especially the colour or size. Sometimes I get a 'flash' of what's there without even trying;
- The location of lost items that do not belong to me. My daughter once lost her 'hanky' when she was small. Something told me to look in the vacuum cleaner tube. I thought it was silly but I looked anyway and there it was stuffed inside one of the tube attachments!
- How someone is really feeling, including actors on TV and people serving in shops or restaurants, even if they are trying to portray something different;
- What song is next on the radio;
- A scenario of the place to which I am going and it turns out to be right;
- Feeling the energy of the people who live in a house when I arrive for my first pet sitting visit. It's as if they are still there because their presence feels so strong. I can tell if they haven't long left. Their energy gradually fades as I do more visits and the house takes on the energy of the animals I'm looking after. I can also tell if someone has been in the house such as a relative visiting or a person doing some work, even before I see the physical signs of this. I can often tell from the moment I put the key in the lock;

- Most of the time, when I look at a photograph, I can tell if a person or animal has passed away since it was taken. Even if it's a group of people or the photo appears at random, they stand out to me like a sore thumb and I know that they are no longer with us. It can be a bit upsetting at times, especially if I discover that they had a tragic death;
- When a lady is pregnant even if I can only see her from behind or above shoulder level;
- What someone looks like and/or the location of their house and what it looks like before I meet them;
- When there is a dog in a house even when there are no external clues;
- When someone has a dog or other animals in their lives when there are no obvious physical signs of this. I can just tell. I believe that I am may be sensing the love they have for their animal in their heart or aura; I sensed this in the lady who once sat next to me in the doctors. I felt her love for her dog in her heart, she then turned to me and within a couple of minutes, she was telling me all about her dog!
- Feeling the energy of a person's thoughts. I was recently in a book shop and I browsed through the pets section, I could feel the energy of a young lady sitting in a chair over by the window. I could hear her intelligent curiosity and tumbling thoughts as she enjoyed poring over a book she was looking at before I even glanced in her direction;
- 'Willing' my husband to turn over in bed when he is snoring and it often works!
- Clairvoyantly seeing the medical issues and areas of soreness or discomfort in people and animals. This is sometimes during a Reiki session but it is usually spontaneous and happens in-person or when I look at a photograph;

- When a cyclist, jogger or dog walker is coming up fast behind me whilst dog walking or I am just about to go around a corner;
- Knowing when the mail is for me, even when the envelope is face down on the mat and I'm not expecting anything;
- Feeling the physical pain and symptoms of others, mainly close relatives but sometimes passing strangers. I don't always know but sometimes I know when it's 'not mine'. This also happens with feelings and moods, especially with family members, even if we are miles apart.

Intuitive Development Exercises

In order to develop your intuition, you could use some of the examples in the 'Intuitive Abilities' section that can become ways of practicing your intuition in everyday life to strengthen and develop it. Play on your own strengths and be creative. Developing your intuition should be enjoyable so make it fun and the more things that you get right, the more your confidence grows. Don't beat yourself up if you are not right all the time. Learn to feel when it is your intuition speaking to you, rather than just your mind trying to guess. Intuition is an energetic flow, like sweeping for information with an internal radar and receiving 'blips' when you are correct. Get to know how it feels when you are receiving something that you know to be true. As you practice, you will get to know what I mean.

If we knew everything about everyone and every situation in this world it would be absolutely overwhelming and impossible to function. We receive the intuitive information that we are meant to receive to help ourselves and others. Most of what we receive is about ourselves and immediate friends and family. We are sometimes intuitively made aware of events around the world and about people we do not know but there is always a reason for this. In my view, it is to make us aware of how our intuition works, what is going on in the world and give us validation for the information we receive to help us develop. The Universe is one huge energetic web and occasionally, we catch glimpses of things that are 'not ours' to help us learn.

Other intuitive exercises in addition to the ones above could include the following:

- Who is it? When your phone bleeps, 'feel' to see who has sent you a text, email or social media message before you check it;
- Day to day decisions – call upon your intuition, even if it's only to choose a sandwich! It's about learning how your intuition FEELS to you so that you can recognise it;
- Remote viewing – try the exercise that I have mentioned above to see if you can sense what colour or type of vehicle is coming toward you along the road. Of course, this should not distract you from your driving. You do not need to go into a meditative state to do this but the road should ideally be a single lane either way at a quiet time of day. Send your intuitive radar up and out in front of you and see what is pinged back. Is it a colour, size, word or pattern? A van, car, lorry or tractor? Practice a few times on each journey when you don't need to concentrate too hard. I also do this whilst walking, except I change it to sense what is approaching from behind me and often laugh to myself when I'm spot on, even down to the name of the company on the vehicle;
- You can do remote viewing for lots of things. See what ideas you come up with;

- What's in the box? Find a nice box that is big enough to place random items into and enlist the help of a friend or family member. Get them to place something into the box out of your line of sight and hearing. Ask them to place the box on your lap and try to intuitively 'feel' what is inside. Your friend could have a go too to keep it interesting;
- People watching – this is always interesting and can be a good way to develop your intuition. When you are walking down the street or sitting outside at a café or restaurant. Look at the people approaching from a distance. Try to feel for what nationality they may be. It is probably best to play this in a busy town or city. As they walk by, you may be able to hear their accent to see if you are correct or not. It may not always work but if they are with someone else, chances are they will be talking;
- Intuitive readings – ask a friend or family member to bring a photo of someone only they know or ask them to introduce you to a willing friend to whom you can give an intuitive reading. Grounding and protection should take place for both of you before and after the reading. You could have set questions to ask or simply see what you are able to intuit. This can be very good for confidence building when you get lots of things right but don't worry if it takes a while to get used to doing things like this and you get things wrong. It's all about practice; the most important thing is to relax and say what you receive without analysing it. Seemingly random and abstract things can often be spot on!
- Ask a friend or family member to place a photograph into a blank envelope and see if you can feel what is on it. Keep it simple such as a person or animal on their own or a particular place or landmark;

- Traditional tests such as reading playing cards from the back or tests such as psychic Zener cards may work for you. Take your time and see what you can pick up from these;
- Anything else you feel drawn to or inquisitive about!

Of course, intuitive development is not simply about knowing which symbol is on the other side of a card; it's about our experiences in everyday life. Find out what works for you and develop it. Understanding your own intuitive sense will encourage it to thrive and strengthen. Keep things varied and be brave. Allow your thinking to be fluid and move with the rhythm of your heart. Close friends and family may be able to help you with this or you can practice in other ways on your own. There are also private social media groups that provide opportunities to practice in a safe and confidential space. You may also find local groups that hold development circles.

During the journey of intuitive development, there may be a mention of the third, fourth and fifth density or dimension. This is a way to describe the raising of our vibration during the spiritual awakening process. I'm not going to write about this in-depth because it is not something that I have fully explored. I prefer to see the process as gradual up to the fifth dimension and beyond, which is a higher form of consciousness in which we become more aware of beings of light such as guides and angels. Some people in the spiritual community believe that this includes extra-terrestrials and inter-dimensional beings but this depends on the experiences of each individual. Basically, the third density is our ego and physical experiences; the higher fourth and fifth densities and beyond are where we become more enlightened and spiritually aware. It can become rather confusing but there is a lot of information about it online for those who wish to delve further into the subject. Meditation helps us to raise our vibration in this way.

Meditation

Meditation is a very simple practice which can enhance your intuitive abilities. It is about quieting the mind to find the stillness amidst the chaos and the silence behind the chatter. The simplest and often most beneficial form of meditation is to sit with a straight back in a chair with your feet flat on the floor or cross-legged with a straight back with a cushion beneath you for support. A straight spine allows Universal energy to flow more efficiently. Your hands can be placed with their palms uppermost on your lap or you might like to put them in a prayer position with your thumbs level with your heart, like in a Reiki gassho meditation. Do what feels comfortable for you. Focus gently on breathing in through your nose and slowly out through your mouth. Do this a few times until you begin to relax then resume breathing normally, still remaining aware of your breath.

Allow yourself to be aware of your thoughts but do not hang on to them; let them go. Gradually, the more you become aware of thoughts arising, the longer the gaps between these thoughts will be. There's no need to get frustrated because you are having thoughts; they are perfectly natural. It is the moments where you can let them go and feel the silence that makes meditation so beneficial.

It is called meditation 'practice' because it takes practice to be able to quiet the mind. You may wish to set aside a dedicated place in your home to meditate or sit outdoors in a tranquil place, such as your garden or quiet place in a local park. When the mind is quiet, we are not thinking about our worries or troubles, we are letting go into that wonderful, tranquil place that is deep within ourselves where complete and utter peace resides.

Set aside a quiet time and place for this practice without distractions. This is time for you and is part of your self-care routine, so give it value and if you live with others, let them know that you are going to meditate and ask not to be disturbed.

It may take a while to get used to but the more you sit and meditate on a daily basis, the more beneficial it will become. Even if it is just five minutes per day at first, persevere and you will begin notice an improvement in your mental, physical and emotional state. The calmness and peace that you find in meditation transition through into every aspect of your life. You will feel a greater sense of stability and calmness, even in stressful situations.

When you start to feel that blissful feeling of peace during your meditation, allow it to rise up, do not resist. If you have not meditated before, it may seem unfamiliar to let go and trust that you are allowed to completely relax on every level. It is not like being asleep. It is a change in your brainwaves of a different kind. Your brain is aware of your surroundings but has slowed down to allow itself to rest. It is a bit like putting yourself on stand-by to realign your energy.

If you have lots of mind-chatter and keep thinking of your shopping list, allow those thoughts to pass by and fall away. This is the part of mediation practice that people find so difficult. Even if it takes a dozen times for those thoughts to stop interfering with your relaxation, do not give up. Make sure that you sit down every day and allow yourself that quiet time to build up your meditation practice. It takes discipline and commitment but it will be worth it when you finally feel that peaceful sensation I am talking about.

When you have got to the point where you come to understand why mediation is so beneficial, you will KNOW. It will also become clear when the benefits of your meditation practice begin to show through in other aspects of your life. It may take a few days, weeks or months but it'll happen. Even after you have established your meditation practice, there may still be days when you find it hard to settle but sit down anyway. Sometimes, the most beneficial meditations are the ones where you initially struggle to relax but if you persevere, your meditation may turn out to be very deep and tranquil.

During meditation you just have to let yourself BE. You do not have to DO anything. That is the whole point. It really is that simple. Meditation gives us peace, calmness, harmony, healing, balance and strength deep within that resonates through your entire energy field. Others will sense this in you as well and will feel relaxed and calm in your presence.

Journal 11.05.15

'I sat in the sunshine with our cat, Monty and completely switched off and felt truly connected with nature in my meditation. I felt a bit low this morning but I realised it's because I push myself to be doing something or feel that I should always be doing something else. I just need to let myself BE!'

Of course, there are other ways to meditate such as playing gentle, soothing background music or following guided mediations. There are also visualisations or you could join a meditation group. First of all though, I would recommend the simple method I have described above. This is one of the best ways to truly quiet your mind but some people may prefer other options. These achieve a similar state of mind to meditation, it depends on personal preference.

If sitting quietly really doesn't work for you, you could try walking in nature, painting, dancing or sitting on the beach listening to the waves crashing. There is more about finding your spiritual flow and channelling in the 'Finding Our Soul Purpose' section in the 'Emotions' chapter. This is also about developing your intuition and growing and flourishing as a person to discover what makes you truly happy.

You never know what you may discover once you have mastered the practice of just allowing yourself to 'be' and letting go into the silent space where we are one with the energy of the Universe, especially on a warm, sunny day:

Journal 15.03.17

'There is nothing quite like an outdoor meditation with the sun pouring down on you and birdsong all around. Monty lay at my feet as huge waves of relaxation and healing rushed through me, magnetising my feet to the ground. My sinuses suddenly cleared and my whole system was cleansed with beautiful light. Wow! Thank you, Universe. It's so good when you can let yourself go in a meditation like that. It's truly healing. I sat there 'recovering' for a few minutes afterwards with orgone spangling all around me. There are still some pinpoints of energy shimmering and popping on this page as I write. I'm so glad I sat there for long enough to relax. I wasn't sure if I would do at first. My third eye started gently buzzing once the waves of relaxation began.'

Spontaneous Meditations

Spontaneous meditations may occur whilst you are out and about once you begin to develop your intuition and strengthen your spiritual connection.

A sudden rush of energy is experienced that floods into every cell of your being and your feet become heavier, as if they want to remain flat on the floor to steady you whilst you connect to the energy and remain grounded.

It is similar feeling to a spiritual 'download' and has the sensation of a sudden rush of intuition starting to flow very strongly and switch on with a very definite burst. Your vibration is raised and your intuitive array expands into higher levels of consciousness, giving you an incredible sense of awareness of how everything around you is connected. You can feel that you are not alone as beings of light and those in spirit step forward to surround you with their love, light and wisdom.

When I feel that I need to ground myself and meditate, I do so if it is possible at the time, depending on where I am. It's not so good if I'm in the middle of a shopping centre! If I am in a quiet place or I can step to one side for a few minutes, I stand with my feet flat on the floor and allow the energy to flow and fill me up. If I can sit down and meditate, this is even better.

If there is nowhere quiet to go, it is still possible to go into a meditative state whilst moving around by becoming aware of the flow of energy and not resisting. Allow it to increase and flood you with joy and motivation to help you feel energised and inspired. Be creative in your endeavours with a sense of gratitude and adventure.

Establishing a Routine

Intuitive development is a life-long practice. When working with intuition, there does not come a day when you can hang up your hat and coat and say that you are done. Intuition won't let you! It is part of who you are.

Getting into a routine is important because developing your intuition takes patience, dedication and consistency. We all have busy lives but we should always make a special effort to find time for the things we love. Being intuitive is a way of life and embracing the magic of intuition can bring such joy and enlightenment. Doing these simple things on a daily basis will enhance your experience of life:

- Grounding and protection;
- Self-care;
- Meditation;
- Keeping an intuitive journal, including logging your dreams;
- Reiki self-treatments and precepts (if you are attuned to Reiki);
- Intuitive development exercises that you enjoy;
- Doing the things you love as often as you are able;
- Keeping an open heart and mind;
- Being your true self.

In addition to these daily practices, there are other spiritual practices that you can try to fit in when the opportunity arises to enrich your life, if these are what you enjoy or feel drawn to:

- Reiki practice with people and animals;
- Animal communication practice;
- Finding your soul purpose;
- Enhancing your spiritual awareness:
- Join spiritual groups locally and on social media that feel safe and supportive;
- Read widely and learn as much you can from spiritual teachers that you like;
- Educate yourself and others without being pushy;
- Find ways to promote your spiritual and intuitive work that feel right for you;
- Participate in spiritual practices to which you feel drawn to enhance your abilities;
- Ask the Universe to send kindred spirits your way, both human and animal;
- Be happy and share it around!
- Always work from your heart.

EMOTIONS

Working From Our Hearts

Evolution blessed humans with superior intellect but sadly, we often neglect to use it. So many people have lost touch with their hearts and have become so reliant upon external sources and technology to provide us with answers and entertainment. We rarely look inward and experience our own infinite world of our deep wisdom and intuition. We are the only species that can grasp abstract concepts and communicate using complex spoken and written language yet our intellect is so easily led astray by the temptations of greed and personal gain.

Our hearts and souls are vast yet most of us keep them tightly grasped to our chest for fear of losing them or of revealing too much of our true character underneath, exposing us to the danger of less scrupulous and underhanded human beings.

Having open hearts, minds and energy centres is perfectly normal yet so many people mock others with a strong spiritual connection or completely misunderstand them, expecting them to provide them with all of the answers to their future instead of taking responsibility for their own lives.

These intuitive abilities and open-hearted attitudes to life are all too often suppressed in our children who are required to conform to the expectations of society, mainly through fear of what others will think. Being naturally open about intuitive abilities is frowned upon by much of modern Western society, mainly because those in power would struggle to maintain control over whole generations who are fully awakened and intuitively aware. They would not be able to continue to amass their fortunes or hold onto power if they were to become transparent and exposed.

True power comes from within, connecting us to the truth and wisdom of the Universe.

The human race has changed and evolved so much, especially over the last few decades. We have advanced scientifically and technologically at a rate of knots yet we still wage war on one another and so many of our leaders are corrupt, intolerant and controlling. We cannot continue this way if we are to flourish and thrive as a species. We desperately need people to continue to awaken and see things as they truly are to raise the vibration of the planet with their new-found energy of peace, love, compassion and wisdom. There may never be perfection in this world but there most certainly does not need to be so much hatred and blatant disregard for the welfare of others and the planet we all share.

Evolved human beings are latecomers to planet Earth yet we somehow became the dominant species. We pride ourselves on our superior intellect yet only use a small portion of our intellectual capabilities, basing most of it on academic achievement, leaving out the most important parts that will bind us together and keep using moving forward as an amazing species with infinite potential.

Intelligence is about a great deal more than academic intellect; it is about the success of a species in its own right and its ability to achieve the right balance to ensure its continued to success by producing healthy off-spring and a good, sustainable living environment and stability for generations to come. If we cannot share and sustain our planet in the way that nature intended, our species is not going to last and we will take many other species down with us.

Intelligence encompasses our hearts, minds and spirits. We all need to have fun and enjoy a few luxuries but when this becomes a self-centred way of life, it can be to the detriment of others in the wider community and world as a whole. This is where our intuition needs to step-in. Our brains have an incredible capacity to do so many amazing things yet so many of us try to use our brains and minds as stand-alone commodities when they are actually part of a system that is based on so much more. We need to expand our repertoire to combine intuition, intellect and our loving, spiritual nature. It is these qualities combined that represent the true power of human nature.

Our superior intellect has helped the human race achieve many amazing things but it can also get in the way of us trusting our intuition and spiritual nature. We could not successfully function without our mind to guide us but it has a tendency to run away with itself, becoming lost in a place of fear and uncertainty. It can get into a state of over-thinking, over-analytical questioning and trying to place logical interpretation on information that should be kept raw in order for it to be helpful so it retains its authenticity and healing and spiritual qualities. This is why working from our hearts is vital when offering healing or being open to intuitive information. The mind can become paranoid and try to convince us that something is not logical and should be ignored but when we listen with our hearts and energetic bodies, it makes perfect sense.

Quieting the mind is essential for intuitive work. The mind is there to keep us rational and safe but we should try to avoid second-guessing intuition once we learn to trust it. Applying common sense and discernment is useful and often necessary in some situations, especially when dealing with a confrontational person or a nervous or aggressive animal. Once we learn to communicate on an energetic level, the information and impressions flow through our mind to make us consciously aware of them and we should 'say what we see' rather than allow the mind to apply analytical processing.

Effective communication is part of working from our hearts. When we only communicate using spoken or written language on a superficial level, it may mean that a lot of the substance and intention behind those words can be missed out or misinterpreted. Enriching our communication by using all of our senses on every level allows for a much deeper connection to give a fuller understanding and meaning to what we are saying and receiving. Having a conversation is about so much more than words. It is the sincerity and authenticity behind those words that give them ultimate power, making it unmistakable when we use communication that encompasses the whole of our being.

Working from our hearts and being loving and compassionate does not mean that we have to become a soft-touch or doormat for those who see us as vulnerable and easily taken advantage of. When we are strong, calm and balanced, we become much more perceptive and aware of those who may wish to do us harm or try to manipulate us to serve their own agenda. We may also feel the need to defend the vulnerable and less fortunate amongst us. This is the heart of a Spiritual Warrior. When we are strong, sure and wise within our own heart and soul, others are unable to move us from this powerful spiritual centre that we have worked hard to achieve. We do not need to use violence or aggression; we can simply remain strong and firm and use our wisdom, love and clarity to deal with any situation that may arise.

We do not have to put others down or judge harshly, we can simply choose to walk away from a situation or use words to state our own truth without harming others to make it clear that we will not be manipulated or bullied. When someone comes to us with toxic or negative energy, they will not be able to use this against us because we will not allow it. They will soon realise that they are getting nowhere. We are able to transmute or neutralise this unpleasant energy by simply being our true selves. Our energy may not be able to change another person but it can be enough to stop them in their tracks when they do not get the desired response and are unable to syphon our energy. A Spiritual Warrior is not someone to be messed with!

Working from our hearts gives us confidence and self-belief. When we work from our hearts, others will notice and sense that we are kind and approachable. This is especially true when working with animals. Being confident is about believing in yourself and your actions. Confident people easily engage the attention and respect of others because they seem unafraid to express themselves in an entertaining and intelligent way without the need to put others down or be critical. They are inspiring because they seem so knowledgeable, passionate and articulate in expressing themselves.

True confidence comes across as sincere, honest and genuine. You cannot fake genuine confidence. It is not cocky, conceited or attention-seeking. It is a beacon that ignites the fire in others and grows in intensity when positive feedback is received. A truly confident person does not need to walk all over others in order to be successful. They will be more inclined to encourage others to find their own sense of confidence and discover ways to lead a more fulfilling life. They are able to share their confidence in this way because they are comfortable with who they are on the deepest level. Real confidence is very different from arrogance or pomposity. These come from our ego but natural, flowing confidence comes from deep within our core. Confidence is an expression of who we are, how we feel, our values and what we believe in. It is a reflection of our true character.

Understanding Our Ego

The ego is our sense of identity as to who we are as a human being in this lifetime. When the ego is unbalanced, it can become controlling and may try to separate us from our true self by telling us that we are superior to and more worthy of success than others. It gives us an inflated sense of self-importance and casts judgements and pity on others. People who too readily listen to their ego often tread all over others to achieve material gains and higher positions in business or politics.

An over-inflated ego works on a superficial basis and not from a place of love. It is detached from our true self and when it takes hold, it can often bring about a sense of fear about losing everything that we start to see as important, such as power over others, material possessions and money, leaving us riddled with insecurity. A balanced ego is aware of its limitations and becomes a thriving cog in a healthy machine, working harmoniously with all of its counterparts.

Of course, we cannot become detached from our ego as it is our self-identity but we can become more aware of when our ego is trying to take over. As we become more spiritually aware, our ego will naturally flow into our new way of working from our hearts and become more humble. The ego centre is in our Solar Plexus. When we work on ourselves holistically on a physical, mental, emotional and spiritual level, our ego will become calm, balanced and not over-inflated, making us aware of who we are as an individual so that we can express this in a balanced and harmonious way. When we work from our hearts and 'Hara', our ego will remain healthy and form part of the cohesive system of who we truly are as an individual.

Our 'Hara' is an energy centre located just below our naval that runs through to the lower back, encompassing the Solar Plexus. It is a gateway for psychic energy. In Japan, it is believed to be the source of our vital spirit and consciousness. The Japanese refer to it as 'Tan-Den'. When working with intuition or energy healing, such as Reiki, the Hara plays a key part.

Even in daily life, we often feel our emotions here, such as when someone says hurtful words, it may feel like a kick in the guts. We also feel joy in our Hara and get the sensation of butterflies here when we fall in love. Keeping the Hara healthy is achieved through practices such as meditation, exercise, martial arts and other disciplines that require concentration and focus to quiet the mind. Our vital energy force of 'ki' should be encouraged to flow freely and remain strong in our Hara, giving us stability and balance. We are emotional creatures and the healthier and more emotionally stable we are, the more we can enjoy life.

Love, Fear and Everything In-between

The source of our emotion comes from one of two places – fear or love.

These are two sides of the same coin and each has their place in the Universe, creating balance. We cannot know love until we have experienced life without it, just as we cannot know heartache without having experienced love. Each experience in our life teaches us something to enable us to keep learning and growing so that we are better able to cope when difficulties arise.

Love is pure energy. It is associated with positive emotions such as joy, passion, acceptance, happiness, exhilaration, empathy, excitement, hope, pleasure and enthusiasm.

To love unconditionally means to expect nothing in return for the love that we feel and express. It requires complete trust and fearlessness. This love has no ending and comes from the infinite depths of our heart and soul. To give and receive unconditional love is a blissful and beautiful thing.

Unconditional love is eternal and infinite and is the purest, most selfless love that there is. Animals love in this way and it is a love that humans are capable of yet we have so many complexities that get in the way. When love has conditions attached, it is not pure love but a mere façade to fool you into giving someone what they need at that time.

Fear is designed as a response to keep us safe from the unfamiliar or threatening but it can become irrational and all-consuming. Feelings of fear can be a sign that something should be avoided at all costs yet it can also arise in situations that are similar to those we have been in before and can hold us back when, in the current instance, there is nothing to be afraid of and we miss out on life-changing opportunities because fear takes over.

Some of the emotions associated with fear include jealousy, envy, paranoia, hate, intolerance, frustration, sadness, despair, guilt, hopelessness and disappointment. These are often referred to as negative emotions or negative energy.

Fear has many pitfalls and when it starts to become our most dominant emotion, many problems can arise because fear can negatively affect the quality of our life. Depression and anxiety often have their roots in fear and it can be a long, hard climb back up to the light. Fear can be destructive when it is on-going, irrational and causes a distorted perception of life.

Emotions are energy in motion. Our thoughts, feelings and intuitive senses all have energy and influence our actions. Some emotions are very difficult to deal with and some people cannot cope with them. They may turn to outside influences such as drugs, alcohol or violence to dull the pain or anger they are feeling. Learning to respond appropriately to our emotions and understand them is much more beneficial than reacting on impulse in a way that we may later regret. Emotions need to be felt and expressed but not in a destructive way. Understanding our own emotions can be even more difficult than dealing with the emotions of someone else.

By developing our intuition, we empower ourselves to feel stronger from within and gain a greater sense of clarity and wisdom. Empowerment is very different from the concept of exerting power over others. Our own personal power gives us strength, confidence and connection with our true self. This is our inner power. Intuition and spiritual energy strengthen us on every level, especially in our aura and chakras, giving us greater stability and emotional balance. We are better placed to understand and deal with our emotions, both past and present, when we are in good health from the physical to the spiritual. We become empowered from within.

Seeking power externally is when we try to gain power over others, material possessions or situations. This is the pursuit of power through our ego and can be taken away from us when those external influences cease to exist or a competitor takes over. Our own personal power cannot be taken away from us. It is the essence of who we are. When we work on ourselves spiritually, we are empowering ourselves to become a better person from within, which will enable us to help others when we feel strong enough to shine our light into the world.

One of the strongest and most potent emotions of all is grief. This naturally flows from the experience of love and is a painful reminder that we are only suffering in grief because we are capable of love. It is a double-edged sword. Grief takes us on a journey of many complex and confusing emotions but it is a natural process and there are lots of people out there who can help us through it, along with the love and support of our family and friends. Guilt is also part of the grieving process, which can be hard to bear. It is often irrational because we have nothing to feel guilty about, which makes it even more painful and confusing.

Love makes us vulnerable and, depending on your life experience, it may be something that some people do their best to avoid. This may explain why some people are afraid to fall in love or even show love towards themselves. Just like grief, it is incredibly powerful and avoiding it can have dire emotional consequences as the person constantly battles with their feelings and may shut themselves away. Emotions are so complex because we experience love, fear and everything in-between and our brain often gets in the way of our hearts by over-analysing it all, rather than allowing our heart and intuition to lead the way.

Journal 02.01.17

'I was looking out of the window at all of the stars and asked what was life about when we all had to suffer so much pain! I received an immediate answer "through suffering we know love and through love, we know suffering. We cannot have one without the other. They are two extremes of the same scale and we cannot truly understand love without suffering."'

Empaths and Highly Sensitive People

Developing our intuition enables us to become more emotionally intelligent. Some people are Empaths, which means they feel the emotions of others as if they are their own. This can be confusing and draining for those who are unaware that the emotions they are experiencing do not belong to them. For developed Empaths, this ability is a gift because they are able to transmute negativity into love and radiate this out into the world. They are aware of what is theirs and what is not. Knowing whether or not you are an Empath is half the battle when it comes to maintaining your emotional and overall health and peace of mind.

No two Empaths are the same yet we share many similar traits and eccentricities. The most common Empath traits are as follows:

- Experiencing the emotions of others as if they are their own;
- Kind and compassionate towards others, especially the vulnerable;
- Deeply moved by scenes of sadness, joy, suffering and wonder in equal measure;
- Strong awareness of subtle and electromagnetic energy;
- Tendency to suffer from anxiety and depression and/or ailments such as irritable bowel syndrome, sensitive skin, chronic fatigue, fibromyalgia and digestive imbalances;
- The ability to discern the truth and easily tell if someone is lying;
- Intuitive, psychic, clairvoyant and mediumship abilities;
- Feeling the physical pain and discomfort of others as if they are their own;
- Strong connection with the energy of the Earth, moon, planets, weather, animals and other natural elements;
- Can feel the energy of people, animals, places and natural elements, often being able to pick up intuitive information such as there being spiritual activity in a location;
- Does not like being in enclosed man-made spaces or crowds;

- High sensitivity to light, sound, loud noises, static electricity, electrical equipment and generally has heightened physical senses;
- Feelings of being homesick, as if they don't belong on this planet;
- Very uncomfortable around inauthentic people, show-offs, bullies and 'fake' people;
- Energy is easily depleted if they do not take good care of their own needs;
- Must have time alone each day to recharge and enjoy the silence;
- Children and animals are drawn towards them, as are people who need a listening ear;
- Some Empaths may feel a stronger connection to certain things and are given an additional title. For example, if an Empath feels a close connection with animals, they are referred to as an Animal Empath. The following types also exist, to name but a few: Plant (Flora), Intuitive, Emotional, Claircognizant (Precognitive), Medical, Medium, Geomantic (connection to the Earth), Psychometric (Sensing things from objects) and Telepathic.

Empaths are often confused with Highly Sensitive People because many of their traits are similar. A Highly Sensitive Person (HSP) is acutely aware of myriad of things including sensing the emotions of others. They might also be highly reactive to sound, touch, light and electromagnetic radiation and dislike crowds and unnatural places. The level of sensitivity varies from person to person and life can become overwhelming for those who are not aware of why they feel things so intensely.

Being sensitive should not be misconstrued as some kind of weakness; it is a potential super-power! Sensing and feeling almost everything around us opens up our energetic connections in a way that can enrich our daily lives and enable us to reach out to help others but we must ensure that we take care of our own needs first and foremost so that our energy levels do not become depleted. We cannot take care of others if we are not feeling fit and well-balanced.

The main difference between an Empath and HSP is that an Empath has the ability to transmute negative energy into positive, loving energy whereas an HSP has a strong awareness of other people's emotions but does not feel them as their own and cannot usually transmute energy. HSPs are also often intuitive and may be referred to as HSiPs, with the 'i' standing for intuitive.

Empaths don't claim to be perfect or better than others. Life can be tough as an Empath, especially if you are unware as to why you often feel so overwhelmed. Empaths function differently to the vast majority of people and see the world with a finely tuned sense of perception. Once they learn to harness their abilities and practice robust self-care, an Empath can lead a wonderful and enriching life but they must always remember not to do too much that will burn out their delicate energetic system.

Some Empaths and HSiPs feel the need to put up energetic barriers or shields to keep negative energy away and cut off contact with people who seem to drain their energy. This may be a useful tool for some but it is often best to start by strengthening yourself from your spiritual core so that such deflection and preventative measures may not be necessary. This comes back to personal power, setting boundaries, self-care and protecting your energy. An

Empath needs to get to know their own energy so that they can become more aware of when they are receiving emotions and intuitive information from others. This can be done by spending lots of time alone in quiet relaxing places, meditating, eating healthily and getting plenty of sleep and moderate exercise. Self-care is essential for an Empath to remain healthy and be able to enhance their abilities to become empowered from within.

When we stand in our own power, we are filled with Universal energy and, as a being of light, our flow of energy will respond to transmute negative energy, not allowing it to affect us. We do not have to place ourselves in situations in which we are uncomfortable but sometimes we can experience growth by stepping out of our comfort zone and realising that something we are unsure about is not so bad after all. This can reduce our fear of unfamiliar situations and allow our confidence to grow. An empowered Empath or HSiP has the ability and strength to maintain their own health and energy levels whilst feeling strong enough to help others.

Be honest about how you REALLY feel in a situation – learn to feel your own truth and when something is right or wrong for you. What 'pings' back – pleasant, unpleasant, neutral? Is it dry, soft, raw, comfortable or uncomfortable? Don't be afraid to admit the truth to yourself, even if it's not what you want to hear. Recognising truth is very powerful; not to over-power others but for you to be discerning and steer clear of dishonesty and trouble.

As the abilities of an Empath develop, they may discover that they have a strong connection with something in particular, such as helping vulnerable people or conservation work. Many people who believe that they are an Empath, often have a variety of traits but the one Empath type that I can most relate to is the 'Animal Empath' or 'Fauna Empath'. Animal Empaths are particularly drawn to animals and have the ability to know how they are feeling and can communicate with them on many levels. I am also highly intuitive, which is why the best description of my qualities and abilities is an 'Intuitive Animal Empath'. Animal Empaths may also sense the mental state of an animal, feel incredibly comfortable and happy in their company and possess the ability to offer them healing. An Animal Empath is a natural 'animal-person' and may prefer the company of animals to other people because they relate to them so well.

Labels such as this are sometimes viewed as restrictive but they help others to understand what someone's strengths, interests and talents are. Giving someone or something a name or label in this way is not intended to place restrictions on them, it is more of a guideline and a means of communication about the services on offer. We are a verbal species and labels can help to point us in the right direction when we are looking for something, just like using tags on a website or social media. Labels aren't all bad, it depends how you use them.

Of course, a person does not have to be an Empath or HSiP in order to develop their intuition or communicate with animals but working with subtle energy on a deep level is greatly enhanced for people with these abilities. All humans have these abilities within them at different levels of development and intensity.

Although my main Empath type seems to be an Intuitive Animal Empath, I am really a combination of all of the types. It is difficult to fathom how someone could possess one particular set of abilities without the support of others. Being an Empath is a wonderful thing but a good self-care routine is vital! Quite a few Empaths seem to be introverted and struggle to find authentic friends who are on the same wavelength. Many of them have a personality type starting with 'INF…'. This doesn't mean that all Empaths are introverts but this does appear to be a common trait.

My personality type is an INFP-T (mediator). I am not usually one to be drawn to tests to find out such things but after INFJ kept coming up on social media groups and I became curious as to whether or not this might apply to me. Some elements of it did but after doing a personality test, the results came back telling me that I am Introverted iNtuitve Feeling Perceiving personality type (introverted feeling with extroverted intuition). There are around 4% of these types and our main traits are that we are genuinely caring, good listeners and like to avoid conflict. We can be hard on ourselves and tend to be perfectionists but also laid back unless our value system is threatened, in which case we become passionately defensive. We choose friends wisely and like to make others feel at ease.

One particular trait pleased me considerably. INFP-T types are usually talented writers but rarely give ourselves credit, even when we do wonderful things! I hope this book is one of those wonderful things. We are good at defining and expressing ourselves in the written word. What a relief; I'm glad I haven't written a book for nothing! In all of this though, the 'T' stands for turbulent which can mean that we are self-conscious perfectionists who are sensitive to stress and hide away when things seem overwhelming. It all makes perfect sense!

Negativity and Dark Nights of the Soul

There will be days when we feel down or depleted in energy. This is only natural when we are spending our lives in a physical body. When negativity seems to take hold and we cannot shake it off, we should start by looking to discover why we may be feeling this way. This is part of embracing our shadow-self so that we learn from our feelings, both good and bad. Such dark periods when we feel low are often referred to as 'dark nights of the soul'. They will pass and we should aim to return to a neutral place and not expect to be ecstatically happy every day of our lives, which would be nice but it's not realistic!

Journal 26.04.16

'I'm sure that depression and anxiety are part of the lives of most, if not all, empaths and light workers. It's as if our human state and logical mind fight against who we truly are sometimes.'

When we manage our expectations and let go of control to trust in the process of the Universe, everything makes a lot more sense. Of course, that does not mean that we should become reckless or irresponsible but that we should trust that life is a learning process and the Universe will only give us the things that we can deal with. The main principle behind letting go and learning to trust is to allow yourself to just 'be' and go with the flow of life without resistance. We cannot control everything and taking a more relaxed approach can help us to release tension and see the things we have been missing when we were holding back.

Worrying is something that most of us suffer from to a greater or lesser degree. Allowing ourselves to worry is futile because we deplete some of the energy we need to live in the present moment by projecting it into a future event or outcome over which we have little or no control. I can't count the times I have dreaded something and spent many sleepless nights worrying about but when it came to it, everything went smoothly and all of that time and energy that I spent worrying could have been used much more effectively elsewhere.

Projecting our energy ahead of time creates a negative feedback loop with something that has not happened yet and is often based on irrational fears and our own anxieties about what may or may not happen. It is hard to get out of the habit of worrying but by focussing on the present moment and remaining open to calmness and positivity, we can relieve ourselves of worry. Meditation and healing therapies that bring about balance and harmony can help us to achieve this, as can indulging in doing the things we love.

Our past experiences and mental constructs are what we are familiar with but they can become distorted into negativity when we are low in energy or feeling anxious. Worry feeds on this so we need to learn to nip it in the bud. If you feel worry rising up, take a step back in order to stop the cycle before it has begun. Do something simple such as having a hot drink, going for a brisk walk, sitting outdoors for a while or, better still, meditate. Anything to get you back into the present time and break the toxic loop of worrying. Focussing on your breathing and calming yourself down will help with this process. Worrying is a different kettle of fish to anxiety though, which we will explore in the next section. Worrying tends to be about something specific, whereas anxiety is often all-encompassing and irrational.

Journal 26.10.16

'I've started to view the ever elusive 'answer' as a continuous work in progress that is to be enjoyed. I'm allowing the energy and passion to flow up through me and for me to not look for it externally but still do lots of research and seek out inspiration that resonates with me. It's a journey but still a process of self-healing. Instead of my logical mind looking for something tangible to cling to in order to make me feel secure, I need to let go of fear and let the Universe bring things to me – to relax and to trust.'

Working from a place of love and gratitude for the greatest and highest good gives us the strength and compassion to help others but this can seem out of reach when we feel low and depleted in energy. During dark nights of the soul, self-care is all the more important. Spend some quiet time with yourself, do the things you love and indulge in nurturing activities. Be kind to yourself. When others know that you love and respect yourself, they are more likely to extend the same courtesy to you instead of taking you for granted.

'Negative' emotions are there to teach us and keep us on the right path. They must be acknowledged and understood. Suppressing emotions closes us off and causes energetic blockages that can lead to illness and dis-ease. We have to learn to deal with them appropriately and find out what they can teach us. Dark nights of the soul help us to better understand ourselves.

There will always be days when we are in a bad mood or feel as though we hate the world. We are complex sentient beings and this becomes magnified as we become more spiritually aware. It does not make us perfect or untouchable. Ignorance, inconsideration and a lack of manners are my pet hates. Most days, I can let them go and don't allow other people to get me riled, yet on other days I turn the air blue and feel myself seething. This often happens when I'm driving so I have to calm myself down and imagine that another driver is not really behind me, driving far too close to my rear bumper! I also tend to shout at politicians on the telly. I try to see if it is my own feelings and behaviour being reflected and if this is the reason why I get angry. I'm a lot calmer than I used to be but we must all remember to give ourselves a break and not expect ourselves to be permanently brimming over with joy. Turning hate into laughter is often the best way to process these feelings. It's hard to stay angry when you're laughing!

For the vast majority of us, life is a balancing act. It is cyclical, fluctuating and peppered with varying degrees of self-doubt, anxiety, depression, joy, euphoria and days with a mixed bag of all of these extremes, especially for the highly sensitive amongst us. One day, we might feel like the world is crashing down and the next we might feel amazing. We should not allow others to set the bar on our expectations by placing rules upon our spiritual awakening or intuitive journey. Living in the moment and acknowledging how we truly feel is the best way to approach life.

Be aware of your inner world, moods and feelings. Do not chastise yourself for feeling down, cynical or jaded. Your bad mood will lift and as you develop along your path, you will get to know why you may be feeling this way and learn to take a step back and stop expecting so much of yourself.

Daily self-care, spiritual practices and keeping an open heart and mind will help you through. We cannot expect to live in a permanent state of euphoria but we should not have to suffer by feeling as though life is just too much on a daily basis. Depression and anxiety can often creep up on us and we should not have to cope alone. Reach out for help if darkness won't release its grip on you. You'll be surprised how many people will rally round in support.

Some people believe that we have to be 'fully healed' in order to help others but we are all works in progress and our life experiences change us on a daily basis. As long as we are looking inward at helping ourselves, we are becoming more self-aware and healing on every level as things come to the surface to be acknowledged and healed. None of us wake up one morning and think 'Oh, wow. I'm fully healed'. That is completely unrealistic, especially for those who have suffered emotional trauma or abuse. If we waited until we were fully healed before we started helping others, we would never help anyone.

I really do not like it when some spiritual teachers insist that we should find a place of peace and happiness and imply that we will feel that way, day in, day out. This sets people up for disappointment and feelings of despair when they continue to be typically human and still sometimes feel down, lost and alone. It is very rare for someone to suddenly be filled with joy every second of the day and night.

Life can throw all manner of challenges our way and even on a good day when everything is going right, we can still feel miserable for no apparent reason and the slightest thing irritates us or leaves us feeling exhausted. Yes, that's right - even the spiritually aware can get depressed. They just experience less of it and tend to spring back more easily because they are aware of how to overcome it and find a brighter place. Depression and anxiety can sneak up on you and take over so being aware of the warning signs is vital for good health.

Depression and Anxiety

We are often led to believe that depression and anxiety should be crushed, squashed and got rid of, which is not very helpful. Their actual purpose is to tell us something. They are part of an alert system to tell us when we are not looking after ourselves properly, are failing to see to our own needs or sacrificing part of ourselves in favour of others. The first port of call when such feelings arise should be a visit to your doctor. It is important to seek medical help initially but doctors do not have all the answers. Dealing with depression and anxiety involves a long process of self-healing and self-discovery but the support of professionals may still be required to enable someone to fully understand how to get back on their feet without their problems getting worse.

When we suppress our true feelings and desires, ignore our own needs or refrain from doing something that we long to do, it can make us miserable and anxious. The same thing can happen when we take on too much and feel overwhelmed, yet we continue to take on more and more pressure without any regard for our own well-being.

It isn't always easy to look on the bright side of life and laugh things off. Life can be very difficult, especially when you have been through challenging times or the pain of losing loved ones. Even the strong and resilient amongst us can suffer from depression and anxiety. When things get tough, we no longer feel safe and secure and some emotions are difficult to handle.

Depression and anxiety seem to be rife yet there is still a stigma attached to them. Is it any wonder that so many people suffer from these debilitating issues? We expect far too much of ourselves and life can often be cruel. When fear begins to consume us and we are unable to escape from its clutches, depression and anxiety can take hold.

Feeling a bit low is very different than suffering from depression, although this may be where it starts if it goes on for any length of time. Depression is all-consuming and often comes in waves, some less bearable than others. When a person is suffering from depression, they rarely recognise this within themselves. Their emotions and sense of self-awareness may have become clouded over as daily life starts to seem hard to bear. Even when a person finally realises what is going on, they may find it difficult to seek help and confide in others because of that mother of all pests, yet again – fear!

There is nothing worse than when someone says to you "Depressed? What have you got to be depressed about?" as if you have a choice in the matter. That is the main problem; it is not usually ABOUT anything in particular. That is why the symptoms can be so hard to shift. Pinpointing where the problems started can be very difficult as it is often a set of circumstances or series of stressful events that cause deep internal distress which bubble under the surface and result in feelings of a loss of control and helplessness. There is so much ignorance about depression and anxiety that the prospect of reaching out for help can seem terrifying.

We are all different and being afflicted by depression and anxiety is a very individual thing. There is often more than one definitive cause. They may be a result of past trauma, chronic stress, abuse or caused by a physical problem within the brain. In many cases though, these two very unpleasant things are trying to tell us something and we need to take notice and listen. Suppressing them will only make them shout louder and may cause further issues to arise.

I am not a medical professional but unfortunately, I do know an awful lot about anxiety and depression from my own personal experience. Seeking help from a doctor takes a great deal of courage, as does admitting to yourself that you are not coping with the rigours of life. Telling friends and family can seem daunting and telling your employer all the more so but bottling things up can be even worse. Once the pressure builds up too much, a critical point is reached and by then, you have become a big, hot mess. Telling someone is the starting point to release the pressure and know that you are no longer suffering alone.

Getting support from a doctor may be of some help but the majority of work comes from within. Learning to manage anxiety and depression is a very steep curve. You may be offered anti-depressant and/or anti-anxiety medication. These can ease the symptoms in the short-term but in the long-term it is much better to discover the reasons behind depression and anxiety so that you can pull yourself out of the vicious cycle from which there seems to be no escape.

Counselling is another form of therapy that may be on offer but it usually involves a long wait to be seen. This can seem like an eternity when you feel as though world around you is crumbling.

Cognitive behavioural therapy may also help but may not always be offered through your doctor.

I sought help for depression in my early twenties. I felt uncomfortable about taking medication so I opted for counselling. My first two sessions consisted of me sobbing and not really making much sense, although this was an immense relief. I attended a couple more sessions and found them helpful but I was much more at ease counselling myself once I got the hang of it. We all have different ways of coping with things and if I can do something my own way, I will. I still give myself regular counselling sessions and enjoy breaking things down so that I can gain a clearer understanding of why I'm feeling a certain way about something.

Depression and anxiety are often lumped together as being similar things but they are not, although they can be related to the same root cause.

For me, depression is like a thick, oozing black sludge that fills my entire being, leaving me lethargic, unable to think straight or complete basic tasks. It is has a low, toxic vibration. Depression affects your whole entire being, not just your mind. Your body becomes a dead weight and your thought processes turn to mush.

Mental fogginess can be a real problem. It can be a simple thing such as turning around to do something in the kitchen then a split second later, it's gone. You have absolutely no idea what you turned around for. The thought has vanished to that place in the ether where all of the missing socks go, along with all of the other thoughts you once had that disappeared because you didn't write them down. So, as you stand there with your mouth open like a salmon, trying to figure it out, nothing comes to you. It is a complete and utter mental fog. Of course, the thought does come back to you eventually; usually when you are halfway along the motorway with no access to a pen. I can easily sit down and write a thousand words but remembering why I opened the kitchen cupboard can be a challenge in itself. This can bring even further feelings of despair and exhaustion.

The fortunate ones amongst us who do not suffer from this debilitating issue often completely misunderstand and think that someone with depression is just being mardy and seeking attention. This is why there is a stigma attached. There is no blood, gore or pimples with depression; it is an invisible illness that takes you down from the inside out. How could anyone really understand unless they have been there?

It is not simply a case of feeling a bit blue; it is like being knocked sideways by a freight train, closely followed by a beating with a meat tenderiser then being left for dead in the gutter with vultures circling overhead. That is what depression is like. That is how it feels. It is not just a mental issue; it also causes physical pain, usually all over the body, especially in the joints, muscles and digestive system, which is often accompanied by severe fatigue and a battle to string your thoughts together. It feels as though depression fills your veins and essential organs with thick, toxic sludge. You long to sleep yet there is an on-going battle with insomnia and a feeling of being uncomfortable in your own skin.

How are you supposed to lead a 'normal' life feeling like that? How are you meant to rationalise anything or find the strength to get up and face the outside world? I don't know, but people do. Life has to go on but some days you feel as if you are a giant boulder with spindly legs. It's exhausting.

Anxiety on the other hand has a high, buzzing, irritating vibration. It is irrational, annoying and sends wobbles of worry, panic and nausea through your gut, making you feel out of control, frantic, freaked out and exhausted. It can go on for days, weeks or months with occasional fits of shaking and panic attacks over stupid things like stressing about emptying the bins or finding two crumbs on the floor after you've cleaned up. The only way to combat it is to step aside, find a way to ground yourself and just breathe. Grab hold of your rational mind if you can and force it to take a look at exactly what it is that made you feel anxious in that given moment and, if you possibly can, laugh at it. I get anxious over such silly things; it's ridiculous but also hideously debilitating. If you have an ounce of rationality available, insist that it comes along to help you to eradicate the anxiety that is rising up in that moment. It won't always work, but when it does, anxiety gets a slap in the face and backs down.

Anxiety has many forms from an outright debilitating panic attack to a small, annoying repetitive thought that burrows its way into your brain, keeping you awake at night, filling every fibre of your being with an intolerable disturbing inability to relax that makes you want to scream 'make it stop!'. It often comes in waves and has many different triggers, whereas depression creeps up on you slowly but can then suddenly lift, leaving you wondering what it was all about. Relieving yourself of as many stressors as possible and curling up in a cocoon are sometimes the only way to let it pass. Even then it can take an excruciatingly long time. It is possible to get on top of these feelings before they escalate once you become aware of them building up.

When you are in the depths of depression or the clutches of anxiety, it is very difficult to apply any kind of rational thought or implement a plan to snap into happy-mode. Most of the time, you do not even realise what is happening for quite some time. Managing the issues and being aware of the early signs are essential.

Self-acceptance is the starting point for self-love and feeling worthy of your own self-care. Do not beat yourself up if you are not ecstatically happy every day. Forgive yourself for being a vulnerable human being with a complex and sensitive heart and mind. Give yourself a hug!

Self-care and self-love can seem so out of reach because feeling guilty is part of depression. I am usually the first to step forward to help in a crisis yet when it comes to my own needs, I feel guilty. We feel guilty because we do not feel worthy. This loop must be broken. Start small and think big in terms of looking after yourself but always manage your expectations. You do not want disappointment to come along and join the party. It is not good company! Take it a day at a time. That's what I do. Every second of our lives is precious; as we all are. You will feel better tomorrow. It is a brand new start. Make the most of the good days and enjoy the simple things.

One of the kindest things you can do for yourself when you are feeling low and overwhelmed is to give yourself permission to have a damn good cry. Sob your socks off and let it all out. I find it particularly hard to let go and release everything but our eyes are designed to produce tears and not allowing them to flow causes us further damage. There is no need to have a public meltdown, choose a time when you are alone in private and allow your feelings to come to the surface. You must let them out and release them. This is part of the healing process of life. Crying is healthy but if you are crying an awful lot all of the time, get some extra support. We all need help when we feel vulnerable and delicate.

The best way to manage depression and anxiety is to deal with them when you are feeling moderately good and have some energy so that you can put measures in place to recognise the signs and not allow yourself to have a sudden slump or head straight into a wall of panic.

The aim is to find a happy medium in which you feel calm, rational and positive. Those of us who are prone to depression and anxiety are easily overwhelmed and should be strict about our self-care routine. We are much less likely to have bad days if we are as healthy as possible.

When I feel a cloud of gloom approaching, I stop what I am doing and begin to question my current life situation and goals or even what I am going to be doing over the next couple of hours. I feel my way into the darkness and see what is rattling around in there. Am I avoiding a certain task? Am I feeling vulnerable because I am in pain? Am I hiding from the truth about something important? Have I been putting something off that needs to be dealt with? Am I having irrational thoughts about something that is not really going to be that bad? Am I tired?

Being kind and honest with yourself is essential here. Take a break and do something gentle and simple that you enjoy. Put off anything that is not essential to bring your stress levels down. Go for a long walk, a jog or simply have an indulgent hot bath or sit on the sofa reading a book. Take a few days off work and do nothing. You really do deserve it!

Depression and anxiety throw many conflicting emotions at us – guilt, self-doubt, confusion, frustration, anger, blame, hate, deep guttural feelings of sadness, despair, hopelessness; the list of negative feelings could go on forever, yet when dawn breaks the following morning, you may feel completely different. It does get better but there will always be bad days, just fewer of them.

The key to maintaining a happy equilibrium comes back to self-love and self-care. Do not feel guilty for looking after number one. We are entitled to our health and happiness. When depression and anxiety come calling, action must be taken. A whole life review may be required with some drastic changes or maybe something as simple as dishing out responsibilities more fairly amongst friends and family to relieve some of the burden. Do not allow yourself to feel responsible for taking on other people's crap. If they are trying to push guilt onto you, recognise it and energetically refuse it. Stay strong. Being honest with yourself is essential. Your loved ones would not want you to struggle on alone and will gladly help once they know you are suffering. It's surprising how many people are suffering in just the same way as you when you open up to them. Knowing you are not alone can make a huge difference.

The Self-saboteur and Leaving Your Comfort Zone

Our comfort zone is not always a great place to be. It can make us feel stuck, frustrated and unable to move forward. It may sometimes seem easier to stay there but we can only learn and grow by taking on new challenges. When we plan on leaving our comfort zone there is one main problem we should all be aware of - the self-saboteur!

The self-saboteur sneaks up on you from behind and tells you that you're not good enough. This mischievous little pest is related to self-doubt and fear. It likes nothing better than to hold you back and keep you in your comfort zone, getting nowhere fast.

The most effective solution is to tell it to 'shut up!' and ignore it. It won't be expecting that! Once the self-saboteur has been sent away to sit quietly in the naughty corner, you can begin to experiment with stepping out of your comfort zone towards happiness.

Learning to recognise your intuitive voice, rather than the voice of the self-saboteur is vital. Intuition is encouraging and positive, whereas the self-saboteur constantly nags and reminds you of your weaknesses. It's like a little devil sitting on your shoulder. Keep ignoring it and you will soon start to rise to a higher vibration.

Once you know your limitations, you can push the boundaries a bit further each time you set out to try new things and enjoy life. Happiness is different for everyone. A feeling of relaxed contentment is blissful to me, especially when I have a clear head and feel well. Finding a happy medium is a realistic goal. Life is about achieving balance in order to create a stable base to hold you firm and steady in a crisis and allow you to fully experience joy when it comes along.

Finding Our Soul Purpose

Our soul purpose is to discover the one or many things that bring us true joy and a sense of effortless flow, in which time has no meaning as we are swept away in the pure delight of whatever it is we are doing. It is the purpose of our soul in this lifetime. This could be something as simple as reading, writing, art, dancing, music, running or spending time with animals. It could be our job, studies or hobby. If it brings us joy, we should do more of it, providing that it does not harm or hinder anyone else. It is a blissful feeling when we do things that are aligned with our soul purpose and unfortunately, the opposite is also true. Even though this may seem like a bad thing, it can actually be helpful in the long-run.

We all have an inner child, which is our creative, curious and inquisitive inner being. When we nurture and respect our inner child, life becomes more exciting and playful. Not in a childish way but in an uplifting and creative way. Listening to our inner child allows us to be more open to possibilities and explore the things we love that nourish our soul and enable us to grow as a person. We started our lives as a child; a time when we were unafraid to express our innermost needs and desires. We can rekindle this exploratory time and once more experience a deep sense of wonder.

It is our true nature to be curious, creative and vibrant and it is also important to remember not to take ourselves too seriously. Laughter and a robust sense of humour are essential to get us through the rigours of life. There is a big difference between being adventurous, playful and child-like than being self-centred and child-ISH. We must nurture, respect and listen to our inner child who may seem upbeat and light-hearted but can also be fierce and brave when we may be unsure about what we really want. Our inner child can become our best friend when we need an extra push in the right direction.

Creative flow can be a very spiritual and cathartic experience in which we lose track of time and we are completely absorbed in what we are doing, as if we are receiving energy and focus from a higher source. In these moments, we are about as close to our soul purpose as we can get. Whether it is dancing, reading, writing, music, cycling, healing, drawing, painting, flying a plane, skydiving or any other activity in which we are excited to engage, this is the feeling that we are searching for.

It's as if we are channelling our creative flow and receiving downloads of exactly what we need at that time. We are in the zone with our true passion, which may change over time or evolve to a whole new level. We may even start a business based on doing the thing that we love, just as I did back in 2011.

Our soul purpose is what we chose to come here to do in our lifetime. Discovering this is not always easy and whilst some people seem to be aware of their soul purpose from a very young age, others may take a whole lifetime to even get close to it. Discovering our soul purpose can be a difficult journey with lots of pitfalls, disappointments and set-backs but all of these are to keep us moving along the right track and not get distracted by things to which we are not really suited. Life as a responsible adult can be difficult as we are faced with having to earn money to put a roof over our heads. We may become stuck in a job that literally feels 'soul destroying' because it is out of alignment with our true soul purpose.

Becoming aligned with our soul purpose is vital for our health and well-being on every level. Spending our days doing things out of a sense of duty, guilt or perceived necessity can drain our energy and make us feel depressed, hopeless and trapped in a cycle of doing the same mundane or stressful thing every day. There will come a point when this is all too much and change HAS to take place, even if this means that we may fall ill, yell at our boss, get fired or have a big row with our partner.

Journal 13.01.17

'Yesterday when I was making dinner, I received a download that said "everything that you love is an expression of your soul. Forcing yourself to do things that do not align with your true soul purpose can bring you heartache, sap your energy and result in poor health". Very true!'

This crisis point can be a catalyst for change. It is eye-opening and although it may seem painful and almost intolerable at the time, it is the Universe giving us a very strong nudge in the right direction. We must start to look for the truth within ourselves, gain a sense of self-worth and learn to place value on our own happiness. As we begin to recover from the experience that has brought about this change, we can start to grow as we are no longer able to tolerate things that do not bring us joy. If anything is not taking us in the right direction, we recognise this deep within ourselves and may also feel it on a physical level, such as tiredness, a headache or stomach pains.

We begin a process of 'soul searching', which is vastly different for everyone. There are infinite variables as to what will make each and every person happy. Finding balance and harmony in our lives is key, even if the journey is sometimes rough. If we can discover a place of positivity within ourselves to guide us and brighten our outlook on life, we take a step into the realm of manifestation and attracting the things into our lives that will take us closer to our soul purpose. This may not always be a full-blown spiritual awakening but it can often start us on a journey of looking for greater fulfilment. Many people are already aligned with their soul purpose and indulge in it every day.

Our soul purpose is not always one definite thing. We are so often conditioned to believe that we have to settle into a steady job or trade and dedicate ourselves to it for the rest of our working lives. This may suit some folk but it doesn't help those who thrive on the excitement of constant change and fresh challenges. Some of us may be accused of drifting and flitting between jobs but spiritual, sensitive and creative people are often easily bored. This boredom can seem excruciatingly painful because there may be a deep longing in our heart to move on and we easily feel trapped and confined. This type of person has to take what they need and move on to their next point of interest to keep them motivated and prevent them feeling depressed or bogged down.

If you are not sure where to start in finding your soul purpose, the following exercise may be useful. It can be expanded to encompass anything you like, from your career aspirations to everyday life, your interest and hobbies. It's ultimately about what sets your heart on fire!

I am a huge fan of lists, mind maps and putting things down on paper, which can provide clarity, healing and a sense of direction. If you have no idea where to start in finding your soul purpose, start with two simple lists – the things you love and the things you dislike. These do not have to be a long list of friends, family and pets; although I'm sure you love many of them. What you are aiming for is the small things of which you may not be aware that bring you moments of joy throughout your day. Putting them all in one place can give you great insight into your own true nature. This can be a starting point for greater expansion into deeper things.

From enjoying the smell of lavender to hang gliding on a cloudless day, writing a list of the things you love can include anything and it is unique to you. If you love it, write it down. If you love staring at the stars, watching old movies on TV or immersing yourself in a nice cappuccino, write it down. This list will be endless and you can keep adding to it. If you're not sure where to start, please see the list below of some of the things that I love in no particular order (some are rather random!):

- Peace and quiet;
- Birdsong, especially first thing in the morning as I'm waking up;
- Croissants and cappuccino;
- Shopping trips with my family;
- Walks in natural places;
- Watching fish swimming around;
- Stroking soft fur;
- The warmth of the sun on my face when it's not too hot;
- The smell of freshly cut grass;
- Cats;
- My family enjoying a meal that I've cooked;
- Music and how it makes me feel;
- Hugging;
- Giving Reiki to animals;
- Giving Reiki to myself;

- Spiritual gift shops, especially ones that sell crystals and wolf figurines;
- Writing;
- Comfy jumpers;
- The sound of expensive sports cars, especially Ferraris;
- Driving with loud 1980s music on;
- Watching my cat have a wash;
- Crisp Autumn air;
- The smell of bonfires;
- Laughing at old British comedy shows on TV;
- Peeling carrots;
- Taking photos of animals and unusual things;
- Keeping a journal;
- Watching the world go by;
- Hot air balloon rides;
- Taking off in a plane (I love the acceleration);
- Meeting a person or animal for the first time and feeling an immediate connection.

I thought I'd better stop there or I'd fill an entire book!

Now for the part that may be a little more difficult in some ways or perhaps not for some of us – writing a list of the things we dislike. I have used the word dislike as opposed to hate because the word 'hate' is a bit strong!

This list doesn't have to be gruesome, heart-wrenching or painful. It can be approached in the same way as writing down the things that you love. Keep it simple and honest. What do you dislike with a passion? What repulses you? Snakes? Rude people? Badly made sandwiches? Annoying sounds? Not being able to finish a project or assignment because you no longer have the motivation? If you don't like it, write it down. You may find that it's even harder to stop writing this list than writing down the things that you love once you get started! To help you along, here is a list of some of the things that I dislike:

- Doing the cleaning (because I usually get obsessive once I start!);
- Ironing;
- Feeling obliged to do something that I really don't want to do;
- People tapping their fingers or chewing loudly;
- Politicians;
- Modern music;
- Having to rush around when I'm not in the mood;
- Custard;
- Egg custard;
- Trifle or anything else that reminds me of custard;
- Seeing bones protruding out of the skin;
- Clowns;
- Morons;
- Tailgaters or people who shouldn't be on the roads because they are too terrified;
- Walking dogs in heavy rain;
- Nasty people;
- Bullies;
- Ignorance;
- Packets that won't open;
- Dishonesty;
- Constant swearing;
- Show-offs and big heads;
- People who are cruel to animals or other people;

- Participating in competitive sports;
- Strange noises in the night;
- Walking into cobwebs;
- Itchy jumpers;
- Gardening;
- Spam calls and emails;
- Things that make me jump;
- Crowds;
- Rooms without windows;
- Glass lifts;
- Not getting a reply from someone when I need an urgent answer;
- Being ignored;
- Lack of manners;
- People who don't listen;
- My body being much older than my mind thinks it is!

This exercise should help you to identify the activities that raise your vibration and those that leave you feeling drained. Finding your soul purpose does not have to be rushed. Ultimately, it is about enjoying the moment that you are in and discovering a sense of blissful flow.

As you add to your list and do more of the things you love, you may find that everything starts to fall into place and synchronicity becomes more frequent. The Universe will ping back at you whatever you give out and the happier and more fulfilled you feel, the more likely it is that you will receive hints and nudges that take you in the right direction – towards finding your soul purpose. Nothing is set in stone and life is fluid and flexible. There is no need to be pulled into drama and tales of woe. Be your true self and value the beautiful soul that you are.

Take from these list making exercises whatever feels right for you. You could turn them into mood boards and cut out pictures or take photographs of the things you love that seem to have a recurring theme. Let your creativity flow and express how you truly feel. The happier you feel, the less likely you are to be affected by negativity and the things that you dislike. Let go of expectation and see what happens. Feel the freedom of being who you truly are, starting with the little things. After a while, they can make a big difference.

There is no shame in following your heart, the rhythm of your own energy and creative flow. This is the very thing that drives us toward our soul purpose and could even be our soul purpose itself, which changes, fluctuates and remains fluid and adaptable over time. We should remain buoyant, impulsive and fired-up if this connects us with our true self and happiness. Living your life without embodying your own passion is not really living at all. Be unapologetically who you are!

Synchronicity and the Law of Attraction

When we send out positivity, we attract it back. This is the law of attraction – like attracts like. If we have a negative, downbeat outlook, we will almost certainly attract or feel drawn to things that are not good for us, such as dead-end jobs, abusive relationships, addictive substances, various illnesses and apparent 'bad luck'. Some people get stuck in a cycle of this way of thinking and feeling. It can become addictive because it feels familiar and safe to be the victim. Not that all bad things and situations that come our way are what we deserve but our thoughts have energy and when we are unhappy and wallowing in misery, our vibrations become very low.

Negativity can become a self-fulfilling prophecy in which we expect bad things to happen and when they do, it reinforces our belief that life is not good and there is no way out, because it is the way life always seems to be for us. We can become consumed by self-pity.

If we can get back up to at least a neutral way of feeling that is calm and level-headed, we can begin to work on raising our vibration high enough to feel positive and happy again. This starts with the little things that make us feel good and building up to do more and more of them until we are on a roll with attracting the things we desire and enjoy. This is hard to imagine when we are down in the doldrums but everyone deserves to be happy and connected to who they truly are on a soul-level.

Do we mentally and emotionally create our own illnesses, diseases and injuries? I believe that sometimes we do but not always. The better we look after ourselves, the less likely we are to become ill. Dis-ease can manifest itself in our aura and work its way in to our physical bodies if we do not acknowledge and deal with our emotions and negative thought patterns but other things such as injuries caused by external factors are another matter entirely. There are an infinite number of timelines and consequences brought about by the billions of other people on our planet, how can we possibly bring all of the things that happen to us onto ourselves? There are timelines converging upon us with every split second but maintaining a positive, healthy outlook on life and looking after ourselves will certainly improve our own lives. There are also natural disasters and accidents over which we have no control.

Manifesting what we want and need in our lives happens gradually over time and the Universe sends us uncanny little clues and pointers along the way. Simple things such as a chance meeting with an old friend who has the same interests as you, seeing the same topic keep coming up on the TV and in magazines until you have to take notice of it and then finding that the local community centre is running classes on it. Through the power of intention and visualising what we would like in our lives as if it is already there, we can create a flow of positivity to make this a reality.

This is similar to the story of how I discovered Reiki or, should I say, how Reiki discovered me. Reiki was first of all mentioned by a colleague when I worked in an office. A year or so later, I kept feeling warm energy building up in my hands whenever someone was ill or seemed distressed. I then kept seeing Reiki mentioned in books and magazines, it was on TV, I saw an article about it, kept hearing people mention it and eventually my daughter brought home a leaflet about Reiki classes at her school. When I rang the lady to find out more, it turned out that we already knew each other from a chance meeting a few years prior. It was a series of constant nudges until I took notice!

Synchronicity was the name given to this phenomenon by Carl Jung, a Swiss psychiatrist and psychoanalyst who had a fascination with this subject, as well as other intriguing intuitive matters such as dreaming.

Journal 13.04.16

With reference to the pain and discomfort in my neck and having to let go of three dog walking clients that were making my problem worse:

'I'm feeling that my problem has been sent to me as a help to nudge me onto the right path, enabling me to do more animal communication and stop me walking dogs that are too much for me.'

Letting go of expectations and discovering the excitement of uncertainty allows us to flourish and trust in the processes of the Universe. It works for our greatest and highest good when we learn to embrace the amazing way our lives unfold in our favour when we take notice of the many messages and nudges in the right direction that we receive. There will be times when things happen that are out of our control but life is one long healing and learning process. We cannot expect perfection but we can expect to be taken on a journey that is right for us to become the fully fledged human being that we were always destined to become.

Déjà vu is another interesting phenomenon in which we seem to receive split-second snatches of the future or we know exactly what someone is going to say or do before it happens. It occurs very quickly but seems to be in slow motion at the same time. It's as if we have been in exactly the same situation before, in the same place at the same time with the same people or set of circumstances, yet this is impossible in the world as we know it. It is a very peculiar yet compelling feeling and is hard to imagine unless you have experienced it yourself. I write any déjà vu occurrences in my journal as it may be the case that it falls into a pattern of other experiences that lead toward an opportunity or interesting life changes. I believe it is connected to synchronicity. It is showing us that we are going in the right direction because we sometimes already know what is about to happen in a given moment.

Our future is never set in stone. There are infinite possibilities and many timelines that change on a daily basis or even in a split second when we open ourselves up to possibilities, opportunities and that warm, positive gut feeling when something is absolutely right for us at that very moment, because this very moment is all we have; everything else is flexible and ever-changing. No-one ever stays the same and the more we can change, adapt and choose to take the path that leads us to greater health and happiness, the better. This all keeps coming back to the same thing – learning to trust and take notice of our intuition. It is much more than a gift - it is what we are born to be – intuitive beings of light. Some of us just forget and need to learn how to rediscover ourselves, shine our light into the world and embrace our heightened awareness to keep low vibrations away.

UNDERSTANDING HUMAN NATURE

Intuitive Imperfections

This is where all the real 'weirdness' starts – trying to understand yourself! I couldn't let this book get published without being absolutely honest about my own true nature and the many quirks of being an Empath and HSiP so that readers can rest assured they are not losing their minds. Being highly sensitive and intuitive can be a rocky road with a multitude of trip hazards but, after every tumble, we get back up stronger and wiser. We are only human and need to be more forgiving of ourselves for not always being beaming vessels of sweetness and light. Spiritual people are not gods or saints with brightly polished halos. We are who we are and sometimes being acutely aware of subtle energy and the pains of life can make us feel as if the older we get, the less we know. We are quite resilient though and once we find a better way of doing things, we learn our lessons well.

In the early days of trying to make sense of your intuitive abilities, it can feel a bit disconcerting as it seems as though you could be going slightly bonkers but can't find anyone to ask in order to make comparisons in case they wrestle you into a strait jacket. You have to find ways to discover if the weird things that you think, feel and experience are natural, human quirks or if there is a strong possibility that a bunch of psychiatrists may come chasing after you armed with a tranquiliser dart. Hopefully, this section will help at least one person feel a bit more 'normal' in their weirdness! The meaning of life? Well, for me it seems to change on a daily basis...

Being an 'Empath', 'Intuitive' or whatever you prefer to call it is not often an easy ride and I have a great many imperfections, as do we all, most of which I have learned to embrace and infuse with a sense of humour. Empaths and HSiPs are so often misunderstood and branded as over-sensitive, even by their nearest and dearest. What people fail to understand is that we constantly have to recalibrate and monitor our own internal state of affairs on a daily basis in order to stay sane and level-headed. The high level of input and barrage of energetic information that we receive every second of the day can be overwhelming as we desperately try to work out what is ours and what is not, trying to make sense of it all.

I have to carefully monitor how I'm feeling on a daily basis so that depression and anxiety don't try to jump me from behind. Maintaining a healthy balance and upbeat attitude often feels like an ongoing battle but most days are good. Daily Reiki self-treatments, meditation and doing the things I love go a long way towards this but there is always a darkness rumbling in the background. This is our shadow-self and we cannot deny its existence. Learning to accept and understand it helps us to become a wise and balanced human being who can truly understand the power of intuition and vast array of benefits it can bring into our lives. Human nature is very complex but intuition can shed a great deal of light on all of our quirks and eccentricities, both good and 'bad'.

Empaths and HSiPs can see the truth in all situations and have a deep desire to save the vulnerable, yet we long to stay at home as much as possible to get away from all the 'noise' of other humans. We become frustrated and upset when people seem to be unable to think for themselves and remain oblivious to the wonder of what is all around them. They sit back and only think of their own problems, seemingly doing nothing towards the betterment of the human race. They rely on others to bolster up their energy levels, supply them with constant entertainment and clutter to fill their minds to block out the desperate cries of their soul as it begs them to live a more fulfilling and substantial life. They are afraid to be alone because the silence is hard to bear as it may force them to face their own painful truths.

Most of the time, us Empaths and HSiPs feel as though we are from a distant planet. Not because we are arrogant or conceited but because we struggle to find a sense of belonging in the human race. We find it difficult to understand how nearly everyone else isn't acutely aware of every nuance and detail of life. We long for elaborate, deep and meaningful conversations that reach into the depths of our soul but kindred spirits are so hard to find. We long to scream to the heavens, 'Please! Come back and take me home!' but we have no idea where home actually is.

Finding ways to understand and connect with other humans is not easy, even when they appear to have the same interest as us. Empaths and HSiPs have a tendency to be self-critical and can seem uncaring and stuck up to non-spiritual people when we struggle to explain ourselves or bungle up our attempts to help others. We have huge hearts but seem aloof and anti-social when we feel drained and have to retreat in order to protect our precious energy. We quite often feel a sense of disconnect from the billions of other people on our planet. All we really long for is a sense of inner peace which so often ends up being inner turmoil. Not because we are mardy or self-centred but because it's so damned hard to understand ourselves, let alone anyone else!

Being an Empath makes you feel as though you are a walking paradox. We are filled with conflicting thoughts, contradictions and incompatible goals and desires. One moment, I am calm, peaceful and light and the next I am a venomous beast spitting hatred at the person tailgating my car or daring to walk rudely across my path in the street! The Reiki principles tell me to be kind to all living things and not to anger. I seem to have mastered these quite well but human nature often gets in the way and after a few years of working with them, I think I finally get the gist. They are about responding from a place of wisdom rather than instantly reacting whilst my ears are still venting out steam; something that is often easier said than done.

I have a complex nature and can be dark and brooding and feel exasperated at the actions of others then the next moment feel relieved and reassured when I meet lovely, genuine people whilst out and about. It's all about perspective and trying to understand why someone behaves in an inconsiderate or selfish way. Perhaps it's nothing personal and they are like that towards everyone? I can most certainly feel it when someone's aura does not resonate comfortably with my own. It could be that our personalities clash, our outlook on life is very different or that they are a person who should be avoided at all costs in order for me to remain safe.

I feel angry towards people who refuse to take responsibility for their actions and endanger or upset others. Being caring and considerate just doesn't seem to be part of their make-up or thought process. They come across as intrinsically selfish in their behaviour but does this accurately represent who they are as a person? Maybe. This is why these days, I allow myself to feel angry and peed off for those few moments but then I return to my calm space inside, always prepared to assert myself and express my true feelings when necessary but not looking to start a fight, just to gain a clearer understanding. A lot of the time, I realise that my initial reaction is because something deep within me is triggered. We are all selfish and rude sometimes; perhaps I didn't like them reflecting this back at me?

Perhaps the person is having bad day or a bad life. We are all different and some people cope better with things than others. It's wiser to walk away than get carried away with raging anger, especially when your reaction may be because someone has touched a raw nerve deep within you and there is danger of a volcanic eruption as past hurt is unleashed. Some people don't want to hear the truth and are not prepared to save themselves, let alone anyone else. A futile confrontation can disrupt a sensitive person's system for days afterward so it is essential that they deal with anger appropriately as part of their self-care routine and maintaining a healthy emotional state. Recognising why you are angry and giving yourself time to heal is much better than receiving further wounds or hurting others with harsh words.

Rude people really get me riled so it's hard to keep a lid on it when they make my blood boil. I strive for good manners and politeness yet cannot keep my mouth shut when someone exasperates me or questions my motives and integrity. I also have a very sharp tongue and swift rebuff for anyone trying to sell me something in the street or waste valuable minutes of my life by ringing me up with a special offer that I don't need. I'm not stupid or naïve. If I want something, I'll already be looking for it. I abhor marketing ploys and heavy-handed sales tactics. They are so obvious to me yet so many people are sucked in by devious sales people who are lacking moral standards and conscience. I don't know how they sleep at night.

If I do get in to an argument, I certainly don't like to attract too much attention and have to find a way to calm things down. Getting angry tends to result in tears of frustration. I have never been one to enjoy the limelight. I don't even like having my photograph taken. I do enjoy the attention of my loved ones though and love to have a good laugh. It's difficult to shut me up when I'm feeling relaxed in the company of friends and family.

I also love words and putting them onto paper, as I'm sure you can tell, but there is a particular phrase that springs to mind – 'if you don't have anything kind to say, don't say anything at all'. Although I struggle to adhere to it, I always try my best. Words can do a great deal of damage and cannot be taken back.

Words can have a great deal of power, in spite of what some old sayings try to get us to believe. Words can harm and words can heal. It is our choice and we should take great care not to wound others with what we say. A kind word can mean so much when someone needs a shoulder to cry on. Sometimes 'empty' words can be as bad as harsh ones. It is just as cruel to say something without substance and make false promises to people when they are feeling vulnerable and are relying on genuine support that turns out to not be forthcoming. We are privileged to be able to communicate with words and should use them respectfully and wisely, both in the spoken and written form.

As with everything in life when lots of people get involved, even peaceful, spiritual work and social media groups are infused with individuals who are attention-seeking, egotistical and confrontational. I have joined many different groups but they always seem to end up arguing over nothing and I quickly retreat! I'm not afraid of a good debate but petty arguments are a waste of time and energy.

It's not always easy to be politically correct, which tends to inhibit freedom of speech, but I do try to consider the feelings of others, even if it may sometimes become a little twisted up in my sense of humour. I endeavour to be honest but not brutally so. If I'm struggling to find something nice to say, I become very quiet. I'd rather quietly duck out of a conversation than be dishonest. Sometimes tact and diplomacy are not enough. If I say something that I do not mean, my face and tone of voice give it away.

I enjoy social occasions with close friends and family but sometimes, as it gets closer to going out, I want to stop at home in my pyjamas instead! Not because I don't enjoy seeing them but because of some deep seated need to stay in the comfort of my own quiet company. I'm a hermit at heart. It's even worse when it comes to meetings with strangers and groups. It's like I want to be gregarious and open to new possibilities but I then turn full circle and hide away where I know it's safe in the bosom of the ones who are nearest and dearest. Being at home wearing my comfy clothes is absolute luxury to me. I'm trying to train myself out of this mind-set though because I usually enjoy things when I make the effort. I have to spread out my social engagements though to give myself plenty of time to recharge in-between and indulge in my favourite pastimes.

I'm a grumpy old fart if someone disrupts my routine, interrupts my creative flow, attempts to rush me or tries to tell me what to do or think. I like to be the master of my own destiny and not feel pressured. Pressure leads to anger, anger leads to stress and stress leads to anxiety! Not one of my favourite places to be. I'm too long in the tooth to be led to where anxiety resides. I've been there, done that and got the whole wardrobe. I refuse to go down that road again. When anxiety starts to rear its ugly head, I back off and do something less stressful instead. Making sure that you have a good laugh on a regular basis helps to keep anxiety at bay.

It is important to me to maintain a finely honed sense of humour. Ranging from a high level of dark sarcasm to utter nonsensical, abstract madness, a sense of humour is vital for survival in the harsh realities of the human world. One of the blights on this world that seems to crop up in all walks of life is the 'idiot'. Not a funny, silly kind of idiot; I mean the kind of idiot who spoils things for everyone else. I am not prejudiced about idiots and fully understand that such a condition transcends race, colour, creed, gender, age, rank, political standing and religion. Being an idiot is a full-time occupation for some people. I'm not simply talking about people who are not the brightest here, I'm referring to the self-absorbed, inconsiderate morons of this world who believe that their needs are far superior to everyone else's and will crush anyone in their path to get their own way. Sadly, too many idiots are revered and held in high regard by the masses who seem to be unable to think for themselves, enjoy shallow pursuits and seem to be oblivious that they are being taken for a ride on someone else's ego trip.

Good luck to the idiots and their minions. The discerning amongst us can see right through you with our B.S.-ometers! It's just a shame that so many of them find their way into positions of power, often because they are voted in by those who blindly follow superficial figures of 'authority' because they only hear what they want to hear. The world is full of inequality based on selfishness and greed. This is why so many more of us need to wake up, smell the coffee and drink it, preferably a strong espresso! It shocks me how so few people are unable to see straight through the garbage fed to us by the media and marketing moguls spouting junk which is readily consumed. Working on our intuition highlights these matters and makes us more aware of how we can improve our chances of encouraging more people to see beyond the B.S.

The Power of Intuition

Intuition has the power to give us greater insight into all aspects of life and help us understand how to better relate to one another and celebrate our differences, rather than seeing them as a source of conflict. Intuition can be a wonderful teacher when it comes to understanding human nature.

I see intuition in a very realistic and pragmatic way, infused with a good dose of magical mysticism. Just like everything else, it can be taken to the extreme but it is up to each individual to make it their own. It's part of who we are and no-one has the right to tell anyone else what to do with it or how to feel about it.

For each and every one of us, intuition will mean something vastly different. The word intuition can strike fear into the hearts of those with a strictly scientific mind yet they use their intuition on a daily basis without giving it a second thought. To others, intuition conjures up images of psychics in a fortune telling booth at the seaside, waving their hands over a misty crystal ball. Yet, within these extremes there is an element of truth but at the same time, they both completely miss the point.

Journal 08.08.15

'I feel sorry for people who aren't in touch with their spiritual, natural and caring side. They're missing out! I know we're all different and I can understand why some people get into the depths of despair but not why they deliberately hurt others or show no concern for our planet. Nor can I understand materialistic or extremely vain people. They must only feel true fulfilment from superficial or external sources but I guess those are the extremes of life.'

Journal 30.10.16

After waking up and feel anxious, I manage to have a relaxing day and feel much better by the evening. I still have days like this, as we all do:

'My mood has lifted and I feel completely better, like the very core of my being shifted back into alignment. I can feel another shift occurring as I'm writing this. It's as if it's a completely different day to this morning. There is still a tiny bit of fear bubbling away in me but it's fading away. It's no wonder people go crazy. Being human can drive you mad!'

Intuition is not some mystical fantasy only reserved for the chosen few or some hard-hitting ability that scientists seem to be unable to prove the existence of. It is an innate and natural ability with which we are all born and, just like our physical senses and plethora of talents that make us all who we are as individuals, intuition is developed to a greater or lesser extent in all of us, depending on our own uniqueness, upbringing and outlook on life.

I'm a 'normal' person who does 'normal' stuff (at first glance!). I've got a husband, two children and a business and house to run. I also help to look after my Mum. If I can nurture and cultivate my intuition, anyone can. It is my love of animals that has led me to where I am today and the sad loss of my father in 2016 that was the catalyst that enhanced my spiritual awakening and inspired me to help others to better understand themselves and how the Universe works. Being spiritual and intuitive is for everyone, in any walk of life. We are not automatons or biological machines; we are spiritual beings who need to remember who we are. Not necessarily by going to church or chanting 'ohm' on a mountain top but by harnessing the strength and amazing depth that it is to be human.

I've never been one to try to convince a sceptic of anything but with intuition it's something that we all use, every day and in every decision that we have to make, no matter how small because intuition is how we FEEL our way through life. It's that kick in our gut when we feel that something just isn't right; that awful moment when we realise someone is deceiving us or that we are in imminent danger; it's that contract that we didn't sign because we 'knew' it wasn't genuine; that road that we didn't take one morning because something 'told' us to take a different route; it's about that feeling when we're buying a new house and just 'know' that a place is right for us. That's where our intuition starts. It is our guide and protector but it can be developed to lead to so much more, yet developing intuition is not for the feint hearted.

Instinct is sometimes compared to intuition but it doesn't quite cut the mustard. Instinct is our fight or flight response in a situation where there is a threat to our well-being. It is an immediate response on a physiological level and just like intuition, it can be our saviour in certain situations but instinct is more of a primal reaction. Intuition is often subtle yet powerful and can tell us things that leave our five physical senses reeling from how we could possibly have 'known' something without it being physically present in front of us.

That is what is so incredible about intuition. A lot of people struggle to believe that it is in all of us as a helpful guide. Intuition may be very quiet in some people but when we bring it to the fore and become good friends with it, we become aware that our intuition is able to tell us things that transcend all logical sense, time and space. Intuition is our connection to so much more than what we are aware of in our physical, every day world.

This is why intuition scares some people; it opens up a vast array of possibilities that lead us into the unknown yet once we develop our intuition, we DO know. Intuition empowers, inspires us and builds our confidence. As our intuition grows, we grow and develop as a person. Intuition is part of us; it is intrinsic to our very nature and this is another place where fear resides. It is very difficult to get one over on someone who has taken the time and effort to develop their intuition. They have strengthened themselves from within and stand in a place of personal power, calmness and wisdom that comes from a good place.

This makes the self-centred and manipulative people of this world hang back. They work from a superficial, controlling perspective. A truly intuitive, successful and confident person can disarm them, leaving them without their usual arsenal of bullying tactics and deception. Their finely honed method of trying to get the upper-hand is rendered useless.

Intuitive people often become walking lie-detectors. They can spot a lie, even a little white one from miles away! Not only do they read facial expression, body language and the nuances of individual characteristics, they also read energy and can tell when a person's outward expression and demeanour belies the truth in the depths of their eyes. Of course, this doesn't necessarily mean that the intuitively aware are all wonderful people. Some people with highly developed intuition use it for all the wrong reasons to serve themselves by deceiving and manipulating others. This type of person may be intuitive but they certainly don't work from their heart or work on expanding their spiritual awareness; if they even know what that is! This is why we need to become discerning about whom we can trust. Our intuition will often step in ahead of our conscious efforts to assess someone's true nature and tell us exactly what we need to know before they have even opened their mouth. There is also a lot that can be said about eye contact.

The eyes really are the windows of our soul. They contain bundles of nerves and activity, making them extremely powerful in enabling perceptive people to see our souls laid bare. It is no wonder that making eye contact with others can feel traumatic for people with social anxiety or if they are painfully shy. Even the brave amongst us may struggle to maintain eye contact with certain people. A look can often say so much more than words ever could. Looking into someone's eyes can be very revealing and lead us to the truth much more quickly than an elaborate conversation.

Being your true self from within gives you the clarity and discernment that so many people are lacking. You may find yourself one step ahead of some people and, because you are wise, you will not become cocky or arrogant. The world becomes your oyster as you shine your light and inspire and empower others to follow their own path. This is how real change begins. It begins from within us all.

Keeping Positivity In Perspective

Don't set yourself up for disappointment by expecting perfection and for every day to smell of roses. Life can be tough. Human beings are resilient and tenacious. We didn't get that way by being push-overs. We learned to embrace our dark side, our shadow-self, in order to build our full characters. That does not mean that we should do horrible things or be cruel to others, it means that to achieve balance, we have to be brave and look into the darker corners of ourselves in order to fill them with light.

The worst thing a person on a spiritual path can do is wear rose tinted spectacles and listen to teachers who insist that every day should be filled with joy and happiness in abundance – er, no. These 'spiritual teachers' have a lot to answer for! They often say these things to get people to go back for more of their teachings in search of non-existent perfection so that they can line their pockets with hard-earned cash from the naïve and vulnerable.

We are not going to love everyone and everything and should not feel bad for not enjoying every moment of every day or having an unpleasant thought about something. We are human and have to keep ourselves safe without feeling pressured to be perfect, pure and immune to feelings of displeasure and the desire to run for the hills when things all become too much.

It is essential to be realistic, even when working with intuition and spiritual matters. I started out believing that it would be all rainbows and unicorns when I began to learn Reiki but I have since realised that opening your heart to the truth about life and offering healing to others can be tough. We must be pragmatic and wise in our pursuit of spiritual bliss. There are many fabulous moments to be spent in Utopia but when it comes down to it, becoming spiritually aware leads us to seek out the truth and, as we all know, the truth can often hurt.

There will be good days and there will be days that are a challenge; there will also be days when it feels as though your heart and soul are torn in two. It is on these days that knock you sideways that you realise developing your spiritual awareness and intuition gives you the strength to get through it and keep your eyes on the light at the other end of the tunnel. Remaining true to yourself and others opens up the channels for pure spiritual information to flow through. Even in the darkest of times it allows us to find hope deep within our core. We are all here on our own journey and when we get broken and battered along the way, we can lift ourselves up feeling stronger, giving support to others and receiving support in return. The road to happiness is not a smooth one and the words of overly optimistic spiritual teachers are open to misinterpretation.

Some days, it can feel as though we have a problem and that we should seek help to change ourselves in some way but in reality, we simply need to go through a process of self-acceptance. Nobody is perfect or bouncing around with great abandon on a daily basis. You don't need to change yourself; you need to love yourself the way you are, even if you can be a bit grumpy on occasion. Allowing ourselves to feel and accept our less socially acceptable emotions means that we can embrace every aspect of our personality and understand our shadow-self. Don't compare yourself to others; you are the one living your life, not them. As I have come to discover, most people who claim to be happy and brimming over with enthusiasm are often bluffing and not only fooling everyone around them, they are also fooling themselves. Happiness is about achieving balance and working on raising our vibrations by focussing on the positive things in life.

When we focus on the positive, uplifting aspects of life to keep ourselves buoyant and moving forward, we are not denying that the darkness exists; we are not turning away from difficult emotions or heartbreak. It means that we are aware of them but we do not allow them to consume us. We can look into them, inspect them, take them to pieces and understand them but not allow them to take away our shine. Dark and unpleasant aspects of our world should not be allowed to compromise our well-being or disrupt our equilibrium nor should they be ignored or brushed under the carpet.

Life is a balance of dark and light so next time you see a harrowing image that burns into your mind or you are struggling to let go of past hurt, take a good look at it, feel it, let it rise up and show you what it is trying to say. Acknowledge its existence and feel in your heart exactly what it means to you. Break it down into why it hurts you, gently allow yourself to understand its significance in your life. Can you deal with it? Do you need help to overcome it? If so, admit this to yourself and find out what action would be to your greatest benefit.

Integrating unpleasant feelings into our system does not mean that we are allowing them to make us miserable. It is similar to forgiveness. We have to acknowledge them in order to let them go.

This is why some people do charity work or choose a career in a caring profession. They cannot sit back and allow something horrible to continue. From the smallest of upsets to major life trauma or seeing images of famine or war, it is our response to these things that matters. We cannot save the world but we can look after our own emotional well-being in order to remain strong enough to respond in a way that we feel to be right. Yes, we should most definitely focus on the things that bring us the most joy and raise our vibrations but this is not a selfish act. It is vital for us to live our everyday lives without being in the depths of despair.

We can choose to be aware of the horrors in life but we do not have to allow them to dictate how we feel. I deliberately avoid images of animal abuse or any other kind of distressing images; not because I don't care but because they hit me like a freight train and become emblazoned on my heart and mind. If there are comments on social media that are deliberately provocative or people are getting into petty arguments, I move along. We all have the right to choose the kind of energy that we wish to interact with. Being aware of unpleasant things doesn't mean you have to allow them to beat you up on an emotional, mental or spiritual level. Protect your energy. It is your right.

Sending out positive vibes and love into the world when we are feeling good is a wonderful thing. Do what you feel drawn to doing in order to make the world a better place and allow yourself to look at what may be holding you back within your own life or past so that you can heal and move on.

Just because someone loves unicorns and rainbows does not mean that they are a big pansy! Those people are often the strongest ones of all. They are prepared to acknowledge and understand the things that would make most people shut down and run a mile. The spiritually aware should never be underestimated. You never know how strong you truly are until you have to face adversity and opened your Spiritual Warrior heart. It is infinite in there.

"Sometimes, you need to go full circle to know where you have been" - this is what I wrote after a period of anxiety and confusion. I had come full circle and realised that after feeling lost for a while, I returned to a state of peace and harmony and understood that the Universe really does have my back, after all. I am never alone.

Staring into the face of anxiety, depression, despair and grief can be incredibly painful but we cannot deny these emotions no more than we can ignore our passions and feelings of love and excitement. They are part of who we are as sentient beings. If we ignore and suppress our emotions instead of facing them, we can never be free to express our true feelings. When we face our fears, we can move forward and know what it is to feel pure love. This is why developing our intuition is not for the feint hearted. It leads us to examine who we truly are and leaves us nowhere to hide.

If each of us were perfect, there could be no diversity. We are all works in progress and must take responsibility for ourselves through self-care, self-love and nurturing our inner child, Spiritual Warrior and embracing our shadow-self.

Journal 31.10.16

'At some point, there was an energetic drop-out when my childhood-self lost connection as I became a teen/adult. It's a long healing process but the more I look at things and attract the answers and way forward, the closer I come to reforming and healing the connection to becoming a fully-fledged

human being to integrate with my true, authentic self and inner child. She is a happy, playful one with a fiercely determined dark side that can show me the way forward to enlightenment. She's always been there but when she gets suppressed and denied what she truly needs, the rest of me becomes ill, dried out and blocked. Not the way to live a full and happy life! It's so simple really. We'll get there in the end.'

Life is full of extremes because everything is on a scale from extremely bad and negative to absolutely wonderful and positive with neutral and 'normal' in-between. The majority of things are neutral which makes the extremes more noticeable. This scale can apply to anything including people, places, incidents, the elements, light, energy, the weather, Earth's climate and how we are feeling on a daily basis.

Journal 05.11.16

'Most people have a neutral energy that I don't seem to repel or absorb but I really notice it lately when I see or am near an enlightened or awakening person and, of course, if someone is out of kilter or has unbalanced, less than pleasant energy. It's all very amazing but can be draining and uncomfortable at times. To me it seems better to be selective receptor than the victim of unpleasant or overwhelming energy or completely closed-off and unaware and unfeeling of life.'

There are infinite possibilities in all aspects of life. One day, life can seem obvious and simple and yet another it can feel overwhelming and filled with mind-blowing complexity. Intuition and spiritual awareness can help us to better understand how the Universe works. The intricacies of the natural world are absolutely fascinating. Nature seems to work to a basic blueprint then throws in some amazing variations, just for good measure to keep things interesting and moving forward.

The Natural Order of Life

There is a natural order to life that manifests itself in our physical world. Within this apparent sense of order, there are processes of a subtle energetic and higher vibrational nature transcending and pervading throughout which can turn everything on its head in a split second. This can make us think twice about a decision or teach us how to cope in a crisis to find our deepest spiritual strength from within. Our intuition enables us to see beyond the physical in this respect by picking up on subtle energy and seeing details within the complexities of life that make things clearer.

Nature finds a way to fill our world with logical systems and repeating patterns that have a seemingly perfect structure, such as the atom or the qualities of crystals such as quartz. These are set within a neat and orderly and set of parameters. Occasionally though, inconsistencies and variables are thrown in to disrupt the flow and force change and adaptation to take place.

Genetics and the diversity of species upon this planet are a perfect example of this. Just occasionally, an albino person or animal is born or the genetic code is disrupted by some other type of mutation. This mutation may suddenly place the animal at an advantage if its natural habitat changes and over the next few generations, the mutation becomes prevalent throughout the species until it is the norm rather than the exception.

Our world and the Universe beyond are filled with details and infinite possibilities. When we develop our intuition, those details and inconsistencies in the natural balance of things that have previously gone unnoticed become more apparent. The intuitively and spiritually aware become more aware of the early warning signs of future events, can sense change in the air and begin to understand the non-linear structure of life to which the vast majority of people are oblivious.

There are also man-made constructs designed to keep us in order amongst the natural systems including formal education, the media, religion and politics. Once we can see past the hype, it all appears superficial and lacking in truth and substance.

Most humans and many of our domestic animals need solid structure and certainty to survive and remain stable but for those of us who strive to explore beyond the veil of 'normality', we get to see and experience the bigger picture, even though we may not always like it. Humans become socially conditioned to think and behave in certain ways and our domestic animal companions often also require structure and routine to cope with living in our man-made environments.

When we receive or experience something extraordinary, we quite often need to take a step back to process the information and learn from what we are receiving. As we begin to become aware of the finer points of how the Universe works, we can see people for who they truly are, even the ones closest to us. Everything is exposed in a new light and we need to understand that although we may have greater awareness, we cannot always execute change in the way that we wish to. To see how the world could be if we all behaved in a more loving and compassionate way makes us want more of the same but some people are just not ‘wired’ that way.

Everyone has the right to free will and not everyone views the world as we do. Our new-found wisdom and awareness should not lead us down the road to arrogance. We should remain humble and continue to learn what it means to be human. Our species is fantastically clever and complex yet still filled with primal instincts and the need to put our own stamp on the world. We are all unique yet intrinsically the same. We all have the same basic needs yet we are layered with many differences and complexities.

Our Difference and Complexities

It can often be particularly hard to understand why there are a great many people who do not seem to be kind, compassionate and considerate in any way. They come across as insensitive, selfish, ignorant and unfeeling. Some are worse than others and are devious, manipulative and abusive. These people can really test us and cause us great upset on a deep level if we allow them to but we can take a step back and learn to accept and understand that they are highly unlikely to ever change or treat others any better than they already do. The way they are is so deeply ingrained, they do not know any other way of behaving or thinking. The more we try to change them, the more resistance we are likely to be met with. They understand us just as little as we understand them. It is literally like a brick wall, or maybe even a titanium one.

People who come across as unpleasant, selfish, arrogant or down-right dangerous are usually disconnected from spiritual energy and can only function as a physical being on a basic level without connection to the higher frequencies of love, compassion and understanding. Their chakras and subtle energy bodies may be blocked or badly distorted. It is hard to say whether or not this is the way they were born or if it is a result of traumatic life experiences or a lack of love in their upbringing. Although it is difficult to understand their often bleak and apparently heartless outlook on life, it is not anyone else's responsibility but their own to seek out healing to unburden themselves from the negativity by which they seem to be consumed. It may be all that they know and are familiar with. Trying to help them when they are not prepared to help themselves is futile.

We are all made up of infinite possibilities. The sheer scale of the energetic and etheric variants, likes and dislikes is mind boggling. As we go through life and come into contact with the energetic make-up of the other living beings, locations and objects, we will feel tugs, repulsions and comfortable neutrality in the vast plethora of the mixture of energetic and emotional subtleties that make up who we are. It's no wonder public places and being away from the safety and familiarity of our own home can seem overwhelming for highly sensitive people.

As an analogy of our energetic bodies and how our subtle energy interacts with the world around us, imagine a dot matrix made up of a multitude of lights on a network that resembles our nervous system. Each one of those lights represents an aspect of ourselves such as our personality traits, life experiences, likes and dislikes, fears and phobias, emotional sensitivities and things that we love. There are many different colours, textures, intensities, sizes and shapes. The lights are all connected in complex ways by lines of energy, weaving in and out. Some individual lights are connected one another and others in groups. When these lights and their connections respond to external energy, some flash up and flare causing reactions in other lights and their respective groups and connections, depending on whether or not we are attracted to or repelled by what we encounter. Some things resonate harmoniously with us; others cause discord, great discomfort or distress.

This matrix of lights represents our energetic being on every level from the physical to the spiritual. Some lights may wither and die if they no longer serve us. Some lights may thrive and expand when we spend time with a loved one or engage in an enjoyable activity. Our lights may also take damage if we experience trauma, if we are not doing the things we love or are suppressing our true desires and needs. These can be repaired over time but may never regain full functionality.

We need to accept that there is a vast array of possibilities and mixture of facets that make up each individual in the human race in order to understand our existence and how human life really works. There are billions of us upon this planet and each one of us is different from the rest, some in more extreme ways than others. Some people will be attracted some aspects of others whereas other people will feel repelled by these same aspects and may find them dull, repulsive or unappealing. This may be on a subtle energetic level. We may not be consciously aware as to why, but we can see the 'light' in certain people and feel inexplicably drawn to them. The opposite is also true. We may not like someone but cannot put our finger on the reason why.

Given the number of personality types and combinations of traits, quirks and eccentricities, it is no wonder that we are all unique. Some people are more complex than others and are more likely to have a higher vibration because they have 'a lot going on'. People of the opposite extreme are likely to have a lower vibration. This does not mean that one is 'good' and the other 'bad', it's simply a matter of how multi-faceted their interests and passions are. A very grounded and slow-paced person can still be deeply loving and wonderful. It is just that they have their own unique approach to life and their energy signature is different to that of others. They have firmly grounded energy.

Many of the decisions that we make come from a place deep in our subconscious and only take a split second. They may seem to come out of nowhere but as we become more spiritually aware, such feelings and subtleties of information become clearer and more noticeable as they are brought to our conscious attention. It is the complex nature of energetic beings and locations that can leave us reeling. This is why we need to understand our own energetic make-up in order to have more awareness and stability in our emotional and spiritual lives, especially when dealing with difficult and seemingly unfeeling people.

Opinions

When I was younger, I was easily swayed by other people's opinions. I would allow them to shout me down and place greater importance on their opinions rather than asserting my own, especially if they were loud and seemed more confident than me. Well, the meeker side of me grew stronger over the years and I learned to value my own opinions and became much more discerning about everyone else's. So, if you're struggling with similar issues with regard to the opinions of others, perhaps think of things in the following way.

There are as many opinions as there are people. All of these people believe their opinions to be right but how can this be possible? When should someone's opinion matter? Why should we listen to the opinion of a particular individual? These are questions that our intuition can answer. When we deeply care for and value the opinion of another person or group of people, we feel it in our hearts. We have to firstly place our trust in someone before their opinion matters and know that they say things because they love, trust and respect us in return.

Opinions are the basis of how one person views the world – their core beliefs based on their education, experiences, personality traits and influences of other people – their opinion is what they believe to be true in their perception as an individual.

The opinion of everyone is valid but we all have every right to disagree. If we were all of the same opinion, the world would be a very dull place. Opinions only become problematic for others when someone tries to force their opinion onto those around them or the world at large. This use of force could be mild, such as someone trying to shout someone else down in a discussion by verbally asserting their opinion more loudly and confidently or, at the opposite extreme, an opinion could be forced onto others through the use of violence or intimidation, such as the threat of harm or taking away things that are valuable to them.

There is always plenty of scope for someone's opinion to be based on incorrect information, gossip or ignorance. This is even more problematic, especially when others of like-mind or inclination collude with this person and form strength in numbers to try and force their shared opinion onto others.

We all need to exert control over our lives and environment in order to feel safe and secure. This is perfectly natural. It is when we try to exert control over others for selfish reasons that it causes problems. Most people are willing to share and let others live their lives in peace but some have to have it all their own way. In the extreme, this is the cause of war and oppression. To a lesser degree, it can still cause misery for those affected by the controlling behaviour of others, usually through fear and manipulation.

Expressing our opinions is our absolute right but we should not expect everyone to agree. Freedom of speech is something that each and every one of us is entitled to but when it harms others or has the potential to cause war or conflict, we should use a great deal of tact, diplomacy and care when choosing our words and put our thoughts and feelings across in an intelligent and articulate way with consideration for how our opinion may affect the lives of others.

Opinions are usually connected to strong emotions and it can be difficult to hear someone's opinion when it is vastly different to our own. There comes a point when we have to agree to disagree and learn how to have a healthy debate without resorting to personal attacks or getting carried away with a battle that we can never win – this is where cognitive dissonance comes into play, which is discussed below. Changing someone's opinion that we believe to be incorrect or harmful can be very difficult indeed. Arming ourselves with facts and evidence to educate someone in order to change their opinion is possible but some people are not for changing and we must learn that to be kind to ourselves by letting them express their opinions but not waste our own time and energy by getting into an argument. We simply have to let them be and imagine if the shoe were on the other foot, would anyone be able to change some of our strongest opinions? Probably not.

Some people have such entrenched beliefs that if anyone attempts to persuade them otherwise or presents them with an argument to question their beliefs, it can cause them deep distress within their core. They will often strongly resist change, never being capable of it and just the mere thought of it is enough to destabilise them. This extreme discomfort at the thought of changing or stepping away from their beliefs is known as cognitive dissonance. This is experienced on a deep psychological level when a person is presented with something that is so at odds with their own constructs or mental, emotional and spiritual make-up, they cannot comprehend alternative ways of thinking or behaving. A sense of internal conflict occurs when what they are being asked to consider something that sets alarm bells ringing. This is why trying to convince a sceptic of anything other than what they already believe is often a waste of time and energy.

An example of cognitive dissonance from my own personal perspective is that of someone trying to persuade me that there is no life after death, we are simply made of physical matter without any emotional capabilities or spiritual depth and everything that I hold dear is simply a product of signals firing in my brain. When we die, that is the end of everything and there is total, empty blackness thereafter. This is something that I am completely unable to comprehend. It sends my brain into stand-by mode because it is so at odds will all of my personal, emotional and spiritual beliefs. The same goes for people of the opposing inclination who refuse to believe anything remotely spiritual unless it has been proven by science and they can be presented with hard, physical evidence of it.

Everyone has their own set of beliefs and anything to the extreme would be hard to swallow.

It may be difficult for us to understand that people with opposing and extreme views will never change, even if doing so may appear to be in their best interests but we have to let others follow their own path, even if it may seem to be to their own detriment. If they are not prepared to consider changing themselves, we should respect their wishes and not disempower them by poking our nose into their business. Of course, common sense should be applied here. If they are going to harm themselves or others, it is our moral and civil responsibility to report it to the appropriate authorities. Discretion is required.

Extreme views of any kind can cause us to become closed-minded, intolerant of others and no longer open to all possibilities. We need to accept that not everyone will always agree with us and sometimes it's better to walk away with our integrity intact and not waste our energy or risk our emotional stability by engaging in a fight that we are unlikely to win. Do what seems healthy and feels right. Agree to disagree and leave it there. If we do feel that we should respond to someone who has got us riled, it is better to wait a while and infuse our response with conscious thought rather than instantly reacting on impulse. Becoming spiritually aware doesn't stop us being human. Extreme spiritual views can cause us to feel guilty about our human nature sometimes. We are not going to like everybody and if we really cannot stand them, we can wish them well on their way and choose to never associate with them again.

Our spiritual awareness will also guide us as to when it is appropriate to step in and help others. We should not disempower anyone by trying to fight their battles for them but we will be unable to stand by when it is obvious that someone needs help, such as getting them out of a situation in which they are being bullied and encouraging them to be strong enough to deal with the situation constructively.

Forgiveness is sometimes essential so that we can let go of hurt and negativity and move forward with our lives. It is about valuing ourselves. This is not to condone the actions of others but to allow ourselves to let go of grudges, thoughts of revenge and emotional blockages. We may also need to forgive ourselves at times so our past actions do not negatively affect our future. We should learn lessons from our past and choose to not repeat the same scenarios in future. We forgive ourselves and others to become a better person with a healthier outlook on life.

We are all human beings and sometimes we should give ourselves a break. We are never going to like everyone or enjoy absolutely everything. If you don't like it, move along. We don't have to ooze hate at everyone. Wish them well on their journey through life and focus on your own needs if you come across someone you dislike. Focus on the positive changes you can make and what you have to offer the world by simply being who you are. Build on your strengths and the rest will all fall into place. Enjoy being you.

Judgements

I see myself as a kind, loving person yet I can find myself being unsympathetic, harsh, judgemental and sometimes generally irritable and peed off. Why? Because I am me; a human who lives by her own truth and allows her feelings to naturally flow. It is how we respond to these feelings that matters. We need to ask ourselves why we are viewing someone in a certain way. Is it because we are afraid of them because they are different? Are they reflecting qualities that we do not like within ourselves? Take some time to reflect so that you can respond through love and wisdom rather than reacting by fighting fire with fire. It will only leave bad feelings if things turn into a fight or argument. There can be some hard lessons to learn but until we accept every aspect of ourselves, we cannot begin to grow and heal from within.

If I feel angry with someone, instantly judge them, immediately dislike them, find myself repulsed, disagree with them, fail to understand them or find them hard to believe, a part of me knows that I cannot change them. I have to walk away and let them be. If I have a gut feeling about someone, it is rarely wrong. We all have our own path and we quite often have to let others walk theirs in order to protect ourselves and continue on our own journey. We cannot save everyone and most people do not ask to be saved. They have their own lessons to learn.

As we become more spiritually aware, we begin to let go of any preconceptions and judgements about ourselves and others. Anything that no longer serves us begins to fall away, albeit people, choices of career or situations that seem to drain our energy. Every aspect of our lives begins to align with our soul purpose and brings greater wisdom, clarity and a more loving approach to life. We no longer have to think about it. We subconsciously become grateful, kind and humble and live our lives this way, although some days will seem easier than others. We no longer have to clamber over others or live in fear of losing what we have worked hard to achieve. We have everything we need from the inside out. We are not perfect, but we are the perfect version of ourselves and are always evolving. Some people may be struggling to get to this stage and we may find ourselves judging them, even though we were once just like them.

Being judgemental is part of human nature. We have to form an opinion or feeling about someone's character when we meet them in order to keep ourselves safe. If someone gives you the creeps or comes across as untrustworthy, your intuition is probably right. We need to examine why we are judging that person and adjust our response and behaviour accordingly. Jumping to conclusions can sometimes turn out badly but it may also save us from harm or being ripped off. We should be realistic. We are not a 'bad' person or 'wrong' for making judgements.

It is the context and response to our own judgements about others that shows our true character. We may be judging someone because they reflect something about ourselves that we do not like or we may be sensing unpleasant energy from the person because they are being dishonest or are out to cause trouble. If we are basing our judgement on stereotypical things such as a person's race, religion or choice of clothing, we may need to see beyond this superficial attitude and look deeper into who they are, rather than rely on our assumptions about them. If we are basing our judgement on their behaviour or comments, we can get a better intuitive feel for that person's true character. It all comes down to discernment and common sense. Are we basing our opinion on our own prejudices or our genuine intuitive feelings? If it is the latter, we should listen to our intuition and do what feels right at the time.

The Energy Exchange of Good

Manners and Kindness

In Reiki we are taught that there should be an exchange of some kind in return for receiving Reiki. This is not because all people who give Reiki are greedy and expect payment but because it shows that the person receiving the Reiki places a value upon it and they are grateful. It can be something as simple as giving a Reiki treatment in return or offering a cup of tea and biscuits to the practitioner after the session. It is a kind gesture to show that their time and attention is appreciated.

In everyday life, this is similar to the exchange of good manners and appreciation of acts of kindness. Even though most of our acts of kindness and politeness are not carried out because we expect something in return, it can hurt when someone does not show their gratitude with a simple 'thank you' or other words or behaviour to show their appreciation. When we hold the door open for someone, go out of our way to help them or stop behind parked cars to let them through and they don't even acknowledge our existence, it can seem painful, as if a little of our energy has become depleted.

Kindness is often associated with being weak. This is not so. Some of the kindest and most generous people are strong-willed, confident and colourful characters. Kindness comes in many forms, from reaching out to those in need to knowing when to be kind to yourself by walking away from a situation; kindness is about inner strength and wisdom. We can be kind to someone by allowing them to find their own way through a problem but be there for them when they ask for support.

Being kind does not mean that we are easily taken advantage of; it means that we are tenacious and self-aware enough to offer kindness in a way that will benefit each person, animal or situation based on its own merits. Kindness means never doing harm and working towards the greatest and highest good of all. It comes from a place of love without judgement or selfish endeavours. Kindness is at the heart of a Spiritual Warrior; taking this world forward in a way that encourages others to think for themselves and feel their own truth by loving and supporting them but never disempowering them by attempting to deny people or animals freedom of choice or to feel that they are not being listened to. We can be as one with others and still allow them to be themselves.

It costs nothing to show good manners and be kind and considerate of others. This comes naturally to the vast majority of us. Simple gestures such as giving up your seat for someone who needs it more than you do or helping someone to pick up their shopping if their bag splits can restore someone's faith in human nature and make their day. There are even some social media sites that encourage random acts of kindness. I know that when I'm having a bad day, it makes such a difference when someone is nice to me, even if it's just the fact that they smiled at me warmly and said 'hello'. Spreading kindness and joy is so simple and is another way we can go about changing the world and even if we are not always shown gratitude in return, it's nice when we do feel appreciated. The energy exchange is then complete and we don't feel as though a little piece of us has been taken away.

Another pet hate of mine is a lack of response from someone and feeling ignored. I try to respond to people as soon as I can if they send me a text, email or voicemail. I take my time if I need to give careful thought to my reply but I very rarely ignore anyone. I don't reply to marketing blurb, things that are clearly spam or potential stalkers on social media but as with good manners, not replying to someone can make them feel as if they have done something wrong, especially if it is a close friend, relative or potential customer. It is better to ask them to hang on for a while if you can't give a full response straight away. Responding shows that you care. If someone seems to need help or is experiencing problems, just having someone around who seems to genuinely care can make a huge difference to them.

Other People's Problems

People with problems seem to gravitate towards Empaths and HSiPs because they are drawn by their energy and authenticity. Protecting our energy in important so that we do not become drained when others approach us to off-load their problems and need a genuine, listening ear.

Problems come in all shapes and sizes. Not everyone is equipped to deal with other people telling them their problems and life story. Trivialising another person's problems doesn't help them to move forward and can make us appear arrogant and unfeeling. We all experience life in our own unique way and can only base things on what we already know and our own perceptions. What may seem overwhelming and insurmountable to one person may be a walk in the park for another.

There are, of course, life's chronic moaners who go on and on about their own suffering simply to gain attention and sympathy from those around them but when someone is genuinely suffering and seems to be unable to cope on their own, it is not at all kind or helpful to say "You wait until you have a REAL problem, then you'll know what it means to suffer!" or "That's your problem, not mine!". That kind of attitude sets us apart and creates further divisions in society.

A better way of dealing with it is to offer them a few pearls of wisdom to empower them to find solutions for themselves. This will build their confidence and make them more self-sufficient in future. Dismissing someone else's problems as if they are of no consequence does nothing to help the state of the human race. It doesn't hurt to be kind and offer a listening ear or helping hand. I have had strangers tell me all their troubles and sometimes cry on my shoulder. It is a great privilege when someone takes me into their trust in this way, even if their problems seem mild in comparison to my own.

We may all need that kind of shoulder one day. No-one should have to suffer alone. We should never be taken for a mug but for a spiritually awakened and empathic person, genuine suffering stands out like a sore thumb and if we feel drawn to help, we should do so in a way that we feel to be right. Discernment and discretion may be required but helping someone to find their own way out of a predicament can allow both parties to learn and grow. Suffering can take place on many different levels. Just because we may have experienced level ten, doesn't mean that someone with a level one problem is not in genuine distress.

I have been through some horrible things in my time and each time I promise myself that I shall never worry or stress over 'trivial' matters again, yet when I have a difficult day or feel that I am unable to cope with the simple things, I remember that I am a complex, emotional human being and that sometimes even the tough cookies of this world need a big hug and a good sob on someone's shoulder, even if it's something small that set it off.

Small things can build up and we need to deal with them one at a time to avoid becoming overwhelmed.

No problem is ever truly trivial because we all experience life in different ways. We live in the here and now and for those few seconds, minutes, hours, days or even longer that we are experiencing genuine stress, anxiety or suffering, we should never be made to feel ashamed for reaching out to others for help or to have a moan. Human beings are social creatures and spreading love and compassion around in this world can never be a bad thing.

We can support one another in many ways. When we develop our intuition, we also become more aware of when those in the world of Spirit step forward to offer love and guidance from higher levels of energetic vibration and consciousness.

THE WORLD OF SPIRIT

What is the 'World of Spirit'?

What is the world of Spirit? I would love to be able to answer this question but if I could, it would take away the mystery of life. When referring to Spirit, I am not referring to God or Heaven in a religious sense, I am referring to the world of subtle energy, higher vibration and infinite levels of consciousness that exist beyond the physical world in which we live our daily lives. Spiritual energy is all around us, vibrating at a higher level and our own spirit and higher consciousness can connect with it at any time in a way that we can comprehend as a physical human being. This comes naturally to some people but takes practice and dedication in others.

There are many interpretations when it comes to talking about spirits and beings of light. We are all beings of light in physical bodies yet somewhere along the way, we lost our conscious awareness of this state of being when we chose to come to Earth in human form. We will be fully reunited with this higher vibration when we transition from our bodies at the end of our physical lifespan.

The world of Spirit is difficult to comprehend because it is not what we are supposed to be focussing on whilst we are here to experience our human lives yet so many of us have an innate curiosity for all things spiritual and to find deeper meaning in life. Many paranormal experiences seem to relate to the world of Spirit, especially ghosts and sensing presences.

Our loved ones who have passed reside in the world of Spirit, as do so many other beings including angels, spirit guides, spirit animals and benevolent beings who have different roles in their own world and ours. I imagine the world of Spirit to look like an iridescent nebula filled with breath-taking beauty and wonder. I was once shown a pink and purple nebula and was told that it is where angels are born. This filled me with great emotion, a lump in my throat and tears of joy falling from my eyes. The only trouble was, I was driving my car at the time!

Allowing spirit energy to come closer to us can be achieved through meditation or simply sitting quietly at a time when you feel relaxed. This is a time when your energy will be calm and your usual mind-chatter will have slowed down. Spirits are pure energy and they find it easier to approach when our minds and bodies are quiet and relaxed but that doesn't mean that they won't pop up to pay us a visit when we least expect it!

The best way for me to explain the world of Spirit as I believe it to be, is to feature my own experiences and journal entries here. Spirit stepped forward to help me and my family through the sudden loss of my father in July 2016. They enabled us to understand that he was at peace and that his energetic presence would never leave us. It is too painful to write about the details here but through a series of profound dreams and messages, Spirit gave us tremendous support.

Time is a healer but the pain of grief ebbs and flows on a daily basis. Some days are good, others are hard to deal with but I never feel alone; even during my lowest points, I can feel the love around me coming from a place that is not of this physical plane. Meditation really helps to enhance this and strengthen the connection, as does walking in nature and spending time with animals. I am eternally grateful and humbled by this connection. It is a real blessing in this often harsh world.

Ghosts, Apparitions and Sensations

Most people go through life having never seen or experienced a ghostly presence. I frequently see things out the corner of my eye and feel spooked but such instances may have a rational explanation, although they do seem very real at the time. Below are some of the most powerful glimpses I have received into the world of Spirit.

Hardwick Hall

My most memorable experience of a ghost was at Hardwick Hall near Chesterfield, England. It was a hot summer's day in around 2008 when we entered the main house and went upstairs. As soon as I entered the first bedroom, I became extremely cold to the bone and everything around me faded out and became muffled. I was drawn to look at the side of the bed and felt a menacing presence watching me. I couldn't see anything with my physical eyes but the penetrating cold in my bones and feeling of foreboding was enough to know I was being observed. It was as if everything around me had slowed down and the only thing in my conscious awareness was the ghostly presence.

I moved through to the next room and I sensed the presence slip through the wall at the back of the room, farthest from the windows. I then felt it rush at me and dash behind one of the curtains. Everyone else seemed to be totally oblivious and I lost track of time. My family had already moved on to the next room. Gradually, the presence of the 'ghost' began to subside but I wanted to stay in the room for a few more minutes out of curiosity. I asked one of the guides if that particular room was haunted. She told me that people had reported shadow figures and that there used to be a door at the same place where I sensed the entity move through the wall!

My Dad's Hotel Ghost

My Dad used to travel a lot when he worked as a technical author at the electricity generating board. He was staying the night at a hotel near Morecambe, England in around 1986 because he was visiting a local power station. He checked in and went to his room to unpack. When he went into the bathroom to freshen up, he heard an almighty crashing and banging sound and came out to discover that the tea tray and its contents were on the floor and the wardrobe door was wide open. He was rather puzzled but tidied it up and went downstairs to dinner. When he returned to his room, the same thing had happened in his absence. Poor Dad was feeling rather spooked by this time. He had rather a fitful sleep and awoke in the night to see a thin strip of vertical white light slowly moving across the foot of his bed. He didn't know what to do so he decided to talk to the 'ghost' and told it that he meant no harm and only wanted to go to sleep.

Eventually the light vanished and he spent the rest of the night with the light on! In the morning, he told the staff in reception and they said, "Ah, so you've met 'Jenny' then?!" The story behind it was that before the building became a hotel, a young lady was confined to that particular room by her father to keep her away from her lover, of whom he strongly disapproved. One stormy night, the young lady's lover was killed out on the roads when he was trying to get to her. The wardrobe door was located where a connecting door used to be between two rooms and this is why it had been flung open. Upon doing some of my own research, it seems that a young lady called Jennifer did indeed live in the house when it was a private residence but I don't know her full story. I shall never forget the look on my Mum's face when Dad rang us to tell the tale!

'Ghost' Crossing the Road

This was taken from my report written on 06.05.15 at 4.30pm:

'An apparition just ran in front of my car and across the road in a nearby village just before the local shop.

It is a windy day with gusts but this was weird and not just tossed up dust. I was driving at around 30mph and I caught sight of a black mist forming on the edge of the kerb on my right as I was heading home.

It rose up to about four feet high in a thin line with a definite 'arm', swiftly got to the centre of the road, became slightly taller and darker then fell away as if dissolving towards the pavement on the other side of the road on my left. It was like half a human silhouette.

It absolutely shocked me and I felt rigid with fear and had a cold shiver. It was hard to continue driving and concentrate but there was nowhere to pull over in the traffic. The music playing in my car seemed to fade into a tunnel and I struggled to take in what I had just seen; playing it over in my mind, wondering what it could have been. It was the distinct shape of it that ruled out dirt in the wind. It wasn't like a whirlwind. It looked like a partial human figure. I did some research but couldn't find anything about anyone being killed on the road along that particular stretch. It'll remain a mystery. I was shaken up for a few hours afterwards.'

'Arm Chair' Ghost

Journal 20.01.16

'I went to see a lady about her cat's behaviour this afternoon. As we sat talking, I couldn't help but keep looking at the arm chair opposite me in the corner. I felt a bit 'spooked' about it, even though it's not an old house (around 20 years old). There were a couple of strange tapping sounds on the top of the cabinet behind the chair, which made me look again. I sensed an energy go across from the chair to the other side of the room (the width of the far end of the room). We still talked and I then saw an orb go from the fireplace, across the front of the arm chair and shoot upwards in front of it. I hadn't mentioned any of this to the lady. We got onto the topic of mediums and she said a local one had visited her with another medium. She picked up on a spirit in the arm chair who also used to cross to the other side of the room. She must have seen my face because

I went all cold! Apparently, it is a relative of her grandma's whom she's never met. Her ex-partner used to feel spooked in the arm chair, as if someone was standing behind him. Other people have seen him and the activity increased when she added her conservatory. The spirit seems to be attached to her rather than the house, mainly in the lounge. I told her what I'd been sensing and she wasn't surprised but I was!'

Hospital Ghost

Journal 27.11.16

'I was waiting for Mum to have her x-rays, I saw a thin, wobbly mist, approximately six feet high, like a heat haze come out of a door into the corridor then vanish. Could it have been a hospital ghost?'

Knowing When Loved Ones Are Around

I often sense the presence of my Dad and other passed family members, friends and pets. They are usually accompanied by an aroma or sensation. The most common ones for my family are the smell of cigarette smoke, perfume and occasionally rotting food! This seems to happen randomly and in different locations. When my Dad is around, I sometimes can smell aftershave and feel gentle touches on my face and hair line.

Sadly, my auntie on Dad's side passed away in December 2016. At her funeral, a huge white dove appeared in the high window above the vicar. It cooed very loudly, announcing its presence as it paraded back and forth bobbing its head. Once it had made sure we were all looking, it swiftly flew away and didn't return. Could this be the spirit of my auntie letting us know she was around? My Dad and his two sisters are now reunited in the spiritual realms and my uncle has sadly now gone to join them. They have visited me in my dreams a few times.

I have looked into developing my mediumship abilities over the past few years and attended a couple of workshops and development circles, which have been very interesting and supportive. They touched me deeply and helped me to grow and remain humble. Below are some of the experiences I have had when loved ones in Spirit have visited or Spirit has touched my life in a beautiful way. I have also included journal entries about other phenomena which are just as fascinating but a little harder to explain. There are some things that we in the physical world are simply not meant to know and this is what keeps the mystery alive. I don't work as a medium but I have had many experiences of that nature, which seem to occur spontaneously.

Journal 15.03.16

'When I was making tea in the kitchen, I turned around from the bread bin to go to the fridge and got whacked in the face by the smell of cigarette smoke! It took a couple of minutes to fade and made me cough.'

Bear mind that none of us smoke and neither do our neighbours! This is usually a sign of the presence of our psychic family friend or my auntie.

Journal 15.04.16

'On Wednesday morning, I was coming out of the supermarket when I suddenly felt the presence of Grandad. He came out of nowhere and said

"aww, Sal" and gave me an energetic hug. I felt so emotional and had to fight back tears as I loaded up the car! Thank you, Grandad! It's an emotional time at the moment but I feel very calm, positive and loved and supported. I'm going in the right direction and the family is too.'

Journal 23.04.16

'My son and I had a very interesting visit to Mum and Dad's tonight. Mum was talking about how she's been smelling perfume around her and who it might be. My son and I both then saw a light orb go from right to left across the light fitting over the dining table. It definitely wasn't from outside. We took some photos. The only unusual thing was that one of them had a golden haze. As we were leaving, my son saw a lady behind him in the hall mirror. He described her in detail including her hair and glasses. It looked like she was from the 1960s. I showed him some photos when we got home and he immediately said it was my Nana (Mum's Mum). There is a photo of her and Grandad with my brother as a baby on his knee from 1966-67. Amazing! My son has my gift. Thank you, Nana!'

Journal 30.08.16

'I was waiting outside a shop in Derby when I spotted a monk dressed in red and orange robes a little further up the street. Suddenly, he was right in front of me, asking for directions to the train station. I told him what he wanted to know then he headed in that direction and seemed to disappear as quickly as he had appeared. It was very busy and I was honoured that he chose to ask me out of all the people around. He had a reassuring, calm presence and brightened up my day.'

Journal 23.01.17

'Just as I started meditating, I heard Monty come into the room, walk around the boxes to my right and rub up them, moving their contents, which crinkled. He then walked around my chair and sat down to my left. I could hear his claws on the carpet. Strange thing was, it turned out that he was still asleep on the landing in exactly the same place as when I'd started!'

Journal 21.02.17

'Something weird woke me up in the middle of the night. It sounded like a cross between the cupboard door above me vibrating at very high speed or someone flicking very quickly through a book with thick pages that was trying to escape from the cupboard. I lay there for a while with my eyes open trying to work out what it could have been but I had no idea! Later on this afternoon, I put the computer on in the study then left the room to get something. There was a sudden 'thwack!' and the photo of Mum and Dad on the study bookcase had fallen over. The support on the back isn't great but it was still in place when I picked it up. I don't know why it fell over or how nothing else around it managed not to fall off. It's rather full on there. Is someone trying to tell me something?'

I do believe that there are some signs that angels and loved ones are visiting us such as pennies, feathers and robins but we mustn't get carried away. There are always going to be feathers and robins around. It's the unusual circumstances that we need to look out for when these occur. If we are out for a walk in the woods, it's perfectly normal to find lots of feathers and see many different birds, it's when we see something out of context that we should take notice.

For instance, if you find a large, white feather in your house after you have just vacuumed and you have previously asked for a sign from the angels or a loved one, it is most likely a gift from them! If a robin redbreast appears right in front of you and seems to say 'hello' and not fly away when you get closer, this could be a loved one. As with everything, take it with a pinch of salt and feel into it with your intuition. Messages from Spirit come with a great depth of love and beautiful energy. You will know when you have had a visit from someone.

My Dad sent me butterflies in the summer in great numbers whenever I asked him to give me a sign. We had a strong connection through cabbage white butterflies and they always showed up, right on cue.

Strange Noises in the Night and Sometimes the Day!

I have always seen, heard and felt strange and inexplicable things that seem to be of a paranormal nature. From seeing shadows over me in bed to something hissing in my face in the night, animal sounds next to my bedside and voices calling my name, there is often something unusual to report in my journal.

Journal 08.05.15

'My daughter and I heard a 'meow' in her bedroom with us. We both believed it was our cat, Monty but he was asleep downstairs! I'm assuming it's Millie or another cat wishing to communicate (from Spirit).'

Journal 07.06.15

'I've seen two small misty apparitions when I've been out dog walking lately (white and fleeting). Also, there's been noise like a squawking parrot by my bedside and a moan like an old woman in the night. Weird! I always attract weird things.'

Journal 22.07.15

'As I started preparing to do my Reiki self-treatment, I suddenly felt surrounded by caring and supportive animal spirits and guides, especially a dog who seemed to be a greyhound or whippet. I asked the animals to give me a physical sign that they were there, such as a sound. Later on, I was suddenly awoken by a 'bark, bark, bark; bark, bark' from behind my head at the back of the bed! I had got my hands on my belly and must have fallen asleep like that. The barking sounded like a collie. It startled me but I wasn't scared. I felt honoured and reassured by the animal spirits! It definitely wasn't coming from outside and it was a friendly bark, as if letting me know that they were there. Thank you!'

I often hear someone cry out 'Muuum!' when the children are both at school. It seems to come from the direction of the stairs. This has also happened when both children were at home and they heard it too. The child sounded very young and we could tell it wasn't coming from outside as we all heard it on the stairs.

I've also heard a man say 'hello' in the hallway when there was no-one at home. I thought it was my husband but he'd already left for work! I cautiously searched the house but only found Monty and the budgies.

I regularly hear distant music and sounds that seem to travel from an unknown origin and sometimes softly spoken words (usually indistinct but sometimes my name or a word or number) and tones and strange sounds at night, especially in my left ear. I also get tones when I sense Spirit around me. Some people would argue that it's tinnitus but it is always accompanied by that 'feeling' and goose bumps. It's very much a feeling of spiritual presence.

Journal 01.06.15

'This morning at 2am, I was awakened by trumpeting sound close to my left ear either right next to my pillow or just above the bedside cabinet. It was a cheerful couple of 'toots' as if there was a happy announcement to be made. I then went to the loo, got back in bed and lay on my right side. As I was nodding off, there was a sharp breath across my left cheek and along the left side of my nose to its tip. I thought it must be my husband breathing on me in his sleep but he was facing away from me towards the wall! I had asked for a sign from the spirits and the angels to let me know they are around just before I went to sleep. The must have decided to give me a sign at 2am!'

Journal 10.09.15

'I keep getting woken up by sudden, loud, sharp breaths in front of my face, especially during or just after Reiki. I also get tickly touches on my face. Not sure if it's me or what but sometimes it sounds like words and it's directly into my face from in front of me.'

I sometimes hear my crystals moving about on my glass shelf:

Journal 01.03.16

'At around 2.30am, I was awakened by what sounded like my crystals chinking on the glass shelf! The wind was blowing and I went to the loo. I turned to face the window when I got back in bed. As soon as I did this, there was a bright, white flash! I opened my eyes again, expecting to hear thunder or rain but nothing happened. Strange! It could've been a solitary flash of lightning. I guess I shall never know.'

Journal 13.03.16

'On the night of 8th March, I was woken up by 'something' scratching at my toes through the duvet. It was a very weird feeling and I've no idea what it was. I've also heard strange snapping and zip type noises close to my left ear as I've been going to sleep. I've also heard a 'mew' and what sounds like my crystals being dragged around their glass shelf.'

Journal 12.09.16

'As I was going to sleep last night, I started to 'hear' things in my left ear, as I often do. It's a bit like white noise intermingled with voices and music. I tried to make out some words. It's a bit like the effect of the spirit box that paranormal investigators use. After a few seconds, I hear "nineteen....fifty....seven" and then it seemed to be music rather than words. It was a woman's voice that said it with a couple of others in the background. I think 1957 was the year Mum and Dad met. After a few minutes, my ear returned to normal....(later that day)...P.S. Mum says she did meet Dad in 1957!'

Orbs and Light Anomalies

There seem to be orbs of light of various colours, intensities and sizes all around us. I have photographed orbs in my house which we believe to be one of our cats in spirit and I have seen flashes and pinpoints of light in trees when I have been out walking. One was even on the path right in front of me when I was out dog walking once. I don't find them scary; their presence gives me comfort and reassurance. I occasionally see them in our bedroom at night. They are usually white but one was bright blue. They may be spirits or plasma beings; we will probably never know. I have also seen shadow anomalies in our house and when out and about. Some have the shape of animals and others are like orbs or butterflies. Here are some of my journal entries about them:

Journal 17.08.15 9.25pm

'After my meditation in the garden, I sat with my eyes open and saw a light anomaly go from the bush where the animals are buried (passed pets) to the edge of the patio. I came indoors after a while because I saw a small, bright flash on the top edge of one of the rocks in front of the shed. I would have said it was a reflection on my glasses, but I wasn't wearing them! I kept seeing other dark and light things flying around. Not sure if they were moths or bats etc. but I left them to it and came in. Hopefully I can meditate outside during the day time soon so I'm not spooked!'

Journal 21.02.15

'We went to Birmingham earlier. In the bookshop, I went over to look at the pet books and a flash of white light caught my eye on a lower shelf to the left. I turned to look and there was a paperback version of the animal communication book I'm reading on my digital reader.'

Journal 18.03.16

'As I was doing Reiki last night, I heard a bird chirrup by the bedroom door then not long after that there was a groan. This scared me a bit. I peeped over into the darkness and a little twinkly light floated across my jewellery box then disappeared.'

Journal 24.05.16

'Today I saw strange anomaly in the sky when I was in the garden at my dog sitting house. The sky was almost clear, apart from the odd cloud. I looked up and saw something glinting very high up; at least 37k feet or more. I wondered if it was a plane, satellite or star but it appeared to be almost stationary for a while and rotating between barely visible, bright and dazzling. It appeared to move slowly in one direction then a bit more in another. I went inside to grab my phone and put it to max zoom. Nothing seemed to appear. It seemed to be sphere one moment then almost triangular the next. It got a little higher and continued to appear to rotate and change shape. It started to cloud over and the object was nearly above the house, going out of view. It remained stationary every so often and, in all, it had made a large zig zag movement since I had first spotted it. I looked at my photos and had captured and image of it one of them. It behaved as if it was under intelligent, deliberate control and was making observations. Interesting!'
Journal 10.08.16

'A few nights ago, my son says that a bright, white orb floated about two feet across his room then vanished. It was about the size of a small apple.'

As you can see, many of these things could have easily been missed but the more often we notice them, the more likely they are to keep occurring.

The world of Spirit often contacts us through our dreams because we are peaceful and receptive and our conscious mind is unlikely to try to intervene. A dream in which Spirit visits us has a very distinct quality to it.

Dreams are one of my favourite topics and feature heavily in my journals. The next chapter explores dreams in great depth.

DREAMS

All About Dreams

Dreams are a powerful source of guidance, healing, intuition and connection to Spirit. You are the best interpreter for your own dreams. One size does not fit all. There are many dream dictionaries and books that offer to interpret our dreams but these are based on folklore and may not always apply in everyday life. You are the one living your life and know yourself best of all. Dreams may often seem cryptic and full of symbology but a pattern may soon reveal itself as the events of the next day or a life situation unfolds.

Dreams come in all shapes and sizes and whilst some people may dream in full technicolour, others may dream in monochrome or not at all. There seem to be many different kinds of dreams, each with their own feel and emotional signature. Dreams can be incredibly healing, touching and inspiring but they can also be absolutely terrifying and leave you frozen with fear in bed. More often than not, if I am unable to recall the precise content of a dream, I shall remember how it felt and this can stay with me for days or sometimes even years! Some dreams tend to slip away before you have got hold of them. Sometimes, trying to remember a dream can be like trying to catch smoke in a fishing net!

Keeping a dream journal, which can be included in your intuitive development journal, is a great way to see patterns forming in your dreams and help you to discover their meaning and how they could help you. It is also a fantastic resource to refer back to when you realise that you've had a detailed predictive dream and have written it all down beforehand. My dreams seem to be cyclical and tail off for a week or two then come back with great luminosity!

The source of our dreams can be anything from the mundane and practical to the spiritual realms and beyond. Our brain needs to rest and heal itself whilst we are sleeping and some of our dreams represent this in the way that they seem to go through the events of the previous day and sort things out. At the opposite extreme, our dreams may involve a visit from a passed loved one in Spirit who seems to look younger and appears fit and healthy in the dream. These dreams have a much stronger emotional resonance than 'sorting' dreams and seem very real indeed. Such dreams can bring us comfort but they can also leave us feeing very emotional and delicate.

Occasionally, and sometimes frequently for some, dreams seem to take us to another dimension in which we have full control of the dream and may feel as if we are actually physically present with the ability to touch things with our own hands. These are lucid dreams and the ability to do this can be developed if you look for resources on the subject. I've only ever had a few dreams like this but once I realise it's a lucid dream and begin to touch things and explore, I am ripped out of the dream and wake up with a jolt in bed!

Types of Dreams

The source and intensity of our dreams can be different every time. The essence and emotional charge of our dreams can stay with us for a very long time, often affecting our mood and outlook for some time afterwards. There are so many different types of dream, I may not be able to list them all but these are some of the varieties that seem to exist:

- Brain-sorting and healing dreams;
- Mish-mash dreams made up of the events of the previous day;
- Recurring dreams that often seem to start in childhood and crop up regularly for years;
- Visits from passed loved ones in Spirit or maybe people you did not know well;
- Feature film movie length dreams in great detail and intensity;
- Annoying dreams that you know were good but the details escape you upon waking and only the essence or the emotion of the dream is left behind;
- Lucid dreams in which you suddenly realise that you are physically present and can control the dream and touch everything with your physical hands but you may suddenly awaken;
- Intuitive and predictive dreams that you recognise by their particular 'feel' and resonance;
- Visits from spirit guides and animals;
- Message dreams that give you life guidance and help you to solve problems;

- Blissful healing dreams that leave you feeling revitalised and positive upon waking;
- Naughty dreams in which we experience romance and passion with just about anybody that our brain seems to throw in there, even if it's rather embarrassing because we know them and feel as though they know about our dream or you wouldn't usually touch them with a ten foot barge pole but you now have strange feelings for them because of your dream, or you may dream about someone famous;
- Scary dreams in which you're trying to get away from something but cannot scream or run;
- Nightmares that leave you feeling frozen with fear or terribly upset, maybe even causing you to wake up sobbing;
- Flying dreams that are incredibly liberating and exhilarating but occasionally there are challenges thrown in that make you work harder or strive to stay up in the air;
- Mundane dreams such as finding yourself cleaning bathrooms or doing the ironing;
- Dreams in which you need the toilet but can't find a decent one nor any privacy;
- Naked dreams in which you find yourself naked or partially clothed or without shoes in public;
- Night terrors or sleep-walking;
- Hallucinations in which you are not sure if you are awake or dreaming. I can remember seeing my budgie on the curtains when I was about nine years old. I watched him for a long time then drifted back to sleep, only to find him safely in his cage the next morning. I have also seen a fox next to my bed and a giant red spider on my pillow, which turned out to be my brain working overtime!
- Eating and drinking dreams;

- Dreams that represent part of your physical body such as dreaming that you are freezing, curled up in the snow and you wake up without any covers on;
- Waking yourself up suddenly because you have 'fallen off the kerb' or kicked a football and your body has actually jolted, waking you up;
- Waking yourself up snoring, talking, laughing or making strange noises;
- Sounds, smells or sensations entering your senses and you dream about them;
- Driving dreams or dreaming that you are driving but the car is invisible and you go really slowly because you have to will it to move along with your mind or legs;
- Falling dreams in which you suddenly jolt as if you have been out of your body and fall back into it with no memory of where you have been;
- Realistic dreams where you get out of bed, get up and get dressed then realise you only dreamt it but then it repeats again but you still find yourself lying in bed and wonder if you are still dreaming or if you have now actually woken up;
- UFO dreams in which there is a UFO or alien invasion which is absolutely terrifying but nobody else really seems bothered despite your insistence that we are being invaded.

Intuitive dreams have a quality all of their own. From simple events that may take place the next day to world disasters, when you first have an intuitive dream it can leave you feeling stunned and amazed. This is why it's important to keep a journal and log your dreams as soon as you wake up or at least make notes so that you can remember and write it down in full later on. Sometimes they are a rather cryptic and use symbolism but you will soon realise how your dream fits into the facts of what you seem to have predicted. It's all very obvious once you realise.

Journal 06.02.16

'Dreams seem to fade fast if they don't have emotional content, humour or a 'dark' feel to them. They must be stored in the medium-term memory then get removed if they are not helpful or significant in any way.'

Getting to know your own dreams is a fascinating process, especially if your dreams have started to become more powerful over time. Keep track of them and cherish your dreams. They often come to us from a higher source when our consciousness is not getting in the way. Dreams are a very pure source of intuitive information.

Sources of Dreams

Some dreams come to us as a one-night package and others form a series over a few weeks, months or maybe even years, sending us a message that may seem cryptic at first but as your life continues to take its twists and turns, the meaning of these dreams can suddenly become abundantly clear. We do not really know where dreams come from, so here is a list of what I believe to be potential sources of our dreams:

- The logical processing part of our brains sorting itself out after a busy day;
- The healing processes of our bodies and brains as they regenerate at night;

- External influences that we are consciously unaware of because we are asleep;
- Guidance from our higher-self and intuition;
- Spirit guides;
- The Spirit world sending us messages and connection with passed loved ones;
- Predictive information through Universal energy;
- Healing from Spirit;
- Deep insecurities and fears from our subconscious and emotional centres;
- Our deepest, secret desires from our subconscious;
- Other sources that remain a mystery!

My Own Dreams

This section could go on forever but it is probably best that I give some examples as an insight into the weird and wonderful world of my dreams. Hopefully, you can relate to some of them and have 'a-ha!' moments in which you realise that you are not alone in the craziness of your dreams. It's all perfectly normal and you can begin to see the point of some of your dreams and how they can be important in guiding you through your life. There really is a deeper meaning to the colourful nightlife of our brain's activity.

I have received many visits from passed loved ones in my dreams. The dream always has a very distinct feeling about it. The person usually looks really well and often younger than when they passed. They stand out against the background and seem to be very peaceful and content. Sometimes they speak and other times their presence is enough for their visit to be complete. The background in the dream is often misty and indistinct because the dream is about the person visiting and not their location. I have had a couple of dreams about famous people who have recently passed that seem very real. I'm not sure why they would choose to visit me but I am very honoured that they seemed to.

Some of my dreams are like feature length films. They should win an award! I have had so many but they can be very rambling so I shall just give an overview of a couple. One was about some German soldiers at a camp during World War II. I seemed to be a spy and was hiding in a wall so I didn't get caught and shot. I escaped in the end with another British spy and we managed to achieve our objectives. In another dream, I was in a bar somewhere and it turned out to be in a sacred, mystical forest. I met many people just like me who were kindred spirits. We witnessed the birth of a 'tree person' which hadn't taken place for hundreds of years. The dream seemed very real and it left me with a wonderful feeling of joy and elation.

The dreams that I enjoy most of all are flying dreams and dreams featuring animals. These have very powerful content for me and often help me to make decisions in life when I realise their true meaning. I often find myself swooping down over the countryside, shooting upwards through the clouds with the greatest of ease or sometimes I struggle to fly and people or zombies are trying to grab my ankles to stop me taking off! Occasionally, I am trying to fly but there are telephone wires or other obstacles in my way but I have to overcome such challenges so that I can fly freely. Flying dreams are usually liberating but there is sometimes an air of frustration or fear.

Animal spirit guides often visit me in dreams and give me emotional support and healing energy to keep me strong. I was once walking around with a huge panther by my side in a dream and everyone else seemed to have big cat guides as well. We had to be careful not to bump into each other or fights could ensue. If I kept my hand on the shoulder of my big cat guide, it strengthened our connection. In another dream, each person had at least five wolves as guides that went around with them. They too would sometimes get into fights so we had to make sure we gave each other a wide berth!

Lucid dreams are so intense and I have only had a few. They give you the most incredible feeling of clarity but are often quickly snatched away. These are the only truly lucid dreams I've ever had. I'm hoping for some more:

Journal 07.12.16

'I found myself looking down into a pool/lake. The water was clear but grey/green like healing volcanic waters. I could see red and cream bricks on the bottom, arranged like parquet flooring but thinner. As I stared down at them, I had the powerful realisation that I was in my dream and had full physical awareness and sensation. It was the most incredible lucid dream I have ever had. I could feel myself buoyant in the water. I splashed at the surface and plunged down into it up to my chin. I had no clothes on and felt complete peace and freedom. I stayed floating there and all I could see was the vast, healing expanse of the grey/green water. It was so beautiful. I think the whole dream was probably only a few seconds long but I shall never forget the feeling of that moment when I realised that I was actually consciously IN one of my dreams! Normally in lucid dreams, I have been able to make decisions about where I go and what I see but nothing like this full, physical immersion in the dream. Amazing!'

Journal 23.12.16

'In my dream, I seemed to be in a horrible, old school hall. There were only a couple of windows and it was quite dark. There was wood panelling on the walls and floor. It was a horrible, slightly greenish wood. After a few minutes, I suddenly realised it was a lucid dream! I was actually, consciously stood there and realised that I was fully aware and present in my dream. I felt that lucid dream 'rush' and reached out to touch the wall but then I was suddenly torn away out of it as if I wasn't allowed to have the experience. It felt as if I fell backwards down a tunnel then awoke suddenly in my own body but was dazed.'

Journal 20.01.17

'I had a lucid dream that I was cycling down a street nearby. I turned around to see if my husband was still behind me but he wasn't. It was dark and as I looked towards the centre of town, I could see two children pulling wheelers up past a fence, a person further back and a man walking a black, fluffy dog crossing the road. That was when I realised I was actually IN the dream and could control it. I told myself to stare at the man with the dog so I could stay in the dream. I very slowly crouched down so I could touch the ground beneath me. Just as I put my fingers onto the tarmac and could feel the ground and some dirt with my fingertips, I was snatched out of the dream and woke up!'

When I was a child, I used to have recurring dreams that a small, toy aeroplane was coming after me. Occasionally, it was a washing machine or vacuum cleaner. They sound a bit tame but the dreams were really scary! These days, I usually have recurring dreams that I'm still doing my exams or have a part-time job:

Journal 17.09.15

'I keep having recurring dreams that I still have a part-time job. For a while, it's a relief but then it becomes a burden and I want to quit but can't seem to get out of it. Another recurring dream is that I have to do my GCSEs all over again and I don't want to. No-one believes that I've already done them, years ago! I also keep dreaming that drone-type alien crafts keep coming down from the sky to get me or at least make me frightened in some way. Scary!'

Journal 28.11.16

'I dreamt last night that I was doing my GCSEs again and asked to stop as I'd already proved myself and didn't want to do it again.'

Journal 28.07.16

'Last night, I dream (as I have before) that I still have a part-time job that I want to give up because it interferes with everything.'

A lot of my dreams are predictive, either directly or cryptically.

The earliest predictive dream that I can recall is from the time when I had just become pregnant with my daughter. I was not aware of this when I had the dream. I was stood in the street somewhere that looked like a city but my focus was drawn to a little boy in the foreground. He looked like a pauper from the Victorian days. He released a dove up into the air and it fluttered up quite high then gracefully tumbled down into my belly. As soon as I woke up, I knew that I was pregnant. We had been trying for eleven months so it was amazing to be blessed with such a poignant dream. I did a pregnancy test the next day that confirmed it. Here are some more recent ones:

Journal 20.08.15

'I had a predictive dream! My daughter ordered a dragon figure for her collection. We've been waiting for it to arrive but I had no idea what it looked like. For some reason, I assumed it was black or grey. I dreamt that it arrived wrapped in brown paper last night. She was opening it excitedly in my dream and I could see lots of beige horns emerging from the top. As it turned out, it DID arrive today and the top of its head is exactly like my dream.'

Journal 23.01.16

'A couple of nights ago, I was cat sitting at the flat I go to, trying to clean out the litter tray in the bathroom but it kept getting covered in stuff in a heap and I was getting annoyed because it was unhygienic. The cats' owner told me it was normal and nothing to worry about. I went cat sitting there tonight and there was an empty packet of toilet tissue and the bathmat in the litter tray covering a poo! There were also a couple of other things piled up on the floor. This reminded me of my dream. I went into the lounge to get a poo bag. When I returned, one of the cats had re-buried the poo under the bathmat! He's never done that before. It was just like my dream.'

Journal 26.03.15

'There's been a terrible plane crash in the Alps which killed 150 people. It's believed that the co-pilot may have done it deliberately. What's strange is how I dreamt about a plane crash and people screaming and crying a couple of nights ago.'

Journal 09.06.15

'I had a dream last night that Mum and Dad came back from holiday early because Mum was uncomfortable for some reason and was upset about it. They were home when I turned up to do the watering but there was a bright red garage door sideways on to their house on their neighbour's side. Dreams can be very puzzling sometimes.'

The next day:

'Mum texted me last night and guess what? They're coming home early because the cottage is uncomfy! They'll be home Friday instead of Saturday. There's only one comfy chair, the bed is uncomfy and the hob doesn't work. I had told the kids about my dream as well as writing it down! I got validation on that one!'.

Journal 27.01.16

'I dreamt that I arrived at one of my dog walks and a man appeared trying to deliver bags of coal. He was an older chap in light overalls. We got in each other's way a bit and there were some other people there who were a bit 'floaty' and I couldn't clearly see them. I asked the man to bring the bags of coal into the house but I didn't know where he should put them as they don't have a coal fire because it's a brand new house! He seemed to be dragging them through the kitchen and into the hall, possibly upstairs. The strange thing was, when I arrived for my dog walk there today, the garden gate was open and there was a bag on the drive. I could see a man in the utility in a high viz jacket. There was a man up a ladder in the garden. I had to go in through the front door instead of the utility because there were two men in there and one in the kitchen. They passed me the lead and treats and I took the dog out for a walk. I had no idea there would be anyone there today. Not quite bags of coal but what a coincidence! They seemed to be fitting a new extractor fan and doing a few other jobs. They

were getting in and out through the front door and the atmosphere was a bit confused and awkward like my dream.'

Journal 24.03.16

'I dreamt that I went to walk my collie client but her owner was at home and kept saying she was going out. There were two men watching her closely to make sure she was safe. I kept walking her but we were indoors, a bit like a leisure centre or old people's home.'

Then a little later on that morning:

'How strange! The collie's owner just texted me to say that I should take her out through the back door today because she's got painters in doing the banisters and stairs. In my dream there were handrails, ramps and stairs. That's why I thought it could be an old people's home. Is this my psychic abilities working again??!'

Journal 27.03.16

'I had a dream last night that I was at a park in the middle of Boston, Massachusetts in the USA. It was really busy and there was some sort of celebration. I said to my husband, "I'm so excited to be in Boston, Massachusetts!" It suddenly swapped to be Central Park in New York City then another city park somewhere. Eventually, I was back in the park in central Boston. There seemed to be ladies with their heads covered in a period costume or head scarf. The dream is a bit vague now but today there was a suicide bombing at a busy park in Pakistan. They targeted the children's' play area. It was terrible. I can't help but feel that my dream was a partial premonition but I didn't sense any danger. The park in the attack was in the city of Lahore. I feel that the connection with the

bombing may have been the reference to Boston because they had the Boston bombings. It kept coming across very clearly.'

Journal 02.06.16

'I had a dream that the only way I could ever be truly happy was to live my life in a log cabin in the woods. The closest thing I could find locally was some static caravans in the nearest village. I was rather disappointed because the leaflet said they only hired them out for one night. The next day, I was giving my son's friend a lift home and he said that he had to be back by 8am because they were going away to the seaside in a static caravan owned by some relatives for one night!'

Journal 22.07.16

'I dreamt that one of the cats I'm looking after came home with a mouse trap stuck to either side of him! The vet managed to help him and put him in a cardboard box for me to take him home. In reality, he was fine but when I got to another cat sit, there were two dead mice waiting for me that the cat brought in! Dreams are so cryptic!'

Journal 12.11.16

'I dreamt last night that I was on the bank of a huge river near a city. Suddenly, there was a massive tidal surge, as if it was the apocalypse. The water flooded around in gigantic swells, ripping out the river banks and suspension cables of a bridge. They flew into the air violently whipping at anything in their path and tearing down structures and human beings. I moved up along the bank towards a high embankment that was more like a wall of a dam. There were a few people around but they didn't even attempt to get away, despite being in a panic. They allowed the flood waters and cables to take them. I continued to climb up the embankment.

It was quickly being eroded away by every swell of flood water yet I felt safe, knowing that I would make it to the top and slightly to the left where I could see a field through a fence. I seemed to be the only one left then the dream ended. In another dream, we seemed to be at a cheap holiday camp on a boat ride on wheels. It shook and jostled us through a tunnel and I was glad to get off.' And following on from this on the 13th November:

'Oh gosh, it seems that my dream about the river on Friday night may have been a premonition or that I sensed the earthquake and tsunami in New Zealand! It happened last night and two people died. It was semi-dark in my dream but I'd forgotten to add that detail in. It must have been horrible to experience because the magnitude was 7.8!'

On the night of 16th November 2016, I dreamt about an old metal framed window held together with plastic and tape. On the 18th, there were high winds and one of the windows was blown out at a local school and also a major factory nearby.

Journal 23.11.16

'Last night I dreamt that Mum was a super-woman. She was hiding in a wall that was covered in tiny red lights set into a black background. I telepathically told her to get out of there because she'd be spotted and 'they' were coming for her. You could make out her outline in the upper left part of the wall because she was blocking out the red lights. The scene then changed to an ancient town and Mum was hiding behind some elaborate carving in another wall. 'They' came along (soldiers like unstoppable monsters) and tore the statues apart like they were made of dust, trying to find Mum. To my relief, Mum seemed to have already got away but the beautiful, ancient monument was destroyed. There were more parts to the dream but they have faded because it was in the middle of the night.'

I had bad, undirected anxiety on the afternoon of 24.11.16 then later on that evening, my Mum rang to say she'd fallen over in her kitchen and broken her arm. I'd also had a dream a few nights before about a white crochet shawl and two of my aunties (both in spirit) arguing about it. This is what I wrote about how it fitted into my dreams:

'When I arrived at Mum's, she asked me to get her white crochet shawl and the ambulance man fetched a crochet white blanket to leave the house, just like in my dream about my aunties a few nights ago. Also, could the dream about Mum being in a wall and blocking out the lights represent the x-rays she had on her arm? Sometimes, I seem to 'predict' things but it's always so cryptic, it's almost impossible to know what it could mean until something happens.'

There also seemed to be a big building with curved windows in my dream on the night of 17.11.16, like a crematorium and the funeral director of my Dad's funeral was there. My auntie on my Dad's side was in the dream and was unwell but she had started out looking glowing and young. Her daughter was upset because she was struggling to look after her. In real life, my auntie passed away in December 2016 after being in a nursing home for a few days.

Journal 28.12.16

'Last night I dreamt that we were driving along when my husband went a bit funny. I managed to persuade him to pull over into a lay-by and stop the car so I could do something to remedy the situation. It seemed like I was applying the handbrake or something. There seemed to be a policeman there but he was no use. As it happened, in real life, the next morning we were on our way out for the day when the sat nav popped off the windscreen. I couldn't reach it whilst we were going along so I had to

ask him to pull over into a lay-by so I could lean forward and put it back on! This happened again a bit further along the road. Just like my dream or what!?'

Journal 01.02.17

'I dreamt that I wanted to give up my part-time job to focus on working with animals. I only worked there 3-4 mornings but was worried about losing a regular income. I'd only been back there a short while after being off sick for a long time and wasn't putting my heart into my work. People had started to notice that things weren't getting done.' Later on that same day, I seemed to find the reason for this dream:

'The owner of one of the dogs I used to walk has asked me to start walking her dog again. I thought she meant the former three days per week but she wanted five, which is too much of a stretch for me so I had to tell her I couldn't manage it. It's been a few months because she's been off sick with a mystery illness and is going back to work full-time soon.'

As you can tell, dreams are a very big part of my intuitive abilities. My journals are full of dreams and I've only written about a few of them here. Some are bizarre and others are terrifying. Some of the worst ones are when people or entities are after me and I am unable to scream or run away. I'm sure that maybe one day I shall fill an entire book with my dreams but some are so strange, I shall keep them to myself!

Of course, having vivid dreams is just one aspect of intuition. Being intuitive and highly sensitive can bring many challenges and lead us to examine the depths of our soul and our own inner conflicts and complexities. Growing up as a sensitive child was quite a confusing time but also had a magical quality to it. Reigniting that magical quality as an adult can light up your life in ways you could never have imagined!

BEING INTUITIVE

My Intuitive Youth

I was born on a wild and windy day in 1976. My parents had been told not to expect any more children after the birth of my brother nine years earlier but there was I, alive and kicking; a big surprise! I have always enjoyed being a little bit different and surprising ever since.

I am very fortunate to have many wonderful memories from my childhood. I was brought up in a loving home in which my parents, brother and grandparents happily supported every interest and idea that I ever had and helped me to explore it to its full potential – until I got bored and swiftly moved on to the next. From horses, to cats, to music, hair and make-up, I have wanted to explore just about anything that most children do. One thing I have always loved most of all was the great outdoors, animals and anything remotely mysterious or spooky. I expressed my latest interests by creating a theme in my bedroom. My walls and wardrobe doors were covered in posters of my latest musical heroes, cats and horses. My room was full of houseplants, cacti and animal ornaments.

As far back as I can remember I preferred my own company to large groups of children my own age. My parents once left me at birthday party featuring a naff puppet show. All of the children around me were in hysterics but I had no idea how they could find it amusing. Don't get me wrong, I'm not a party-pooper but I always felt different and enjoyed the company of older children, adults and animals and hated to be in crowds or feeling pressured to follow the masses. I had a few friends and preferred quality over quantity. I needed my own space and hated drama and confrontation. I was highly sensitive and very aware of my own likes and dislikes, especially when it came to how I liked to spend my spare time.

I would happily walk miles through fields and streams with water pouring over the top of my wellies, stop to say 'hello' to cows and horses and run along the beach investigating rock pools on holiday. Confined, unnatural places drained me and left me feeling depressed. I needed to be somewhere light and bright for my own well-being, preferably with a furry or feathered companion or two. I enjoyed watching thunderstorms, gazing at the stars and visiting old buildings in the hope of seeing a ghost, yet I was terrified of vacuum cleaners, lifts and anything that resembled a clown! Some of my fondest memories are of when I was spending time with my close family, friends and animals. Everywhere I went, my heart would light up if there was an animal around and the day would take a brighter turn if I could befriend them.

One of the most noticeable things for me was my awareness of the energy of buildings, locations, people, animals and objects. I would often hide behind my mother or father if I didn't like somebody. Going around the shops with me was a bit of a nightmare. I would run at the sight or sound of a vacuum cleaner and hated busy places, lifts, cigarette smoke and was easily bored. One of my famous sayings that drove my mother mad was 'I'm bored, can we go now?'

My earliest memory is of me sitting in an orange washing basket, laughing and giggling at around 18 months of age. Moving on from this, my next memory is of our family cat, Lucky. She was a black and white cat with amazing green eyes and a face shaped like a Siamese with a voice to match. Lucky used to sit on my lap and completely fill it. She had a wonderful nature and was very calm and loving. She was the 'cat'alyst for my love of animals and soon a gorgeous black rabbit called 'Smoo' also joined our family. I am told that he was called 'Smoo' because I was too young to say the word 'smooth' properly when I first stroked him.

Looking back through family photo albums is a real pleasure for me. I have so many wonderful memories and to capture them in photographs is absolutely precious. There are so many in which I am with animals. Whether I was on holiday, a day trip or in our back garden, there are dozens of photos of me surrounded by animals. They bring so much joy!

We also had a variety of other animals over the years, including three budgies, another rabbit, guinea pig, hamster and two pigeons who used to visit every day. Later on, as I approached my teenage years, we had a very bold ginger cat named Dave. He was a real character who mellowed with age and lived until I was in my mid-20s.

Everywhere I went, I felt a sense of emptiness unless there was an animal around. I would stop and interact with every animal I met and I still do to this day. Their energy has always resonated with me and brought me great love, comfort and gratitude.

We had some very interesting, friendly neighbours living next-door-but-one when I was very young. The lady who lived there was a psychic medium and healer. The neighbours in-between us were not so nice. They seemed to dislike most people and animals and used to throw things at Lucky if she dared to venture into their garden. They also used to shout at my brother sometimes when he was playing outdoors.

I have a very clear memory of the nice lady from next-door-but-one bringing round a bamboo cross and placing it on our wall to bless us against our evil neighbours and keep their bad energy away. This put the wind up me a bit but it was nice to have some extra protection.

It was around this time that I can remember having my first vivid dream. The scary, horrible lady neighbour had put me into a lift. She was wearing a long, black dress and was cackling like a witch. She seemed to be in the lift with me but was outside the doors and the lift was falling at a terrifying rate. Just before it hit the ground I woke up. This made me even more terrified of her. From that point on, if I could hear her vacuuming, I would go to the bottom of the garden to get away from the scary droning noise.

The nice psychic lady had a lovely daughter who was a few years older than me and used to come round to entertain me when my Mum wanted to get on with a few jobs. We used to play dress-up, sing songs and dance. She used to tell me fascinating stories about the work her Mum did and all about spirits, UFOs and aliens. I would listen to her for hours.

One day when she came round, there was a violent thunderstorm and we made a den near the window and hid under some white sheets. Not long after that she spotted a cigar shaped UFO over our back garden. I was only about six at the time but I still thought it was exciting and nowhere near as scary as a vacuum cleaner.

When I was a little bit older, my Dad started suffering from depression due to pressures at work. One day, our psychic neighbour came round and gave him some healing. She gently placed her hands over his head and warm, wonderful healing energy filled his entire being. A few days later, he was almost back to his normal self and his work situation improved. I can remember hearing him laugh for the first time in months when he told me a bed time story. It was an incredible feeling and will always stay in my memory.

My first day at school is another clear memory. I thought school was great fun because we played 'shops' with empty bottles and packets and pretend money. I soon made friends with a few people and took a swift dislike to a couple of them who turned out to be bullies and liked to pull the legs off daddy-long-legs. I could get the measure of people very quickly but was shy around strangers and didn't like speaking out in front of the class or when we put on plays. I liked to blend into the background and observe.

I was very easily bored and my favourite subjects revolved around animals and nature. I also loved words and writing stories. When I was about five or six years old, I wrote a story about a butterfly who lived in a grey, drab world because an evil witch had taken all of the colour away. One day, he found a magic box and flew through it to become a beautiful butterfly with all of the colours of the rainbow.

He helped to turn the land back into a myriad of amazing colour once more and defeated the evil witch. My teacher was impressed and thought I'd copied it from somewhere else!

After a few years, we moved away to a larger house so that my Mum's parents could move into a granny flat upstairs. We still kept in touch with our former neighbours (not the scary ones!). Sadly, the psychic lady passed away a few years after but her daughter has inherited her gift as a psychic medium. I met up with her in 2015 after many years of us not seeing each other. We had a wonderful time and the years were wiped away. As we walked along together, we suddenly felt the presence of her Mum walking between us. It was an amazing moment and we have continued to meet up since then.

We lived in a friend's house for a few weeks during the move because our house sold quickly. I loved it there because the garden backed on to a field with young cows and guinea fowl. I'd often climb over the fence to visit them and sometimes play with a girl from a few gardens along. I went to a different infants school for a while at which we learnt more about nature and spent lots of time outdoors. I liked that too because I would walk through fields to get there.

The summer holidays soon came around and we moved to our new house with my grandparents. It seemed like a magical place and had a big garden to play in. There are so many happy memories from the years we spent there. We grew loads of our own fruit and veg and I'd spend hours playing outside in all weathers. My friends loved it too and always ended up at our house for tea!

The house was in an elevated position and you could see for miles front and back. I'd spend many hours gazing out of the windows, watching the world go by and the seasons changing. I'd also spend lots of time in our street playing on my bike and roller-skating. I can't count how many times I'd fall over though! I had lots of friends I used to play out with but they were quite often mean and I'd run back home to spend time in my own company.

The only problem was that my sensitivity went into overdrive at night. I was scared to sleep on my own because my dreams were so vivid and I'd sometimes have hallucinations. I'd dream about aliens that smelt of acrid static and dark entities that would chase me but I was unable to scream or run away. I sometimes also felt afraid in my room during the daytime but not very often. It wasn't an old house but it sometimes had peculiar energy.

I started junior school in the year that we moved there and absolutely hated it. I was bullied from the outset. Not just by the pupils but by the teachers as well. I was quiet and hated confrontation so I struggled to stick up for myself because I was far too polite for my own good. I did manage to get into a fight with one boy though and I won. I'd had enough of him that day and he never bullied me again after that. It was quite a strict school with a religious undertone. Once they decided that you didn't fit, they made life very uncomfortable. I'd often feign illness so I didn't have to go and they pulled my Mum up about my attendance record. I did usually have genuine stomach aches though because of the tension. It was a very happy day when I left that place. On the up-side, I made a few good friends along the way.

I loved my grandparents living with us. They were very loving and I'd often get into their cosy bed in the mornings with them to have a snooze. Christmas time was wonderful and our whole family would come over for a get-together. I got used to them always being there, steady as rocks.

I started secondary school in 1987, four years after moving house and really enjoyed it. I made some very close friends. We had a good laugh and the years flew by. We're still in touch though but live quite far away from each other. I shall never find good friends like them again. We grew up together.

Sadly, my Nana and Grandad both passed away during the 1990s and my brother got married and left home. The house was a bit too big for just the three of us so my parents planned a move back to Derby.

I did well at school but spent quite a few years drifting in an out of unsatisfying jobs and courses.
After some mild and vague soul-searching, I decided that I wanted to work with animals and get a degree. Ecology popped out at me so I started a Science Foundation course with the Open University and, despite actually finding that boring too, I somehow scraped a pass. I took more of an interest in psychology after that but decided not to continue studying for a degree whilst I was working. I needed to be with animals and nurture my spiritual side but I had many years of the 'wrong job' to come before I realised that I absolutely had to do this for the good of my health!

I was struck down by glandular fever when I was 18 and have never been the same since. I was bed-ridden for three weeks and it took months to regain my energy. I ended up having my tonsils removed in 2002 after suffering from chronic throat infections, which improved my quality of life considerably and gave me a lot more energy.

In 1995, I heard on the grapevine through some family friends that there was a young man looking for love. As soon as I heard his name, I 'knew' I was going to marry him. Not because I am a psychopathic stalker, but because I am intuitive! I didn't really know I was intuitive back then though.

Anyway, we got on really well, soon moved into together and got married in 1997. Our daughter came along three years later and our son almost four years after that. Our family was complete! Of course, we had some animal companions along the way. We adopted our cats Millie and Mandy from a local animal charity in 1997 and also had a hamster called Spicy. Later on, my daughter had a hamster called Bubbles and we kept two chickens called Midnight and Moonlight and two noisy budgies, Karma and Coconut. Sadly, they are all no longer with us but they remain forever in our hearts.

We now share our lives with Monty, a gorgeous black and white cat who chose to come and live with us in 2009.

I've had many different jobs over the years and ended up in secretarial and accounting work. After having to work for several horrible bosses, I was finally given a forcible nudge by the Universe in 2011 to leave my dull and mind-numbing office job and start my own business as a pet sitter. What a great decision. Thank you, Universe!

My intuition and enthusiasm developed rapidly once I spread my wings and my business seemed to effortlessly grow as all of the right people came along at the right time. I also did some cleaning for a couple of years for extra money to support my pet sitting business but it grew too much and I eventually let it go so I could focus on animals. I started learning Reiki in 2012 and it was life-changing. I was drawn to it because I could feel healing energy in my hands but needed something to give me clarity and direction.

By March 2015, I was a Reiki Master Teacher and also learning about animal behaviour and communication. My spiritual and intuitive development has gone from strength to strength and continues to flourish. Life is good but can still seem a little overwhelming at times. Achieving balance and remaining calm often seem like a major feat but most days I feel good and I am always open to learning more about myself and those around me. There is so much to explore and opportunities are abundant, you just have to remain open, humble and aware.

Receiving and Perceiving Intuitive Information

My intuition can strike at any time. Whether I am driving along in the car or lost in the depths of a complex dream, intuition often comes along with its many messages and insights, for which I am very grateful. It is such a simple word yet it is infinite and vast in its expression and connections. There is so much to learn from intuition and making it part of your life is a beautiful thing.

Our intuitive sense can become blocked and distorted if we experience stress, illness or resist its influence. This is not a rule of thumb, however. Intuition is often at its most powerful for me during difficult times when I need all the support I can get.

Receiving intuitive information and learning how to perceive it takes a lot of practice, as does learning to trust in the processes of the Universe. I shall always remain a humble and willing student of intuition because at first, I was way off the mark and went along with all the stereotypical expectations and hype that most people believe about being 'psychic'.

When I first started delving into the world of psychic development, I believed that I would see apparitions with my physical eyes and experience everything first-hand with my five physical senses. I expected great things and instant results with spirits queuing up at my door to speak through me and help me to predict the future. Er, no. That did NOT happen so I started to educate myself and read as many psychic, intuitive and spiritual books that I could get my hands on. Even then, I still didn't quite 'get it' until the day in 2009 when I started to feel the energy buzzing in my hands. I was no longer able to tolerate being stuck in an office job and was becoming much more emotionally sensitive, especially around vulnerable people and animals. My Empath senses became stronger and by 2011, I took the leap and left work. This was the turning point.

After many years of experience and learning to allow my abilities to naturally unfold, I have come to realise how intuition works. It begins from the inside out and is not about impressing other people by giving mind-blowing psychic readings, it is based on a pure spiritual connection through subtle energy and higher levels of consciousness. I have seen unexplained things with my physical eyes and other senses but the majority of my experiences flow through me as energy and information received through my third eye. Dreams are also a big source of intuitive information for me and give me life guidance, even if it is sometimes rather cryptic.

Reiki opened all of this up for me but intuitive development is different for everyone and other spiritual practices can have the same effect.

I find that intuition is cyclical and seems to be at its strongest every 2-3 weeks unless something stressful occurs, which can knock everything sideways. As soon as I feel my intuitive antenna 'switch on', I flow into the sensation to enhance it and my intuition begins to work at maximum efficiency and capacity. During this heightened time, I receive lots of intuitive information, my dreams gain greater clarity and I feel very well, as if my cheeks are glowing and it's easy to smile about the small things. My third eye opens and becomes more active, protected by my inner strength, spirit and the light of Reiki and the Universe.

This usually marks the start of a highly creative and inspired period of time during which I make the most of my good energy flow and remain open to allow inspiration and ideas to flow through unhindered by logical thought. This gradually slides into a state of calmness then a week or two of feeling 'normal' or sometimes a bit low before my intuition flows more strongly again and the cycle repeats itself. This could be hormonal or related to the cycles of the moon. I love to meditate in the light of the full moon! Our cat is also energised around this time.

I feel that there is a matrix of intuition like an infinite net that is visible through the third eye. When I use my third eye, I can have my physical eyes open or closed. It's more of a sensation of looking but receiving information through my third eye/crown chakra and directly into my brain to be interpreted. When 'looking' intuitively in this kind of way, the matrix of intuition appears to be flexible and easily moulded by objects, scenes, words and shapes. I use it for everything, such as seeing if there is an obstruction around the corner when I am driving, before it comes into view. The part of the brain that interprets the incoming intuitive information seems to be in the visual cortex, as if you are using your physical eyes but you are not. It is a different place to imagination or remembering what something looks like.

I also often feel a push or pull from my heart centre and/or solar plexus when intuiting information. It may also affect my whole aura or if it is a communication from the world of Spirit, my crown chakra may become lively and I experience gentle whirling sensations as information comes through. This can also happen during meditation and Reiki. It is important to close it back up to a comfortable position afterwards by using visualisation techniques so that it is not left fully open and vulnerable. We need to look after the good health of our chakras and energy centres.

Intuition tells the truth; there is no other way it can be. When working with intuition and feeling drawn to the truth about something, it stands out against everything else light a bright light. The truth is undeniable and everything else fades into the background. There is a sense of knowing that comes with intuition that is unmistakable, no matter how small the details. At its strongest, intuition brings the truth through encompassing all of the senses, from the physical to the ethereal, there is absolutely no doubt and the trust placed in intuition is absolute. When you get that feeling in every fibre of your being about being absolutely right, you lose all fear of saying what you feel to be true and you know that what comes out of your mouth is something that you could not have known but for your intuition. It is a comforting, humbling and deeply emotional feeling to be able to offer that level of confirmation, especially when it is information about a passed loved one and it brings validation to someone that the person or animal they lost is still very much alive in spirit.

Positive and negative aspects of my abilities:

- Euphoria and joy at my abilities and sense of 'knowing';
- Seeing the truth in people and situations – personal and in the media;
- Easily bored and unable to finish some projects, courses or books as they become mentally and physically draining;
- Unable to stay in a job for a long time or struggling on a daily basis, especially if working with or for unpleasant people (psychic vampires!);
- Irrational anxiety and erratic energy patterns if I am doing something that is not right for me or is out of place with my interests or passions at that time;
- Becoming physically ill if I do not listen to my instincts or intuition for some reason (denial, sense of duty or not wanting to let someone down, unable to say 'No');
- Self-sacrificing in favour of others to the point where I become mentally and physically drained because I try too hard and need to feel in control or that I am pleasing others even though they would manage without my input;
- Wanting to be more sociable and gregarious but when it comes to the crunch I would rather stay and home and curl up on the sofa with a good book;
- Unable to understand why some people are so cruel, selfish and ignorant;
- Depression and anxiety (mild to moderate, especially during hormonal times), hopelessness (for myself, family or the whole world that I can't change) which eventually leads to hope, finding strength and the determination to find true

happiness and make a difference in the world, even if it is only a small one;

- It is hard to accept that I cannot change the way some humans think and treat other humans, the planet and all of its inhabitants but we all have a role to play and the more 'good' people who try to make a difference, the better;
- Overcoming and managing most of the above by maintaining inner strength and calm through the ways I have suggested in this book and keeping a pure and harmonious energy flow (most of the time!);
- Making sense of my past by being fully connected with the present;
- Feeling drawn to unusual and creative people, objects and locations, especially if they get their beauty from nature such as rustic creations, hand-made jewellery and clothing, new age, mystical art and figures, woodland, mountains, sweeping landscapes and places of historical and spiritual interest;
- I love music but it absolutely has to be the right kind to match my mood and be deep and meaningful, well-structured and harmonious or have a strong emotional connection to good times in my past. I hope no-one ever needs to watch my dash cam footage as they will hear me singing loudly in the car with blaring music on; I love to dance but don't do it so much these days – I really should though!
- I am highly sensitive to subtle energy and Reiki. I love to offer Reiki to others but when I started to attend Reiki shares, I found them too intense. Receiving Reiki from other humans feels overwhelming and it makes my legs shake. I guess that makes me a bad patient for my own healing system! Animals give me Reiki in return when I offer them

healing and I also give myself daily Reiki. These options seem to suit me better.

The mistake many people make is to try to put themselves into a box in order to form an identity. If I tried to put myself into a box, it would need to have many different holes from which I could escape so I could get into a different box several times a day, depending on how I was feeling and what or who was inspiring me at the time.

Some people get a job and stay in the same job until the day they retire with hardly a word of complaint. Me? No way! The thought of this fills me with a pit of dread and makes me feel like running for the hills, screaming very loudly all the way. I am a 'go with the flow' person. My mother will vouch for the fact that I have never settled down and followed one path or stuck with a job or interest for any longer than the length of time I needed to glean what I wanted from it and move on.

Most people would recoil in horror at this and have visions of me bumming around and never taking on any responsibility. They couldn't be more wrong. I have been married for just over twenty years at the time of writing this book and have two teenage children. I have run my own business for over six years and am continuing to add to the services that I offer. My life is filled with responsibility but it is the right kind of fluid and every-changing responsibility upon which I thrive.

I am a Reiki Master Teacher, Animal Communicator, Empath, Intuitive, pet sitter and dog walker and, because I have now written a book, I am very happy to add author to the list.

There are many fascinating and curious aspects to being intuitive and working with subtle energy. Below are some of the phenomena that I experience and peculiar things that have happened to me. Life is very rarely dull when it comes to being intuitive!

Empathic pains and sensations

I often experience the aches, pains and sensations of other people, usually those of my own family members but it sometimes also happens with strangers.

Journal 20.09.16

'When I was out dog walking, my right eye became irritated for no apparent reason. It lasted a couple of seconds then was gone. A minute or so later, the dog I was walking started rubbing his face along on the right side, as if he had an itchy eye! A few minutes later, we passed a jogger and I immediately got a sharp pain in my left knee. It lasted for a couple of steps then was gone. The jogger was panting heavily and really pushing himself so I wondered if it was his pain I was feeling. I hardly ever get any pain or discomfort in my left knee.'

Journal 27.11.16

Three days after Mum broke her right arm at the shoulder joint:

'When I was sat with Mum in hospital, my right shoulder began to twinge. Not long after, I got a deep, sharp pain right inside my shoulder joint at the top of my arm. It faded then happened again. It was then that I realised I was picking up on Mum's pain! I forgot about it then stood up to try to

make the telly work and got a very sharp pain in the same place and had to sit down. It happened again a couple of times but stopped after I left.'

Journal 20.01.17

'In the gym when I took Mum for her physio, there was a lady doing some exercises. I wondered what was wrong with her because she seemed young and fit. I kept 'seeing' a black rectangular shape in her left ankle. It turned out that her dog pulled her over a few months ago and she broke her left ankle. They'd fixed it with pins and a plate. Ouch! This must have been what I could intuitively see.'

A Sense of 'Knowing'

A very fascinating aspect of developing our intuition is the phenomenon of precognition. I have always had a sense of 'knowing' things that very few other people pick up on. On the morning of the London bombings in 2002, I had a very uneasy feeling like I was sensing mass terror and I was unable to shake it off. When I arrived at work that morning, I found out about the attacks that had been unfolding in London.

My sense of knowing also extends to my business. I often know when my clients are going to book or contact me out of the blue. My dreams also sometimes tell me messages or I 'see' certain client's faces or their house at random and they contact me within a day or two. They just pop into my head. I also often know when a client is going to cancel, change their plans or if my day is going to be completely altered.

If I wish to know the outcome of a situation, I can usually intuitively sense what will happen by feeling forwards in time with my energy 'probe' and 'seeing' the outcome or sensing success, blankness or no return of the 'ping' so I get a feel for what may happen.

I also often have very uneasy and anxious feelings or symptoms of illness then it turns out that my children are ill in the middle of the night or when they are at school. I often wake up in the night knowing that one of them is about to be sick and I get there just in time to comfort them. I occasionally get random stomach pains, headaches and nausea, only to later find out that I was experiencing these sensations at the exact same time as one of my children or another close relative. I also 'come out in sympathy' for my Mum with some of her ailments. I've also occasionally experienced this with passing strangers. This seems to be a trait of being an Empath. Here are some journal entries about my sense of 'knowing':

Journal 02.02.16

'I've been looking at photos in one of my social media groups and seeing who I felt drawn to. There was an older lady in party clothes. I could feel a Liverpudlian accent coming out of her mouth and a few other indistinct details. When I looked at the comments from other readers, it turned out she was from Liverpool and I got it right about some other aspects of her personality.'

Journal 21.02.15

'When I was cat sitting earlier, I was fussing the cat on my lap when I heard a voice in my mind say "they're coming back early". I thought this was strange because her owners were in Mexico and wouldn't be early.

Turns out that I've just had a text to say her owner's parents are bringing the kids home early tomorrow so I only need to do one more visit in the morning! What a coincidence! (or I should simply trust that my intuition is definitely getting stronger).'

Journal 12.08.15

'Earlier on, I was watching a TV show about dogs. An image of a dog came up and suddenly a voice in my head said "It's Sally". It wasn't my own voice but it was very certain. On the telly they then said "This is 14 year old Sally". Amazing! These instances definitely crop up when I do more meditation, eat less meat and do lots of Reiki at night. I'm very grateful for these abilities, even the subtle ones.'

Journal 06.09.15

'I fell asleep in the car on the way home yesterday (in the passenger seat!). Something warned me about the black car and I woke up with a jolt a split second before my husband honked the horn at a black car that pulled out in front of us.'

Journal 26.02.16

'Today I have been doing my usual road scanning and got a few things spot on and surprised myself (silver car, red saloon car, bus, white van with blue writing etc.) I even did some whilst dog walking. I was 'shown' a silver van with a spiral in red or blue and I got a specific name beginning with an 's'. I asked where I'd see this and told on a roundabout near Overseal. Sure enough, a tyre van with a very similar name was coming over the island on the way there. I smiled to myself but it was blue and no silver or spirals. I did my next dog walk and as I pulled out of their

driveway, there was a silver van with a big blue spiral on its side! Amazing!'

Journal 15.03.16

'I was reversing out of a gateway and something told me to be careful of the people and the dog. I reversed out slowly and, lo and behold, there were two people walking a small, black dog!'

Journal 26.03.16

'On Thursday, I was driving into town over the bridge. A big lorry cab drove up alongside me and I heard the word 'silo'. As the lorry drove forwards, I could see it was carrying a long, white silo on its trailer! Another amazing insight.'

Journal 03.05.16

'I felt my psychic sensing array firmly switch ON, big time. I looked up, over and ahead and around the corner and 'saw' and old, weird mustard coloured thing. There was a cream Mini so I was puzzled. Next thing, I really ugly old campervan appeared. It was burgundy with a really old, yukky raised mustard roof! I sensed again as I approached the next village and saw a large, green and cream lorry. Guess what? There was a large green and cream lorry turning into the yard as I came over the brow of the hill. Next, I could see a building site with a lorry with lots of pipes or metal tubes, possibly pumping concrete. I never actually saw a lorry but I passed the building site where there are going to be log cabins and they had put down fresh concrete into the base of each plot.'

Journal 31.05.16

'It's so reassuring when I get clear messages. It's also fascinating how they come in different forms – visual, auditory, words, images, colours, smells, feelings, sensations, emotions, dreams, the list goes on!'

Journal 20.09.16

'When I was walking the dog from down the road who doesn't like other dogs, we had just passed our house and I was 'told' to cross the road, which we don't usually do. I listened to the voice and saw that we would have blindly bumped into a man with a dog if we hadn't. That would not have gone down well!'

Journal 03.10.16

'I was just walking back from the chiropractor's when I stepped onto the pavement quickly outside the day nursery because I heard a lorry coming up the road behind me. I heard a voice say "it's the food delivery service for the retirement village" A few seconds later the lorry went past and it was exactly that. How's about that for validation?!'

Journal 30.01.17

'On my way to my next dog walk, as I turned left around the big bend onto the bypass, a sudden image of a big, blue lorry with things sticking out of the top flashed into my mind. A split-second later, I turned onto the straight and there it was; a big, blue empty car transporter with black metal framework all over it that stuck out at the top. Voila! Intuition can be random but astounding.'

There are many more entries like this in my journals but I won't bore you with them all! You can get the gist from these. Give it a try yourself and you'll have your own.

I often get a sense of the layout of the land, which is probably from the hidden ley lines beneath our feet and I can 'see' underground features such as water pipes and feel that roads or pavements 'shouldn't be there' because they were placed over beautiful countryside or land with strong energy. This usually happens subconsciously and is brought to my attention by my intuition even when I'm not thinking about it. I occasionally feel unbalanced when walking in certain areas or along footpaths where there are strong magnetic fields.

When I am walking along, I also sometimes know when I am going to be asked for directions or that I'll see people I know. I once 'saw' one of my neighbours pull up alongside me in her car and talk to me then, a couple of minutes later, she did exactly that. The same thing happened the next day whilst I was out dog walking. I knew a van was going to stop and that the driver would ask me for directions to a local business. This also happened with a lady in a car a couple of weeks prior. It's as if I can feel their thoughts before they reach me! I must look approachable.

Journal 11.06.15

'There are some things that I've 'known' lately. I knew that one of my clients would increase my dog walks to three days per week and she has. I've known what's going to happen a lot when I'm driving over the past day or two, such as when to slow down and brake when there's no obvious hazard and if I'll be able to pull out at a junction easily or that someone would stop and let me out. There have been a few other things as well but I can't remember most of them. I think we all 'know' things from time to time but it's nice to feel I can trust my intuition have help from my guides, angels and the Universe!'

Journal 25.03.16

'A couple of days ago, I thought about the African masks on the wall at one of my cat sitting houses but I kept seeing one being taken off the wall. When I arrived for my first visit today, all of the masks were on a chair and they'd been replaced by Easter decorations!'

I also 'knew' they would turn their old bathroom into a study a couple of days before I went round for a more recent visit and walked in to discover the room full of beautiful, bespoke fitted office furniture!

Journal 29.06.16

'I was sitting in reception at my son's school and it was very busy and there were lots of pupils, staff and teachers coming in. Suddenly, as one man approach the door, a voice said 'that's his history teacher'. My son had often mentioned him as he sounds like quite a character. Just after he'd walked past us, my son turned to me and said 'that was my history teacher'.'

Journal 24.10.16

'I was watching a show with the kids and there was a celebrity behind a door that the presenter was about to open. I 'saw' a young woman with blond hair down to her shoulders. He opened the door that's exactly what she looked like!'

I also often hear cats' claws on the kitchen floor or study carpet and I turn around to greet Monty but he isn't there, he's asleep somewhere else. I also see shadow cats and tails going through doorways. My son sees them too. I once saw one going through the garden gate I got home but Monty came for his food from the opposite direction. The tail I saw was completely black and upright and there were no other cats around at the time.

During readings and sometimes spontaneously, I often receive names as the 'shape' of a word in my mind that seems to come from a higher source, the word starts to form and then becomes something distinct and I know it's right because I feel it to be true. This ranges from the names of animals or people in photographs who are in spirit to more simple things such as the name of an estate agent on a well-known property auction show on television. I was once sat there watching telly whilst eating my soup and a lady started walking around a property that was up for auction. A name started forming in my mind. I heard a feint voice saying 'Ma...Ma...Marissa....no, Melissa', with great emphasis on the 'Melissa'. The next moment, the lady's name popped up on the screen and it was Melissa! I said 'thank you' for the insight and swore to myself in amazement. Intuition crops up when you least expect it, just to let you know it is still there.

Seeing and Sensing Subtle Energy

Subtle energy can live up to its name and be very subtle but when you're highly sensitive, it can make itself known in no uncertain terms!

I am able to see my own aura as a white or blue glow and the Reiki in my hands is visible to me as a pale and swirling smoke when I have my eyes open. When I place my hands over my closed eyes, the Reiki appears as either bright, sparkling white or a green matrix or colours such as vivid purple.

I feel very drawn to working with crystals and I have a strong connection with my Ruby Zoizite tumbled stone. I can see her red aura, sense her character and she rolls across my hand with the power of intention. None of my other crystals behave in this way. I also have a selenite wand, which is very soothing and healing when I hold it in my hands for a while. I wear a rose quartz pendant and also one containing black tourmaline which enhance my ability to radiate loving energy and transmute negative energy into something more pleasant. Their properties are highly beneficial when worn in crowded places.

I can hear electrical equipment and unnatural sources of electromagnetic radiation such as stereo systems, computers, televisions, wi-fi hubs, transformers, chargers, microwaves etc. I can hear their high-pitched tones, even when they are on stand-by and feel their aura, even if others don't seem to be able to.

I build up a lot of static electricity and often receive shocks from my children, animals, car doors, hand rails etc. The kids often complain to me about my electric personality!

I feel very connected to the wind and weather. I feel a rush of excitement when I hear the wind blowing through the gap in the window and around the house. My connection to everything on Earth and the whole Universe is very strong. I am especially attracted to people and animals of like-mind, soul and spirit and often sense and dream about energy shifts and tremors on Earth, the weather, alignments of the planets, phases of the moon and solar flares etc. The halo around the moon is often clearly visible to me as a red or orange glow yet most people I know only see white.

My calm energy can often diffuse other people's anger, frustration, impatience, intolerance and ignorance and infuse it with love, peace and sensitivity, when it seems appropriate and safe to do so. I am a good listener and letting someone know that their voice is being heard can greatly ease their frustration and anger.

I often ask for help from the Universe if I have too much work scheduled and it seems overwhelming. This seems to get sent out to my clients energetically and people start to cancel once I've sent the thought/feeling out there. I don't want them to all suddenly cancel their bookings though! It's a healthy balance I'm aiming for.

Journal 17.09.15 2.39pm

'I just went outside looking for Monty but he wasn't there. When I looked over at the bushes in front of the shed 'Monty's toilet' area, I thought it was raining very finely. I got a little closer and I could still see the shimmering effect, as I got closer, it stopped. I looked around the rest of the garden and couldn't see it. I've had this happen to me before. It first started when I was about six years old and it appeared to be raining inside our dining room in front of the window. The effect is very different from seeing 'orgone' or Reiki energy that I often see. I wonder if it's still a form of energy that I'm noticing. It isn't raining. It's more like a stripy heat haze effect, even when it's cold.'

Journal 17.08.16

'I just stood up to watch the moon rising over the roof of the house over the back and saw the most amazing effect. I softened by gaze and stared at the glow of the moon and could see a layer of energy in line with the edge of the roof. As I continued to gaze, the layer suddenly started buzzing with energy, a bit like a heat haze but much more lively and faster. It must be

the energy of the sunlight reflecting off the moon. How exciting! I kept looking back at it and the effect was still there.'

Seeing The Same Thing Twice

Some people and objects seem to be 'repeated'. I've often experienced the strange phenomenon of seeing the same person, in exactly the same clothes with the same bag or pushchair walking along the same street or in the same direction to where I last saw them within a few seconds of the first time I saw them. It's as if they are a stooge and just dropped in there to form part of a background scene. I once saw a Chinese man in a red t-shirt with a newspaper standing in a shop doorway. He had a small wispy beard. I was shocked to see him standing in another doorway about three shops along the road. I immediately blurted this out to my family as we drove along but they clearly thought I was going mad and didn't take much notice.

I also once saw a distinctive woman with a pink pram go into a shop then reappear a minute or so later from further down the street. I was waiting outside the shop she had first gone into and could not work out how she got past me and then came back towards me in from the opposite direction so quickly. This type of occurrence usually happens too fast to gain photographic evidence and it is always hard to believe what you just saw but you cannot deny that it happened as it would ever have crossed your mind unless it did.

The same phenomenon also occasionally occurs with vehicles and is especially noticeable when they have an unusual private number plate or distinctive features. I once had a motorhome drive past me with distinctive stickers on it and a few seconds later, the same vehicle pulled out in front of me from a side road. There is no way it could have got down there in that time frame. It also happened with a little black car with white stripes and a few other cars that drove past me once then came past me again from the same direction a couple of minutes later. It didn't seem possible!

UFO Sightings

Although the topic of UFOs is not directly related to intuition, I have seen too many to just leave them out of this book. There is a great deal of speculation about the existence of life on other planets and from different dimensions. We will probably never know the real truth but I have seen many Unidentified Flying Objects and tend not to believe many stories, photos or videos unless I get that 'feeling' of truth about them. I believe what I can see with my own eyes and sometimes even then I sometimes find a rational explanation. Below are my UFO sightings that I have not yet managed to debunk!

Red Wisp UFO (Approx. 1986)

When I was about ten years old, I saw a peculiar red wisp out of my bedroom window that appeared to be over the railway line to the left of our house. It looked a bit like a rocket but was barely discernible in the bright sunlight. It rose up with a smoky red trail behind it and flew around erratically in and up and down fashion for a few minutes then seemed to vanish. My Grandad also saw it and neither of us knew what it might be. It was too slow for a flare or rocket and left us with an eerie feeling.

UFO with Multiple Lights (Approx 1999/2000)

The report below was in response to someone's sighting on a UFO website on 4th May 2015:

I was so pleased to read your sighting. I had a similar one several years ago that I never reported because I could hardly believe it myself. My husband and I were travelling home from Derby at about 9.30pm and it had just gone dark. We spotted a bright search light over the fields just after Ticknall (on the bend near the Foremarke turning). As we got closer, the search light went out and a very long object became visible hovering low over the field. It was about three times longer than a helicopter, was silent and had coloured lights flashing along its length. It followed alongside our car behind the hedgerow for about 100 yards then shot off at tremendous speed and was nowhere in sight after that. My husband only caught a glimpse of it because he was driving but it left me shaking like a jelly. I was amazed but rather scared!

Bright Orange Light and Silver Orb UFOs 26.03.12

This is my report that I entered onto a UFO website: Last night I was looking out of our open bedroom window at around 10.30pm at the moon and stars when a very bright orange light shot up across the moon and Venus, made a loop and shot back down again before it promptly vanished. This all happened in a split second. It reminded me of a huge firefly. I was very surprised and can't imagine what it could have been. I would have said it was some space junk or a meteor but given the fact it didn't move in a straight line, it probably wasn't. I also saw a white/sliver orb at around 4.30pm earlier that day floating behind the roof tops at the back of our house. It was highly reflective and travelled in a straight line for about a minute then gradually began to descend near the telephone mast in the fields down the road just before I lost sight of it. As it flew, it seemed to jerk around a little. As a rough estimate, it was probably the size of a beach ball and flew at around 100-200 feet in the air. I thought it might have been a gull at first but I soon realised it was round or oval in shape and appeared to be able to control its own flight path.

Bright Light UFO 29.04.15

I was looking at the bright moon out of the study window when I noticed a bright, white light between the two houses over the back directly opposite. It seemed to be two lights close together, slowly blinking on and off. It was not a familiar sight and I started to feel concerned. At first, the lights were vertical then they slowly moved to a horizontal position, side by side.

I called my husband to come and look then him and my son came into the study. We got the binoculars and could see two lights with nothing in-between. They remained motionless for a while and I tried to film them/it on my mobile phone but could only get a small dot because it's not good in the dark. There was no sound from the lights.

It became apparent that the lights seemed to be on one object. After a couple of minutes, it began to move slowly upwards the suddenly jolted up what seemed like a couple of hundred feet and stopped.

After that, it slowly began to float towards our house, silently. As it did so, a further two smaller lights appeared towards the rear of the craft and right side of it. All of the lights where a pure, brilliant white. As it slowly and silently flew over our house, we could only see the lights through the binoculars but not the actual craft itself.

We all ran into our master bedroom to see it fly over the front of our house. As it appeared over the front, heading North West, it had the same appearance as it did when it was coming towards us with only bright white lights visible but it now looked as though they were reflecting off the dull/matt pale grey metallic surface of the craft but the shape was hard to make out. It appeared to be a bulbous disc shape. It seemed as though the white lights may have been oscillating around the craft, giving it a blinking, shimmering effect. It was quite scary and unsettling. If I had to estimate its size, I would say it was about the size of a 'medium' private jet at around 1,000 to 2,000 feet in the air.

My daughter was scared and didn't want to look. It seemed to climb a little higher then vanish. There weren't any clouds in the sky above us and we hadn't heard it make a sound. We have a lot of planes and helicopters fly over our house and they are loud and have green, white (with a yellow tint) and red navigation lights. When military craft fly over, they have one steady red light.

Looking at the craft through binoculars made me feel sick and nervous because it had such an unfamiliar appearance. This craft seemed to be capable of making small, jerky movements, sudden vertical movements and move at speed whilst making no sound.

Journal 15.08.15 9.30pm

'Just saw an extremely bright, golden light go over the trees and gradually disappear behind the houses over the back. It stayed bright and vivid like a star and did not behave like a Chinese lantern. It was as bright as the anomaly we saw a few weeks ago except it was one light and was gold, not

white. Thought it could be an iridium flare but it was too low to be a satellite.'

'Tarpaulin' UFO 16.04.16

I was in a muddy field, surrounded by horses at one of my animal communication courses. I spotted something big and black 'flying' over the trees in the distance. Our tutor was talking to us and I didn't want to interrupt by shouting 'look!' so I kept it to myself. I watched the movement of the anomaly as best I could and felt quite unsettled by it, as if it knew I was looking at it. It seemed to have the shape of wings but wasn't flapping and was much larger than a crow or other bird. It had an eerie, menacing, fluid motion to it. I wondered if it was loose tarpaulin or other material but it seemed to be following a certain flight path that was not randomly being tossed around.

There was hardly any wind so I don't know how it was being propelled, unless there was a therm higher up in the sky. It appeared to be about a couple of hundred feet in the air and seemed to be changing shape. It kept the same trajectory, although it did appear to be gaining height as it flew. It was quite fast and very black against the blue sky. Everyone else was facing the opposite direction to me and they were focussed on the lesson. I watched the anomaly fly over the trees and eventually go out of sight. I had never seen anything like it before or since. I just wish I'd had my phone with me but taking photos or video would also have interrupted the lesson. It will remain a mystery but even thinking about it now is a little creepy.

Déjà vu

I have experienced déjà vu a number of times. It seems to occur around trivial matters and links conversations with times, places and images that seem to have happened before but couldn't have done.

Journal 25.08.16

'I had a couple of incidences of déjà vu yesterday. One when I was walking alongside Mum on her scooter. I have definitely been in that situation before – even though I haven't! Another was when I was walking somewhere else and also when I was sat in the lounge looking at something. Life is so peculiar.'

Out of Body Experiences

Some people try to conjure up out of body experiences at will but I don't particularly like the feeling! Here are a couple of them I've had in which I seem to have left my physical body for a few moments:

Journal 26.02.16

'Last night, I went to the loo and then when I got back into bed, all of a sudden I found myself floating down the stairs quite fast towards the front door in purple-black, swirling darkness. Next thing, I was above my body, lying on my back falling into shadows. I was definitely out of my body and shouting that I didn't want to die and wanted to go back into my body immediately! I suddenly fell and was back in my body but I couldn't feel it for a while. I was saying weird stuff and had my arm in the air (or so I thought!). Eventually, I came to and was exhausted so I fell back to sleep.'

Journal 23.01.17

'I woke up half way through my Reiki session last night with my hands on my stomach with a start, wondering why I was in bed, in the dark with a man next to me! After a moment of panic and a sharp intake of breath, it was as if I was suddenly placed back into my life and I remembered everything. Before that moment, it was a total blank, as if I was in a completely unfamiliar place. Did I go back to source or a parallel existence during my Reiki treatment? Strange!'

Animal Communication and Reiki

Animal communication and Reiki are in intrinsic part of my nature and intuitive abilities. The remaining chapters of this book are dedicated to them and our fascinating connection with all life through Universal energy.

COMMUNICATION WITH ALL LIFE

Our Connection with Animals and Nature

Connecting with the Earth and all of its creatures on a deep energetic level is an incredibly beautiful and healing experience. To be as one with the roots of our very nature can unlock our true potential as human beings and fill us with spiritual nourishment to our core. Our lives become enriched with the wisdom of our ancestors and the multitude of animals and plants that have flourished on our planet since the first signs of life.

Meditation, spending time in natural environments and the company of animals raises our vibration and uplifts even the heaviest of hearts. Breathing fresh air and feeling the warmth of the sunshine on our skin remind us that it is the simple things that can be the most fulfilling.

Opening our hearts, minds and energy systems to connecting with animals and nature is literally life-changing and in these chapters we explore the infinite potential that this can bring on every level, from the physical to the spiritual. We are the most highly developed mammals of all yet many of us seem to forget who we truly are and neglect to nurture our soul. Once we remember to do this, everything else will fall into place.

In the chapters that follow, we explore communicating with all life through intuition, physical interaction, science and the healing power of Reiki.

Animals have their own unique capacity to win our hearts and they have certainly won mine. It would be a wonderful world if everyone felt this way about animals but sadly they do not.

Human beings constantly invade and destroy the natural habitat of wild animals as if it is our absolute right to do so. Trees, plants, animals, the oceans and the planet itself all suffer. We always take far in excess of what we need. This is why listening to the animals is so important. They know exactly 'how it is' on every level and their level of understanding goes far deeper than our own. Each species forms an energetic network and unique energy that works in harmony with their surroundings.

Animal communication is not just for fire-side fun or storytelling; it is about getting to the heart of the matter and making this world a far better place by listening to the ones who remain silently affected by the consistent greed and over-development of the human race.

We are connected to all forms of life and can communicate with everything from the wind, plants and trees to the energy of the near-perfect structure of crystals, rocks, the ocean, Earth and subtle energy throughout the Universe that connects us to higher forms of consciousness and the spiritual realms.

We are unlikely to suddenly find ourselves surrounded by wild animals and trees that have uprooted themselves to converse with us but it is possible to open our hearts to communicate with all life and feel the energy of everything around us. When animals and other living beings sense that we come to them for the greatest and highest good, they may be willing to share their wisdom and show us what it truly means to be as one with the Universe.

As human beings, it is all too easy to forget that we are mammals and have the same primal instincts as most other animals. In the face of perceived danger, our fight or flight instinct kicks in and we may lash out or run away. Human beings are capable of a great many atrocities and despite our higher intellect we remain territorial, aggressive, predatory, fearful of the unknown and may behave unpredictably when we feel threatened or confused. The upside of this is that we do have a choice as to how we behave and respond in situations of conflict, threat and fear. We are intelligent and resourceful creatures who often show signs of great altruism and problem-solving skills, even when a situation seems hopeless and out of control. It is about taking responsibility for ourselves and our thoughts and actions.

Journal 11.06.16

'I feel that we were all put here for protection under the Earth's atmosphere but humans got a bit too ambitious and some of us lost our way and became consumed with hate, fear and war. Eventually, more of us will become enlightened and the animals and nature will be our teachers.'

Those in power are beginning to feel the energy amongst the billions of people on this planet who are no longer prepared to put up with being down trodden in order to feed the greedy fat-cats that run some of our countries. Corruption and greed run riot but when we stand together, no longer willing to feed the monster, we can bring about change through the power of our spiritual strength as individuals working together to raise the vibration of the planet to make this world a better place in which there is fairness, balance and trust. Changing the world begins with loving and nurturing ourselves as individuals. We cannot serve from an empty vessel.

As more of us become awakened and aware, our energy is more closely aligned with the energy of our animal companions and the natural world. When we are open and raising our vibrations by working from our hearts, we are able to protect and offer healing to more animals than ever before and pass our legacy on to future generations by teaching them love, respect and compassion toward animals. Communicating with and understanding them on a deep, spiritual and energetic level will become the norm rather than the exception.

Many animals often seem to carry out greater acts of love and compassion than some humans may ever do in our lifetime but we should not give up on the human race. We are continually evolving and in present time, more and more of us seem to be awakening and are dealing with oppression and unfairness with greater clarity, insight and wisdom. We should aim to be the better person in a bad situation. Not in the way of a soft push-over, but to bring balance and harmony and instil these qualities in others by listening and placing realistic options on the table that allow us to celebrate our differences rather than approach things from a divisive point of view. Animals need us to show them love, trust and respect but we also need to extend these toward our own species.

Trust, Love and Respect

I find it hard to be forgiving towards fellow humans when they seem to misunderstand animals and treat them harshly out of frustration or ignorance but I have to remember that it wasn't so long ago that I made similar mistakes, simply because I was being a typical human and failing to see things from the animal's perspective. It wasn't until I learned more about animal behaviour and worked on my animal communication skills that I realised there was a much better and kinder way to relate to them in situations that many humans struggle with such as dogs pulling on leads and cats peeing in strange places. It's about working from the inside out and understanding how animals think, feel and learn.

Humans are highly intelligent but the way some people treat animals goes far beyond them simply being a little ignorant or lacking in awareness. Some of what I have written in the following chapters may seem a little harsh towards my own species but it has to be said. Animals deserve a lot better when it comes to their interactions with some humans. Earning trust is the starting point and that trust needs to continue for life. Once trust is broken, it's very hard to get it back.

Animals are very adept at knowing who they can trust. They recognise people who are intuitively developed with open hearts and minds. They can feel it in their energy field. The spiritually aware and intuitive amongst us stand out like beacons of light to animals; it is an energetic language that they naturally understand.

Trust begins by showing respect and this starts by showing an animal that you respect their personal space from the outset.

Animals are capable of feeling a wide range of emotions but they find it much easier to live in the moment and do not have to hide their feelings behind a shroud of deception and manipulation in order to protect their vulnerable emotional core in the same way that some people do. Animals are very clear-cut and tell it like it is. They are much more likely to try to hide physical pain or discomfort as a survival instinct than try to conceal how they are feeling on an emotional level. Animals are masters of emotion. Their language is based on subtle energy because they are naturally in touch with the finer points of life.

Animals are usually unwilling to connect with us when we approach them from our ego. They may feel that it is insincere and wish to have no part in it. When we approach an animal from our ego, we may see them as pitiful and believe we can help them to recover from a place of suffering because we are superior and can work wonders that they couldn't possibly imagine. This is not a loving approach. Animals should be shown love and respect in order to feel safe in opening up to us.

Trust is the foundation of a loving relationship. Without trust, there is nothing upon which to build mutual respect and affection. Love can still exist without trust but the chances of a healthy and happy relationship are very slim.

When working with animals, it is vital to instil trust in the first instance. Everything else is built upon this. If an animal can learn that it is safe to approach you and that you will always treat them with love and respect, a beautiful friendship can form.

With animals, first impressions really do count. Approaching an animal in the correct way is vital, especially if they are nervous or afraid. Every species is different but when approaching any animal, it is wise to do this from a slightly sideways angle as approaching them head on can seem threatening and scary. Crouching down a few feet away and allowing them to approach you is usually the best way, unless there is a possibility that may become aggressive. Always offer an escape route; never make an animal feel trapped. Softly spoken words and only touching them when they instigate it may also help to build trust.

Animals don't hang onto the past and they don't make devious plans for the future. It may look like they are planning your demise if you do not feed them on time but animals are alert and aware in the present moment, taking in the sights, sounds and energy around them to work out their next move. This does not mean that they remain unaffected by past trauma or suffering. They can still have issues on a psychological level, it's just that they don't plot revenge or hang onto grudges like humans do or go over and over scenarios in their mind.

Responding to their own emotional state and reading the feelings of others is a fast and fluid process for animals. This takes place on a different level than it does for humans and doesn't get caught up in a big knotted mess in their solar plexus like it can do for us, nor does it get caught up in logical processing, trying to apply rational thought or a vast multitude of possible outcomes that all seem to be steeped in negativity. Animals have a much purer and clearer energy flow and are not subject to social conditioning. They take complexity out of the equation and see things as they truly are without barriers, judgements or hidden agendas. If an animal loves you, they will let you know.

Journal 04.11.16

'When I was walking Millie, one of my client's golden retrievers today, a man in his twenties was walking past us and Millie turned to him to say 'hello'. The man crouched down and asked her name, gently fussed around her head and ears. It was a magical moment; the man looked as though he really needed this interaction today. He said how beautiful she was then said 'thank you very much' with the utmost sincerity and carried on his way. He had a long winter coat on, dark hair and short dark beard. I could 'see' that he had a beautiful soul. It was if he appeared suddenly out of nowhere then was gone again.'

We need to show respect to our animals for who they really are and set them up for success. Domesticated animals such as cats and dogs are predatory in nature and still retain all of their basic instincts, just as humans do. These instincts become diluted when they are well socialised and lovingly shown how to live happily in our domestic environments. We must learn why they behave as they do and adapt our own lives and ways of thinking to take their needs and instincts into account.

This is where animal communication starts; with their basic needs, body language and behaviour. From there on in, we can get to know the animal as an individual and the amazing and surprising differences between the members of each species. Just like human beings, no two animals are the same.

Horsey Humour

At the sanctuary where I did one of my animal healing courses, there are many different rescued horses and ponies. One little pony is very bold and cheeky. I connected with him energetically and he said to me "I'm the best looking one! Ha ha ha ha....!" His laughter was really funny and high-pitched. I shall never forget it!

Animals are intuitive beings, just like us, but they have not become detached from their intuitive and spiritual connection like many humans have. When human-animal relations go wrong and the animals are accused of being badly behaved, it is most often due to a misunderstanding on the part of the human. Not necessarily because they are being mean or too demanding but because they are imposing their human way of thinking on the animal and expect it to behave as they 'command' it to. This is known as anthropomorphism, in which people view animals as having human thoughts and characteristics. This does a great disservice to the animal and reflects badly on us because animals deserve better.

Some people also dress animals up and treat them like babies or train them to do silly tricks. It's good that they are loved but this often causes animals stress and frustration. They are our companions, not toys. We should not expect animals to conform to our wishes when it goes against their instincts and natural needs and desires. They place their trust in us and we should honour this. Being an animal guardian is a big responsibility. They are not human and, although some of their behaviour may appear similar, they have very different needs and a language all their own. Whilst they may understand a good deal of our human repertoire, some of it may seem scary and filled with mixed messages. Making an effort to learn about the natural inclinations and behaviour of our animal companions can help us to reduce the stress levels in their lives and bring out their true character, without the need to force them into a frilly frock or parade them around like a baby. When animal behaviour problems do arise, there are still people who believe that their pet is deliberately trying to destroy their home as some form of hate campaign or that they are seeking world dominance.

Animals do not try to dominate us or do things out of malice. The vast majority of the time, the behaviour that we may view as being 'bad' or 'unacceptable' is perfectly normal for the animal and they may be struggling to cope living in a human environment and could potentially be highly stressed. They do not know any other way to behave because the humans have not shown them. Kind, force-free training and behaviour modification should be requested from a qualified behaviour professional to give the animal the best chance to become well-balanced and live a happy and relaxed life. A veterinary check-up should also be carried out to rule out any potential medical issues. Prevention is better than cure and people should be prepared to take the time to meet all of their animals' needs as soon as they welcome them into their home.

Wild animals can show an amazing amount of trust when they need help. There was once an injured baby magpie in our garden. Its distressed parents were circling overhead for a couple of hours but we couldn't catch it because it kept running away and hiding when we tried to get near. We thought that it had managed to fly away in the end so we thought no more about it that night.

The next morning, it was raining heavily. I went out in my car for a little while and when I returned, the baby magpie was standing in the middle of the driveway looking bedraggled and soaking wet. I slowly approached it and it didn't move. I gently reached out and we made eye contact. I could feel that it desperately needed help and was willing to trust me in order to get it. I gently put my hand around it, picked it up and held it to me. I placed it in our cat's carrier and took it to the local wildlife centre where it was nursed back to health.

I shall never forget that feeling of utter humility and gratitude for the young magpie allowing me to help it. Its parents returned later on that morning to look for it but gave up their search after a day or two. I told them that their baby was safe but it was sad to still hear them calling for it but at least it was being well cared-for.

Animals need us to be their trustworthy and honest guides. All too often, the voice of the animals goes unheard and we should endeavour to help them whenever we can. This is why as responsible animal communicators and healers, we should aim to learn as much as we can about animal care and behaviour so that we are better able to perceive life through their eyes and encourage others to do the same.

The Language of Animals

The vast majority of language in our domestic animals is silent. Animals such as cats, dogs and horses predominantly express themselves through body language, facial expressions, subtle energy, movement and telepathy. Vocalisations are generally reserved for specific intra-species communication such as during mating rituals, territorial disputes and rearing young. Many of our domestic animals reserve a repertoire of audible sounds to get their humans to do their bidding!

The use of scent and visual markers is also an important part of animal language, especially when claiming territory and leaving scent messages about sexual receptivity.

When an animal communicates with a human being, we can make things a lot easier for them by showing that we are open, receptive and ready to listen. FEEL how the animal is communicating with you. What is the animal communicating to you on a physical, mental, emotional and spiritual level? What kind of vibration are they giving off? Are they happy and relaxed? Are they scared? Would they like you to crouch down so that you do not seem so intimidating?

Quieting the mind and approaching an animal with calm and loving energy from our hearts is a starting point. Slowing down our mind and our movements will help to put them at ease. The animal may start to communicate by offering a little eye contact and a body posture that shows that they may be willing to trust you if you offer them the same courtesy. A state of mutual trust.

Animals do not judge others in the same way that humans do. They make an assessment as to whether or not that person or animal is safe to approach but do not pile on the requirement to socially conform or have the same morals and principles as them. Sociable species just want to get along. They don"t see the superficial differences; they only see the heart and soul of the other being when making the decision as to whether or not they should interact. Animals have so much to teach us and we could learn a great deal more about life by perceiving things in the way that they do. We all possess that innate deep wisdom; we just need to listen to it more often.

An animal will look for physical and visual cues from a human, as well as reading their energy and sensing what is going on in their mind and heart. Reading the subtle nuances of animal behaviour comes naturally to some people but not others. Some people think that dogs are smiling when they narrow their eyes and slightly pull back their gums to show a little of their teeth. This is not the case. This is a sign that they are afraid and uncomfortable. This is why it is important to learn about animal behaviour on a physical level when working with animals professionally or welcoming an animal into your home. This is all part of listening to the animal.

An animal that is willing to interact with you and welcome you into their space will have a relaxed body posture and facial muscles. As an example, a dog that is feeling relaxed will have soft facial features, a fairly loose body posture and their tail will probably wag around and around without any stiffness to it. If the dog is not relaxed, it may show the whites of its eyes, be panting a little, have a rigid body and its tail may wag slightly side to side in a low position. These are signs of uncertainty and fear and can sometimes be missed by humans. A dog who displays these signals may seem to bite without warning but to the trained eye, the warning signs are very apparent.

The power of touch can have amazing effects. It can be reassuring and healing but some animals do not like to be touched or enjoy a little contact from humans but only on their terms. Asking permission to touch energetically and combining this with non-threatening body language will be greatly appreciated by an animal. Looking for signs and sensing when an animal has had enough is important to earn their trust and prevent an aggressive response.

This is why listening to animals is so important. By listening to them, we are showing respect and they are more likely to trust us and incidences of aggression can be avoided.

Learning to Listen is Vital

Actively listening to what an animal or person is trying to communicate involves much more than our ears. Being fully present and engaged in what someone is saying and acknowledging and appropriately responding to what they are expressing is actively listening.

There is nothing worse than feeling ignored or overlooked when we need to explain ourselves or have someone understand our inner most thoughts and feelings. A listening ear can be very healing and help us to work our way through a problem simply by saying how we feel about it.

Active listening involves opening up our hearts, minds, senses and energy to the person or animal that needs us to listen. They will not only express themselves through words or sounds but will also do this through body language, facial expressions, eye contact and the energy they are exuding as they get things off their chest and tell you how they are feeling.

We should acknowledge what they are saying without interrupting and reflect back what they have told us so far when there are appropriate pauses, to show that we have listened to what is being said. This is important when listening to a person but with animals, listening is rather different.

When we open a channel for animal communication from a place of love and trust, they will feel safe and relaxed in our company and a special bond is formed.

Listening to an animal is also part of training, helping them to settle into a new home or making them feel at ease in a new environment. If a human would like an animal to behave in a certain way or change its behaviour, they must listen to how the animal feels and responds. Animals will not just unquestionably respond to commands or 'corrections' from human beings. They need to know that there is some benefit to what they are doing and that it is enjoyable. Part of being a good trainer or guardian is to listen to the animal to gauge how they are responding to and understanding what is being asked of them. Clear communication, love and trust go a long way.

Our demeanour and approach to animals is the first thing we should consider. Establishing trust, good communication and working with the natural inclination of each animal need to be taken into account. What makes them tick? I feel my way in see them as a soul, animal, species, breed, individual and what they would benefit from learning and the reasons why. What does an animal NEED to be taught by a human in order to live a long and happy life? I allow our interaction to flow and feel the subtle energy at work. Mutual respect is soon established and an understanding that both of us need our own personal space. Firm but fair boundaries should be established, just as when two human beings first get to know each other.

Many humans make the mistake of believing that a relationship with an animal is one-sided with the human TELLING the animal what to do then getting angry when it refuses to obey. Why should it? It's up to humans to understand the animal and work with them intelligently. They won't know what is expected of them unless we communicate in a way they understand. All else is futile and of no benefit to anyone. Adapting the pace and format of training and behaviour modification to match the progress that the animal is making is vital to success. Taking a few steps back until they have grasped a previous stage may sometimes be necessary. Training an animal is about forming a partnership with good communication on both sides. It does not involve dominance or the human assuming the position of 'Alpha'. Managing the animal's living environment and changing routines and other lifestyle factors can also make a big difference.

Animal Intelligence

Wild animals are intelligent in terms of their natural habitat and survival requirements. Domesticated animals retain these qualities to a certain degree but most have evolved and adapted their intelligence to gain the most that they can from their human companions and domestic environments.

A human who does not understand animals may assume that an animal is not intelligent because they do not think or behave as a human would when faced with a typically human problem or situation. This is not an accurate interpretation of how animal intelligence works.

A cat does not know how to drive a car or understand the purpose of a television yet it can wrap a human being around its paw and navigate its neighbourhood with stealth and precision in the blink of an eye. Animals know what mood we are in, if we are safe to approach or if we are suffering from illness before we have even had chance to think about it.

Animals are highly intelligent within the bounds of their own species and very often their intellect and intuition expands way beyond this. They are adaptable and flexible. Emotional, spiritual and energetic intelligence are enhanced in animals because they live in the moment and sense things of both a physical and energetic nature long before most human beings do. They are immersed in Universal energy and not confined by the rigid boundaries of logic and reason. Animals are excellent at problem solving but they will only do so when they see some benefit in using their valuable time and energy on a task.

Not all animals wish to interact with humans, no matter how much intuitive or spiritual energy they resonate. We are in physical bodies in a physical world and the instincts of animals are incredibly strong. It is only on extremely rare occasions that a wild animal will choose to trust a human being when they do not see them as a threat. Even some domestic animals are choosy about which humans they wish to associate with. They can be highly perceptive and discerning and their intuition is usually spot-on. The vibration of some animals and humans simply do not resonate harmoniously, just as with some human to human interactions. We are not always immediately comfortable with everyone we meet, including those of different species.

Some species of wild animals start out tame as babies but when they reach adolescence, many become aggressive and wary around humans as their wild-side begins to flourish. It has taken many thousands of years for the majority of our domesticated pets and livestock animals to feel comfortable around humans. Even then, they must be properly socialised with human beings from a very young age in order to not be 'feral' and skittish in our company. We should never assume that it is our right to force our attention and affection onto animals. They are highly intelligent, sentient beings and it is a humbling privilege when they choose to trust us, whether it is through good socialisation or a wild animal choosing to approach us.

Working with animals is an education in itself. There are so many species of animals and yet, within each species, there are yet many differences still; no two animals are the same. In the rest of this chapter, I write about the species of animals that I understand the most but that feeling of interconnectedness is ever present with all animals.

We expect an awful lot from our domestic animals, of which cats and dogs make up the vast majority.

Animals that have been shaped and moulded by humans over thousands of years have become completely reliant on us to show them how to behave in our human world. There are those who become feral and have to learn to fend for themselves but they usually have a tough life and are often persecuted and abused when they are irresponsibly left to breed beyond the bounds of reason, causing birth defects, out of control populations riddled with parasites, diseases and many other health problems.

Domestic animals behave the way they do because of human intervention. Often bred purely for desirable 'looks' over the past couple of hundred years, consideration for temperament and good health is often last on the list. Some animals are bred to do jobs and have traits adapted to carry out specific tasks such as flushing out game, herding sheep, guarding livestock or killing vermin.

The animals with whom we share our lives have become 'humanised' because we are responsible for their existence and the traits that they exhibit, both good and bad. We cannot breed all of the 'wildness' out of our animal companions and livestock. They will always retain natural instincts and behaviour to a greater or lesser degree.

We expect domestic animals to be compliant model citizens and when they display perfectly normal behaviour for their species, some people are up in arms about it, punishing the animal and 'showing it who's boss' by trying to suppress the behaviour as if it is wrong. It is not wrong. Animals need to be shown how to behave and what is expected of them when they live in our homes or workplaces in a kind and understanding way.

They do not come pre-programmed with an internal set of etiquette guidelines and obedience commands. Human beings have to show their furry or feathery companions the way. After all, they may have an ancestry going back many thousands of years but they are a long way off from their wild forefathers. Species that came about through human intervention are the responsibility of humans yet all too often they are badly let down and misunderstood by those who brought about their existence.

We should be grateful for our domestic animals; each time we are in their company, we are graced by the presence of a wild animal that has become tame enough to tolerate human companionship through a few genetic twists and a lot of nurture.

So many humans know so very little about the animals with whom they choose to share their lives. Nature never intended dogs to be carried around in handbags covered in a layer of bling and cats were never meant to cope with being cooped up indoors without ever experiencing the exhilarating freedom of the great outdoors.

Giving a home to an animal is a huge responsibility. Cats and dogs are complex sentient beings, just like humans and many other animals. They have a wide range of needs that must be met on many different levels in order for them to live a happy, healthy and abundant life.

Knowing how animals are truly feeling takes time, patience, education and an open heart and mind. It is essential to further our understanding of our closest companions and enable us to appreciate the finer points of how the natural world really works.

Connecting with Cats

I love all animals but it is with cats that I feel the strongest connection. I was brought up with cats and am comfortable with every nuance and quirk of their nature. Cats and I experience a merging of energy that is beautiful and sacred. There is something about cats that draws me in and connects to my soul. The way they look, the way they move and the way they are so self-assured and well-equipped to do what their species was intended to do has a magical and mysterious quality to it. There is nothing quite like a cat.

I like dogs but cats are who I am. They sing to my soul, endlessly repeating with an uplifting resonance. I am cat; my personality is cat. Their precision, poise and grace have me captivated. Cats are our connection to all things spiritual. Once you understand all things cat, they have you hooked for an eternity and feature in nearly everything you do.

Whilst it is possible for a human to train a cat in the same way as a dog, it is much more likely to occur the other way around. Cats are notoriously adept at getting humans to do their bidding.

My cat, Monty owns my heart and soul, which means that I obey his silent commands without hesitation, not realising what I am doing until it is too late.

It is no wonder that these stunningly beautiful, adaptable and highly intelligent creatures have been both the subject of worship and objects of fear and persecution since they decided to live within the vicinity of humans thousands of years ago.

Cats even have a special repertoire of vocalisations purely set aside for communicating with their humans. Most adult cats do not communicate vocally with one another unless is it related to mating, rearing kittens or territorial disputes, whereas kittens soon learn that humans are very responsive to the sounds that they make and use meows, chirrups, purrs and various other sounds to their advantage.

The power of a cat's purr can be quite phenomenal. Scientists have been struggling to locate the source of the purr for decades. It seems to have many purposes. A queen will purr to comfort her kittens and let them know she is close by. A purr can be a sign of happiness and contentment but cats also purr when they are in pain or feeling stressed as a way of comforting themselves.

Monty has a few different kinds of purr. He has a light purr to show his delight at finding a comfortable spot to sleep; a stronger purr for when he is enjoying some fuss or a good brush and also a persuasive, deep guttural purr for those moments when he is staring at you, trying to persuade you to feed him.

Felines also have a special language that is sometimes missed on humans. Slow blinking, head boops and nudges all form part of feline communication and are usually affectionate in nature. A cat who is pleased to see you will usually trot towards you with a raised tail and wind around your legs. A lot of feline communication is in the form of body language, territorial marking with scent and visual markers such as scratching with their claws.

Cats do not like to be stared at, although it seems to be perfectly acceptable for them to stare at humans when they want something. Offering a nervous cat a few slow blinks will often reassure them that you are not a threat. Slow blinks are vital if you wish to earn the trust of a cat. If you have never slowly closed and opened your eyes a few times when a cat is looking at you, I suggest that you try it. Slow blinks are a must in feline society. They indicate trust, a relaxed demeanour and that the blinker wishes to be their friend.

When a cat offers you slow blinks in return, or maybe even a wink, it is a very uplifting and humbling moment. However, please do not assume that this means you can just rush in and schmoosh them on the cheeks. A return of the slow blinks is just the tentative beginning of building a relationship with a cat. Cats like to know who they are dealing with and prefer to have the option to approach someone to greet them, rather than have a person charge up to them, pick them up and force their affections upon them. This will often result in the well-meaning person being scratched to pieces or bitten by a disgruntled kitty.

Approaching a cat should begin with the person crouching down low and offering a few slow blinks. If these blinks are returned by the cat, a hand should slowly be offered from a sideways angle for the cat to sniff. Always ensure that the cat has an escape route should it choose to run away. If the cat finds the hand acceptable, it may offer a cheek to be rubbed. Softly rub the cheek and perhaps behind an ear, closely monitoring the cat's facial expression and tail movements.

If the cat's face looks relaxed and the tail is still, you are in with a good chance of making a feline friend. If the cat has its ears back, even slightly and the tail is flicking, beware! Terminate the fuss and allow the cat to carry on its way. Cats command respect and more fool the human who does not adhere to this protocol.

Part of the appeal of cats is their interdependent nature and the fact that they like to keep themselves fastidiously clean, unless they are in poor health. They are usually solitary creatures in the wild, relying on their hunting skills and tenacity to stay alive but some wild cats, such as the lion, form social groups to increase their chances of successful hunting and reproduction.

Feral cats are domestic cats without a home. Some may be terrified of people because they were not socialised as kittens. They tend to live in large groups if there is an abundant supply of food and often get along well, spending time grooming one another and curling up together for a snooze. In locations where there are large populations of feral cats, charities often operate trap, neuter and return schemes to ensure that the place is not overrun with cats.

The same goes for domestic cats who do have a home. It is essential to get them neutered because numbers of cats can escalate so quickly, resulting in a wide variety of problems. Responsible cat guardians should ensure that their cats are neutered as soon as they reach breeding age at around four months.

Domestic cats get a bad reputation as being anti-social and aloof yet there are many domestic cats who form deep and affectionate bonds with members of all species, especially if they were brought up together. Anyone who has ever spent their life with a cat will know how strong this bond can be. Cats are unique creatures and make wonderful companions. It's a shame that some people do not like cats. They are missing out!

Understanding Dogs

Dogs are a different kettle of fish to cats yet they share many similarities (although I'm sure most dogs and dog 'people' would disagree!). Both are often food-orientated and like to get their own way. They know how to work it with the big, sad eyes routine and like to find a warm place to sleep. Ultimately, even though most dogs are 'trained', they still know how to get their humans to give in to their whims without hardly lifting a paw.

When I first started out as a dog walker and pet sitter, I was a little afraid of dogs, especially when they barked or became over-excited. After many years of working with them and meeting many teachers of the canine variety, my fear subsided to a loving understanding and appreciation for the wonder and depth of unconditional love that is the domestic dog.

Dogs come in so many different shapes and sizes, it's hard to fathom that they are all of the same species. Having met and gotten to know many of the 'vicious' breeds, I soon realised that nearly everything I had been led to believe about dogs was untrue and a load of old poppycock. Out of all the dogs who have graced my path, it has been some of the most common 'family-friendly' breeds that have turned out to behave in the most aggressive and unpredictable ways.

I have known a Rottweiler who is soft as grease, several soppy Staffies and some very calm and polite German Shepherds. I have come to understand what most kinds of bark mean and that low growls and grumbling are usually a form of self-expression, rather than the threat of an imminent danger. It's about looking at the body language and context of canine communication in order to interpret its meaning.

A few years ago, I would not have appreciated that when a Golden Retriever the size of a small bear growls and grumbles with a toy in his mouth, he is actually telling me that he is excited to see me and hasn't really done much all morning except sleep; when a Greyhound runs up to me and starts chattering his teeth, it's a sign of affection rather than dislike, and when a large Border Collie nearly knocks me flying, she is simply trying to get close enough to my face to lick it because she loves me.

What saddens me is that even to this day, so many people completely misunderstand dogs and rely on training methods based on dominance and asserting themselves as leader of the pack. Such methods are something out of the ark and are not even supported by science, let alone working from a spiritual perspective. Dogs use a lot of subtle body language to communicate how they are feeling, including calming signals such as lip licking, turning their head away and yawning, to name but a few. So many cases of canine aggression could have been avoided if the humans or other animals involved knew how to recognise what the dogs was telling them.

We should set dogs up for success from the outset because we ask a lot of them by expecting them to fit in nicely within our domestic environments. I have found myself in some very uncomfortable situations in which people who do not seem to understand their dogs use punishments and yell at them in a failed attempt to exert some control. They become highly stressed and frustrated because they genuinely don't know what to do, despite seeming to love their dog very dearly. It's heart-breaking to see this kind of behaviour when it is unnecessary, bad for their relationship and often the result of mis-information spread by so-called dog whisperers and old-fashioned dog trainers.

It is not the exertion of control that is needed, it is a well-balanced and loving relationship that allows dogs the freedom to choose to behave in the way that we wish them to because they are intelligent enough to understand what is expected of them if we tell them in the right way. Kind, force-free methods are essential for long-term reliable results. When there is love and respect between dog and human guardian, anything is possible. Puppies start to learn from the moment they are born and once they can see and hear properly, training can begin. It does not have to be intensive, demanding training; it should be fun, light-hearted and engaging for both the dog and human. Short bursts of training, several times a day are required. Consistency, patience and understanding are the key.

All of the different breeds of dog came about because man required them to do specific tasks over the millennia, especially during the past couple of hundred years. Specific breeds have the specific traits for which they were bred yet some people fail to understand this and end up adopting a dog that is totally unsuitable for their particular home environment and circumstances. This is often the reason behind the majority of canine behaviour problems and dogs being given up to rescue centres. Many dogs are adopted because of their good looks but people are unprepared for the emotional and behavioural baggage that tags along with such cuteness.

A dog really is for life and a lot of hard work and patience goes into helping a dog become well-rounded, calm and willing to listen to its human family. Dogs are not born with an inbuilt set of commands but this is what some people expect. Puppies need to be well-socialised and habituated to a domestic environment from a very young age before training even begins in earnest. The demands are high on domestic dogs and it's up to the humans to meet their needs.

There are many dogs with jobs such as guide dogs and assistance dogs. They seem to take to such roles with all their heart. This is because dogs have massive hearts filled with unconditional love. They are very wise, spiritual and intelligent animals with a wide range of emotions. Dogs form strong bonds with humans when they are used to having them around and also make firm friends with other species.

When it comes to working with dogs as a healer and animal communicator, they are usually the most receptive species. This is probably due to their genetic predisposition to work well with humans and form close connections. Out of all the dogs to whom I have offered Reiki, not one of them has ever refused. It doesn't take long for them to lie down with me and happily accept the healing energy and communicate with me on a subtle level. It is an honour and privilege and I am grateful to every one of them.

Other Species

There are so many millions of animal species besides cats and dogs that it's impossible to mention them all here. I connect with animals of all shapes and sizes and find their energy easy to relate to but in this section, I have narrowed it down to the ones I have come to know over the years.

During my childhood, I was crazy about horses and ponies. I had riding lessons on a horse called 'Dream' and amassed an abundant collection of toy ponies and fancy equine models complete with miniature stables and riders. My obsession levelled out after a few years but horses will always have a special place in my heart. I have the utmost love and respect for these majestic and spiritual creatures.

I have worked with many horses during my Reiki and animal communication training and they have all been patient and kind. It's hard to even contemplate how anyone could mistreat animals but horses and ponies often suffer terrible abuse and neglect, especially when it comes to using them as a way of making money. Fortunately, there are also many people who absolutely love horses and it's refreshing to know that many horse trainers now use natural horsemanship, rather than outdated training methods.

I also love birds and find birdsong so calming and healing. I have known some highly intelligent and friendly birds during my time. We kept chickens for a couple of years but sadly, they didn't live very long. Midnight and Moonlight were two cunning and adventurous hens who kept us on our toes and liked to come into the house to eat the cats' food! There was a mutual respect between chicken and cat but I do believe that it was the cats who were more afraid than the chickens. We also shared our lives with Karma and Coconut, two extremely noisy budgies who were unafraid to express themselves verbally! They liked nothing better than to yell whilst you were trying to watch telly.

I also enjoy the company of fish and other sea creatures. They are very calming and have deep wisdom and connection to our planet. Rabbits, rodents, cavies, spiders, insects, plants and trees, to mention but a few are all amazing and we should never take them for granted. I've known many rabbits, guinea pigs, hamsters and gerbils. I can feel the energy of even the smallest insect or spider. The way that spiders weave their webs and manage to not stick to them is a feat in itself. I find this fascinating, despite my intense dislike of cobwebs, which used to be an outright phobia. When I was a child, I once sent a piercing scream around my friend's housing estate when I accidentally walked through a cobweb at the playground. I speak to spiders in the same way that I speak to any other animal that I meet. I really don't care what people think. I know that they hear me. I rescue spiders out of our house with my hands (I live in the UK so this is usually safe!) and explain to them what I am doing. I have to put them quite far out of the way though because Monty likes to eat them!

There are so many fascinating animals and adaptations amongst the species on our planet. Some of them look 'alien'. All animals seem to have a close connection to electromagnetic fields and seem to find their way around the world so easily. The way the starlings fly so effortlessly and freely in a murmuration always has me captivated. Other animals such as some marine species and bats use sonar and echo location as naturally as we use our eyes and other creatures are able to see extremes of the spectrum of light way beyond human capabilities. There must be so many species we are yet to discover. It's just a shame that we do not show more love and respect to our planet so that no more species become endangered or extinct.

MY CONNECTION WITH ANIMALS

What Animals Mean To Me

It's hard to put into words how much animals mean to me. If I spend time without animals, my heart aches and I feel a dried up, aching cavernous abyss begin to slowly eat away at me from the inside. I absolutely have to spend time with animals, every day. For me, simply being in the presence of an animal is healing. They resonate a natural healing and therapeutic energy.

My closest, deepest animal bond of all is with our cat, Monty. He is a solid wall of black and white feline muscle with a big, delicate warm heart. His presence melts away all of my problems and resonates with my soul. I can even see his aura in the right light.

Whenever I come across an animal, there is an immediate, uplifting joy that is so magical, it nourishes my soul and an energetic connection is formed. It is a deep and ancient understanding of love and respect as to how we should approach each other, which flows naturally and effortlessly. Innate instructions lie deep within our

DNA about how we should communicate and respond on every level, without the need for spoken words or the interference of ego. This connection is profound and humbling, every time. From dog to cat to horse or even the tiniest fly or plant, I feel that love, respect and connection. Our vibration is on the same frequency.

When I see an animal, I feel a rising up of my vibrations from my centre as shimmering, gold and white particles of energy. This is an uplifting and energising sensation filled with joy and a sense of true, deep connection and understanding.

You may ask if this occurs with every human being that I meet, seeing as, after all, we are animals. The simple answer is no, not with every human. Human beings are much more guarded than animals and often hide behind many layers of complex social conditioning, anxieties and self-protection to avoid being hurt or having their true nature exposed.

There are a great many humans with whom I form an instant connection but it is much more complex than with animals. I often find myself raising my own barriers slightly, playing a game of reading their energy with great caution, just in case I need to suddenly protect myself as they may seem approachable at first but could turn out to be faking their sincerity to serve their own agenda.

This is not the case with animals. I am able to instantly read their energy because they do not hide behind their ego nor create false façade to impress others. If an animal is dangerous or potentially aggressive, it will be immediately obvious to me and a close encounter can be avoided. Their physical expressions and energetic signals seem to be fluid and resonate with a language that I naturally understand. This comes from years of spending time with animals and my ability to receive intuitive and subtle information through my aura and the Universal energy that surrounds us and vibrates within us all.

I believe that this is the reason I am better able to carry out intuitive readings of human beings in photographs. A purer energetic connection is formed this way as there is no distraction from physical cues or changes in demeanour, which may be intended to conceal the truth or distort the intuitive information being received.

The same applies to a certain extent with animals but often a stronger connection can be formed in-person because sometimes, especially with a friendly or deeply spiritual animal, an incredible amount of free-flowing intuitive information and healing energy can be channelled. Animals usually let their guard down and understand how Universal energy and healing works. This can also happen when I meet an animal for the first time, purely by chance. It is a beautiful, amazing and humbling gift for which I shall be eternally grateful.

This special connection is with all species. I find fish especially mesmerising and spiritual. When we visited San Diego a few years ago, there were some beautiful silvery fish who swam together in perfect formation in a hypnotic fashion. I sat next to their aquarium and they moved closer to me, swimming effortless together in synchronisation. I could have stayed there all day, sharing in their wonderful energy. They did not seem distressed about being in captivity and seemed well cared for.

Sadly, that is not always the case. Recently, at our local garden centre, I came up to one tank in the aquatic section in which there seemed to be too many fish for their size. The fish were shimmering red and blue in colour and as I got closer, I could hear them telling me that they were taken from the ocean and did not know where they were. They wanted to go home. It made my heart ache. All of the other fish seemed quite content but the energy of these particular fish was different; they seemed to resonate a high level of intelligence and awareness. Here are a few journal entries about animals:

Journal 10.05.15

'It's a quiet day tomorrow (as far as I know!), so I shall be writing up my animal Reiki and communication experiences so far. I'll write a book about it one day and also one about intuition and paranormal experiences.'

Journal 25.03.16

'At Lincoln Castle, I sensed the presence of a dog. I thought it may be in spirit but then a miniature schnauzer appeared from behind someone in front of us. I know when animals are around!'

Journal 25.06.16

'In the book I'm reading, there's a photo of a gorgeous husky mix dog called Sparkey. As soon as I saw him, I saw lots and lots of green, green grass, like my face was in it! I could smell fresh cut grass. On further reading, it turns out he was a former stray who'd been living in the fields!'

Intuitive Information About Animals, People and Places

My intuitive experiences in relation to animals can be very powerful. Here are some examples of the things I intuitively know about animals, their humans and if an animal is present in a particular place:

- I can sense if an animal is unwell or has had a recent stressful experience or injury;
- When a dog I am walking is going to go to the toilet even when it is in a different place every time and there are no obvious physical signs beforehand;
- How to approach animals in general and for each individual based on what I am sensing or feeling from them;
- When they are stressed, excited or going to have a 'mad half hour' before they show physical signs of this. This is often also the case with aggression, especially when an animal 'freezes' or there are very subtle changes in facial expression and demeanour (in-person and in videos);
- If an animal permits me to touch them and genuinely wishes me to pet them;
- If someone loves a dog, cat or other animal whether the animal is living or in spirit;
- If there is an animal in the vicinity or nearby, especially a dog(s). This was very handy when I was delivering leaflets and I could sense a dog on the other side of the letterbox or in the garden before I saw or heard them. I only once got badly caught out when I heard a dull thud and sensed

tension but ignored it and a dog bit my finger. I can also sense dogs, people and bikes, sometimes cats around corners or on driveways or in bushes etc;

- I can sense whether or not an animal is comfortable with a person, situation or other animal or if they wish to move away;
- What an animal would like to do next; sometimes through body language, sometimes through 'reading their thoughts', usually spontaneously;
- If a dog is going to pull on the lead because they have spotted or sensed something and the split second they are going to stop and sniff (synchronised lead walking with a dog);
- Thoughts, feelings, emotional state, physical health, family members and their energy, household dynamics and who animal best relates to or does not get along with;
- Animals that I know often pop into my head when I least expect it to say 'hello'. Sometimes they come with a message. Sadly, one dog who turned out to be very ill and had to be put to sleep came to me out of the blue about a week beforehand. It was as if he wanted to tell me something but didn't know how to say it. He'd never come to me telepathically before and none of us knew he was seriously ill at the time;
- The character of a dog says a lot about the humans with whom it lives;
- I can tell if an animal is mis-matched with the energy of its human companions. This does not mean that they do not love each other but sometimes a high-energy dog may live with slow-paced humans. Dogs are often responsive and easy to train for me but its guardians may be surprised by this because they won't 'behave' for them. It is often a case

of them not being on the same level and misunderstanding each other.

This list could be endless but it illustrates what intuition is able to tell us. These intuitive insights can be incredibly loud, bright and obvious yet at other times it is hard to tell if they are 'real' or my imagination. More often than not though, something will happen to affirm what I am sensing, leaving me gobsmacked at the subtle power of intuition.

One Paw Led to Another

I have always had a special connection with animals from the moment I was born, especially with my cat, Lucky and other childhood pets. I became a pet sitter through my love of animals and this rapidly developed into a desire to learn as much as possible about the animals in my care.

Since starting my pet sitting business, I have achieved qualifications in Reiki for animals, animal communication and Diplomas in Advanced Canine and Feline Behaviour Management. My true vocation is working with animals holistically so that every angle is covered in helping their guardians to improve their lives. This involves intuition, Reiki and animal communication supported by scientific and practical knowledge.

I became an Accredited Animal Behaviourist in 2016 but working in the animal behaviour industry is not always comfortable for a highly sensitive and intuitive person. All of the politics and red tape can be very off-putting, not to mention the bickering between organisations and different schools of thought. I much prefer to work intuitively, supported by my scientific and practical knowledge as and when required.

I have done lots of voluntary work over the years for members of private social media groups, local animal rescue centres and practised my skills on various animal communication courses. I only ever got one reading completely wrong but picked up on the most amazing details in others, such as coat colour relating to a medical condition, people, places, names, symptoms and connections to the symptoms of some of the animal's human companions in Spirit. Practice and validation are an essential part of the process and I never stop learning. There is always an element of self-doubt that creeps in, no matter how many successful readings you have done.

Some animals only seem to need one Reiki or communication session to feel better and others need regular healing to help them stay healthy as they get older or keep painful symptoms at bay. I gave Reiki to one dog who had been grieving the loss of his female companion and had been following his human guardian around the house but was unable to climb the stairs due to arthritis so he would sit and bark whenever she went upstairs. He was a sweet soul and I could feel the depth of his loving heart when I offered Reiki to him. Our session was quite long and his guardian rang me the next day to say she was amazed with the results. He had stopped following her around, was a lot more relaxed and standing squarely on his shoulders, rather than leaning to one side. I love the power of Reiki!

Journal 02.02.15

'I feel so spiritually connected to animals and privileged to be taken into their trust. It's an honour that I get to work with them every day and have a special cat like Monty who chooses to live with us!'

It is very heart-warming and a great privilege that so many animals and their human guardians have placed their trust in me to take good care of them. I have had to reduce my workload due to a few health issues, including a painful neck. There is a real sense of mutual gratitude between my pet sitting clients and I. It was hard to give up some of my dog walks when my neck got really bad. The bond with my furry clients is often so strong that it's very difficult to say goodbye when times change.

I have had some very interesting and sometimes stressful experiences with a wide variety of animals over the years but I'm so glad I became a pet sitter. It has led me to this point and I have met so many wonderful animals and people who will always have a place in my heart. It is truly amazing to have a special bond with an animal who isn't 'yours'. You receive their unconditional love and trust. It isn't always easy, but being a pet sitter can be a real blessing.

Spiritual and healing work with animals is even more incredible. Once I started learning Reiki, my intuition flourished and I became much more open on a spiritual level. My latest animal teacher and healer is a very special dog named Majiq. Right from the moment I saw her photograph, she leapt out at me with her energy and told me that I had lots to learn! She is an older dog with a few health issues and each Reiki and communication session is full of surprises. I always have lots to write about in my reports. She seems to give me healing in return, for which I am very grateful.

Majiq can be quite the comedienne and we often share laughter together in our Reiki space. She once told me that we were going for a walk in the middle of a Reiki session and even showed me the exact path the way in which we were going to happily run along together. I described the path to her guardians and it turned out to be one of her favourite walking places. In another session, she showed me the image of a large steak. It took a couple of minutes for the image to fade. I wasn't sure if she even liked steak but the image was very clear. I mentioned it to her guardian and he told me that she'd been treated to a piece of sirloin steak for dinner the day before!

The Science of Animal Behaviour

From the spiritual to the scientific, both ends of the spectrum need to be considered when working with animals to give us a broad understanding of their behaviour and how they perceive the world. This gives us the best opportunity to offer animals the help they need in times of trouble without us becoming too conceited and assuming that we know everything. The last thing we want to do is leave animals without their freedom of choice but neither do we want to see them suffering. Science and spirituality can work hand in paw if we allow them to but it's not always easy when intuition and scientific knowledge seem to come from different places and can cause internal conflict.

The beauty of animal communication and Reiki is that they come directly through intuitive and spiritual channels without the interference of the human mind. It is a pure, clear connection without restriction, allowing a continuous flow of energy from an infinite source until the right amount of information or healing has been received at that particular point in time in relation to that particular being or situation. This transcends what we have come to know as 'real' here on Earth and blows the laws of physics out of the water.

Science, on the other hand, is created by humanity and requires internal processing through completely different channels, sending energy inward into our logical mind and memory banks to extract theories, knowledge and information we have learned from the minds of other humans. This then has to be sifted through, checked, checked again, applied to see if it fits, see if it works, see if it is correct, see if it is safe, put it through some more logical and analytical processing, do some further research, ensure that this is correct then eventually write it all down to make sense of it on paper and go through the entire application process once more or maybe even several times. Phew! It's exhausting; especially for a person naturally inclined to refer to their intuition yet some people absolutely love science for these very reasons.

I often feel as though science is a swear word. Science and I have a love-hate relationship. My rebellious inner child hates it with a passion yet my analytical mind welcomes it with open arms! This often causes almost intolerable internal conflict within me on a daily basis. On some days, studying the science behind animal behaviour makes me feel invigorated and enthused yet on other days, putting my head into a complex piece of scientific research leaves me feeling frustrated and despairing. It's as if it blocks up my intuitive channels and I feel as though my energy is being drained. I try to bring the two together but they often seem poles apart.

My intuitive and animal communication abilities usually steer the way with my behavioural knowledge following along in a supporting role. A good dose of the spiritual with a dash of science describes it perfectly. Trying to explain to a purely scientific person that an animal is a beautiful soul with a purpose in a physical body would fall on deaf ears but this concept is second-nature to me. The behaviour of some animals defies explanation and they seem far beyond typical for their particular species. These are the deeply spiritual and enigmatic ones who come here to serve a powerful purpose and when you meet one, you KNOW. Some are serene and gentle; others make you stand back and take a deep breath. Humans are not always superior. We should remain very humble and respectful around animals. They can teach us an awful lot.

Working with animals and their humans has made me come to realise that science can only go so far, in the same way as orthodox medicine. The opposite of course also applies. Reiki and animal communication can only go so far when dealing with serious behavioural issues that pose a danger to others or the animal itself. When it comes to most cases of animals with behavioural issues or physical, mental and emotional problems, the use of intuition, Reiki and animal communication can make inroads into a problem that seems almost impossible to solve with conventional methods. Animal welfare should always be paramount and a veterinary check-up should always be the first option with any concerns about an animal's behaviour or well-being.

Just as the appliance of science and logic can instantly solve some behavioural cases, so too can opening up my intuitive array and picking up on emotional dynamics. If the needs of an animal aren't being met and there is upset and discord within the family or household that are having an impact on everyone concerned, the energy of this can be palpable. Sometimes, a simple change in demeanour or approaching an animal differently can be incredibly effective. Some aspects of animal behaviour are about applying basic common sense and others require a combined effort from all aspects of my intuitive and practical toolkit. No two cases are the same and the unexpected should always be expected, because that's what usually happens!

Only recently, I joined a social media group about observing body language in animals but in the photos and videos I was looking at, although I did see the visual signs, I could clearly hear and sense what the animals were feeling intuitively much more strongly than their communication through body language. I distinctly heard one dog saying 'Why won't you give me what I want?!' This is yet more inspiration for me to continue honing my animal communication skills and also delve into as many ways as I can to learn about animal behaviour. One thing leads to another and even when I am endeavouring to learn about science, along comes another opportunity to learn from my intuitive abilities, which is where my strengths clearly lie:

Journal 31.10.16

'My key strengths are helping owners to better understand their dogs, communicate more effectively on every level and be aware of emotions and how the dog is feeling, the dynamic of the household and relationships. I understand training techniques and behaviour modification but I just don't connect well with them in a real life situation. It makes my gut tighten up, my energy retreat and I feel agitated and anxious about it. Working from the heart with pure energy, communication and feelings creates a peaceful, clear flow; my intuition comes 'online'; I receive messages from Spirit; Reiki will start to flow and

tingle in my hands. It's a pure and natural connection and I can see and feel my time line growing in that direction. The other way creates a block, panic, upset stomach and headache. I'm going with the flow...much nicer than trying to force myself into the wrong box!'

I feel that it is important to ensure that I understand as much as humanly possible about the behaviour of the animals whose welfare is placed into my hands, even if it is only for a short time. There is no greater motivation than making a positive difference to improve and enhance the lives of both my human and furry clients in as many ways as possible.

I continue to study animal behaviour at degree level and keep my toe in the water with regard to the latest scientific theories. Whilst most of it is interesting and engaging, some of the methods used to glean the results of certain experiments in the name of 'research' make my stomach churn and my heart ache. Thankfully, methods of studying animal behaviour from a scientific perspective are no longer cruel and animal welfare is paramount. Subjecting animals to electric shocks and distressing scenarios is very much frowned upon but there are still some branches of science that carry out cruel experiments in the name of human progress. I won't go into those here though as my book will go off on a tangent and probably never return.

Combining intuition, animal communication and Reiki with scientific knowledge is considered irresponsible by some trainers and behaviourists but that is the way I work and the results speak for themselves. Each case has to be approached on an individual basis. Reiki and animal communication can achieve some amazing things but animal welfare and the safety of everyone concerned should be paramount. Working holistically to take absolutely everything about the animal into account including its health, background and living environment provides the best chance for diagnosing the reasons for the unwanted behaviour and finding kind, respectful and realistic ways to resolve it.

In many cases that I have been asked to resolve, it becomes clear that the animal has come into that person's life for a particular reason on a spiritual level. Behaviour consultations are not cut and dried. There are so many variables of a physical, emotional, mental and spiritual nature. I have been to see clients whose personality and emotional make-up seem to be completely at odds with the animal in their care yet I feel that is the reason they have been sent to them. By bringing them together and balancing their energy, they can both grow and develop their relationship and strengthen their bond.

Some people may say that intuition has no place in animal behaviour work but it certainly has a place in working with stressed out guardians and inter-species relations. Remaining sensitive and supportive is a vital part of my work. Living with an animal that is experiencing behaviour problems is far from easy and my aim is to set everyone up for success whilst remaining realistic and non-judgemental.

There are many schools of thought when it comes to training animals and modifying behaviour. Some strike horror into the hearts and minds of deeply caring behaviour professionals who only have the animals' best interests at heart. Punitive and aversive methods should have no place in the world of animal behaviour and training, yet sadly, there are a great many 'experts' who advocate such things. Being an Animal Communicator and Reiki Master Teacher makes me ultra-sensitive to many of the horror stories I hear about animals being mistreated and punished for what is often normal behaviour.

Choosing Wisely on Behalf of Our Animals

The label of an 'expert' is dangerous thing. Anyone can call themselves an animal behaviourist or trainer and some of the more unscrupulous kinds are only in it for the money, not because they care about animals and stressed-out humans. People expect 'experts' to have all the answers and provide a quick fix. When you sit down with a new client for a couple of hours and explain to them the intricacies, time, patience and planning it will take to try to resolve their animal's behavioural issues, most of them don't want to know. They still expect you to tell them a fast and simple solution because that is what they have seen on the telly or been told by a friend.

There are then the 'experts' who do suggest quick fixes that are inherently neither effective nor humane and naïve owners blindly trust them because they are an 'expert' and must be right, even though they are not entirely convinced or comfortable with their suggestions. It must be a good thing if an expert says it's ok to force your dog down into an 'Alpha' roll or fit your dog with an electric shock collar or choke chain, right? WRONG! It's going to ruin your relationship with your dog and probably make matters worse or create other issues.

These same experts tend to argue with all the other experts and, somehow, all of them are right at the same time about everything - but what about the animals? How are they supposed to find any room amongst the huge egos of all these experts? At present, anyone can claim to be an animal behaviourist which can result in a great deal of damage being done by uneducated people who are only out to make money from unsuspecting and often desperate animal guardians.

Attempts are being made to regulate the industry but even if it does become regulated, there is still a good chance that old-school methods will be used unless there is a robust force-free policy in place. Even then, the use of words when it comes to describing which methods are acceptable and which are not can become another grey area. Thankfully, there are many behaviourists who are deeply caring and despair with some aspects of the profession. The organisations of which they are members passionately seek to promote kind, humane, force-free methods of training and behaviour modification, supported by scientific knowledge. They are often asked by desperate animal guardians to pick up the pieces left behind by the previous animal behaviour 'professional' who claimed to be more highly qualified but used out-dated, unpleasant methods which made matters worse. There needs to be an overhaul of the industry to actively oust the myth that pack theory, dominance and being the 'Alpha' have any place in animal training and behaviour modification.

Setting out to dominate or take control of an animal from a disciplinary mind-set is asking for trouble and is often detrimental to the welfare of the animal and the animal-human bond. In the end, the animal will either shut down or become aggressive through fear, confusion or frustration. Sadly, in some cases, this results in animals being euthanised due to behaviour problems which were brought about by ignorant humans. Ascribing to such theories is just an excuse to mistreat an animal because the so-called professional is lacking in knowledge and compassion for animals. Their work is based on boosting their own ego, bank balance and reputation for working miracles with quick fixes. This kind of attitude is holding the industry back and keeping it in the dark ages.

It is vital to be knowledgeable and fully informed when dealing with the resolution of animal behaviour problems. It is the interpretation of information that makes it all the more important for people to really do their homework and find a caring, honest and experienced behaviourist or other caring animal professional. They should work with the animal's best interests at heart. When this is combined with the appropriate scientifically based behaviour modification methods, it can work wonders. Many animal behaviour problems are complex in nature and a great deal of knowledge and experience is required. Care should still be taken though when it comes to scientific theories. They can soon become outdated and it is easy for those using out-dated methods to hide behind the façade that what they are doing is supported by science. Many cruel things are done to animals in the name of science so it is not always a good thing. When science and compassion for animals work together, that is the right kind of science.

The same of course applies to animal communicators, healers and veterinary surgeons. It is important to be fully informed and discerning when choosing professionals to look after our animal companions. They cannot speak for themselves and we should choose wisely on their behalf. Just because someone is a member of an organisation or has a list of qualifications as long as their arm, it does not mean that they are the right choice for you and your animal. Meet them, observe how they interact with your animal, speak to their previous clients and do some research to back-up your choice. Word of mouth and recommendations may be a good place to start. Also, make sure they are insured and that their knowledge is up-to-date and based on treating the animal kindly. Most of all, make sure that your animal likes them. If they are very cautious and nervous around them or the person seems to want to take charge and talks about dominance, scrub them off your list of options. Do what feels right in your heart - your animal will be sure to thank you for it in the long-term.

Combining Intuition and Scientific Information

As an Animal Communicator and Empath, it saddens and sometimes angers me when science comes along and has to 'prove' something that is stark-staringly obvious about animals. It's as if the some scientists feel this is necessary because animal lovers have previously been unable to work this out for themselves without science stepping in to save the day.

As a spiritual person, it is easy to dismiss scientific theories because we feel that most of it is obvious as we already have such a deep connection with animals. I have found myself doing this many times then I come to realise that perhaps I'm being stubborn and ignorant by making such assumptions. Knowledge of topics such as genetics, psychology, nutrition, anatomy, pathology and the neurological functioning of animals is essential for professionals working to resolve animal behaviour issues. The same also applies for animal healers and communicators. Learning as much as possible about animals from the right sources can only be a good thing. One of the most important fundamentals when it comes to training and behaviour modification is the concept of positive reinforcement.

Positive reinforcement is a scientific term but most of its principles come naturally to those with an affinity for animals. Its basic principle is that rewarding an animal for carrying out an action or sequence of behaviour will make it more likely to be repeated. It is part of the four quadrants of operant conditioning. I won't go into too much detail here but the other three quadrants are negative reinforcement, negative punishment and positive punishment.

Negative reinforcement is when something unpleasant ceases when an animal behaves in a desired way; negative punishment is when something that the animal likes is taken away when it behaves in an undesirable way (eg. being ignored when it jumps up for attention) and positive punishment is when something unpleasant is added to stop an animal from behaving in an undesirable way.

Kind, reward-based training is based on positive reinforcement and occasionally negative punishment (which doesn't cause the animal any harm as it's not really a punishment; it simply gives them a moment to pause and think about what they should do, ie. stop jumping up, for which they are rewarded through positive reinforcement). It is the other two quadrants of negative reinforcement and positive punishment that should not be used as they can cause distress to an animal and damage the human-animal bond.

Being kind and working energetically and empathically to communicate with an animal to encourage it to change its behaviour seem be second nature to me but there is always room to learn more and I don't know everything; nobody does. Most aspects of positive reinforcement have their basis in common sense and showing compassion towards animals. It really isn't rocket science but it is a science of sorts! Training animals isn't always easy and when tried and tested scientific theories don't work on animals who are mischievous, independent thinkers, it can be hilarious! Even the brightest scientific minds can easily be outwitted by an animal who is already one step ahead.

Science can sometimes seem cold-hearted and clinical without a second thought for the emotional lives of animals yet it can attempt to embrace spiritual and deeply emotional aspects of life with the intention of proving that there is an intuitive and spiritual side to animal behaviour. This goes some way towards bridging the gap between the strictly scientific and human-orientated view of animals and the gentler, easy flowing nature of the spiritual aspects of life. It is difficult to apply scientific theories when you can hear the thoughts of the animal you are with and they are sharing an energetic space with you in which you can feel their emotions. It's a strange sensation!

I have learned so much about canine and feline behaviour over the past few years that is has become part of my psyche and subtle energy system. The scientific information has been assimilated and broken down to fit into my intuitive nature and memory banks as if it has always been there. As much as I find some scientific discoveries laughable because they are so obvious, I must continue to tell myself that I need scientific information as much as the next person, if not more so. Some people will only listen to scientific explanations and theories and dismiss anything less. It is vital to have a wide knowledge base so that I can help as many animals as possible through my work.

I am discerning when it comes to scientific information and only take what I feel comfortable with. If it seems too harsh and cold, I leave it; if it captures my interest and I want to learn more, I allow it to reel me in. Scientific knowledge and intuitive information both have their own unique qualities but they can work together well when blended in the right quantities and proportions. Intuition and spirituality can be taken to extremes in the same way that science can. For me, being intuitive about scientific information is just as important as the subject matter itself. As with all things in life, it must resonate with my own inner truth or I kick it to the kerb.

ANIMAL COMMUNICATION

What Is Animal Communication?

So, how do you communicate with animals? You're doing it already! Our relationships with animals can be so deep and intense because they love unconditionally. They are pure beings of light and do not hide behind layers of complex emotions and self-protection as humans often do. Loving an animal is a very powerful, mutual bond. Animals are sent into our lives for a reason, usually to teach us something and give us deep healing on every level. When we form this bond with an animal, it is a heart and soul connection. A lot of animal communication is spontaneous and as you become more accustomed to it, you'll notice that you receive things from animals as they pass by or stop to say 'hello'.

Journal 01.04.16

'When I was cat sitting, the big fluffy cat with vibrant green eyes was teasing me. He likes fuss but only on his terms. He mews like a little kitten, even though he's a few years old. He usually dashes around when I try to touch him and rolls about then runs away. Today, he teased me all the way to the greenhouse in the garden then stopped, looked directly into my eyes

and I heard him say "you're welcome now". I reached out my hand, expecting him to flirt and run away but he stayed still and let me give him lots of fuss on his head and neck. I was amazed!'

Journal 20.01.17

'When Paddy the Golden Retriever and I arrived back at his front door after our walk, I snuck him an extra treat. It broke up and went everywhere. He efficiently sucked up the crumbs and I then noticed a small bit was left behind. I automatically said to him telepathically "there's a bit more there, look" and raised my eyebrows. He looked me in the eye and 'heard' me, then said "oo, is there?" and immediately gobbled it up.'

We fall in sync with one another, knowing each other's nuances, moods, body language, facial expressions and subtleties of every move with effortless flow. This is how I know you already communicating with your animal! Your relationship has become so familiar and normal to you, that you believe that animal communication is something different that is only available to the chosen few. Not so. All you have to do is become aware of how you are already communicating with your animal and find the peace and calm within to enhance this and take it to the next level. If you feel that your animal is trying to tell you something and you think that you can hear words, feel sensations or are receiving images, don't doubt yourself. You know them best of all!

Communicating with your own animal is rather different from communicating with animals with whom you are unfamiliar. Animal communication comes naturally to some people but it can be developed and enhanced from any level. Practice and validation are the key elements to develop your abilities. This is sometimes easier with other people's animals because they can come up with questions that give a validating answer. When wishing to receive validation from your own animal, perhaps ask them to come over and lick your hand, look at you or do something else to indicate that they understand you. Most of the time, you may simply feel it in your heart and know that you are both linked together with your intimate bond and subtle energy.

Communication with your own animal can be something as simple as feeling them stare at you from behind; sensing when they are approaching or when they walk in the room before you can see them. Their approach can be like an energetic 'ding!' like a little bell announcing their arrival, or a radar sending you their energetic signature. This can also happen when animals visit us from Spirit. We may feel their energy or see their face in our minds. Some people may see orbs, feel sensations or catch glimpses of an animal out the corner of their eye.

Animals are often one step ahead and can see what is going on in our minds before we have spoken a single word. Next time you tell your cat or dog that you are just going to take a ride in the car when you are really going to take them to the vet's, they'll probably turn tail and hide because they see the images in your mind that tell the real story.

Quite often, the dogs I am walking turn around to look at me when I silently communicate with them using words and images or send them an image of which way we will be going on our walk and they go that way without any physical cues. I also have a strong connection with our cat and we do so many things without words it becomes the norm but to other people, they would probably wonder how we know what the other one means without obvious verbal or physical signals. It simply flows. They also let me know when they are feeling unwell and often seem to understand what I say:

Journal 08.06.15

'When I arrived to walk Lily, she seemed fine and happy so I took her for a walk as normal. She wasn't keen on going out and lay down in the road, but this often happens! She usually gets up when offered a treat. On the way back, she kept eating grass which made me think she perhaps had an upset tummy. About half way back she was very slow. Lily normally likes to saunter but she was extra-slow today. A voice in my head said to hurry up and get her home before she went off her legs. Lily flopped heavily on the floor when we got back. She looked really sad and looked straight into my eyes and said how her tummy hurt and she felt bad. It was as if I heard her words! Her owner told me that she'd had an upset tummy but had seemed better that morning. My intuition and her clear communication amazed me. I can definitely 'hear' animals! Fortunately, Lily was soon back to normal.'

Journal 01.07.16

'I just looked at a photo of a little dog on one of my group pages and wanted to bark in a high-pitched way, straining forwards. I clicked on the article and it said that the dog's problems were barking and lunging at children and the neighbour. Also, when I was dog sitting, Izzie the golden retriever was begging for treats and almost got up on my lap when I sat down. I told her to go and play on the lawn because I had none and she instantly did so. I only said it quietly. Animals really do understand what we say (unless they are stubborn or distracted by something far more interesting!).'

During one of my animal communication courses, a little Border Terrier came to visit us with her humans. She went around happily greeting us all and enjoyed a good tickle under her chin and around her ears. I 'asked' her if she would like me to tickle her tummy. She seemed to move down slightly sideways but wouldn't go down any further than putting her shoulder onto the floor. I asked her why she didn't want to lie down and was amazed to receive the reply "I like to be the right way up". After we had all given our feedback on the session, it was confirmed that she hadn't had the best start in life because of complications at birth. This meant that she did not want to be upside down because she had problems with balance and co-ordination. This affirmed what she had said to me and gave me some confidence-building validation.

Animal communication can be astounding but it doesn't mean that every animal will wish to engage with us or that communicating with them will suddenly result in a remarkable change in character or behaviour. Change in any animal takes time, patience and understanding.

It is important to keep an open heart and mind when working as an animal healer or communicator but people should also be realistic. As with all aspects of spiritual and intuitive work, animal communication is not always easy. People often contact a professional Animal Communicator when they are concerned about their animal or they are very ill. It is very important to remain calm and caring but also protect your energy through grounding and protection. Animal communication is a beautiful thing but it can also be very painful when you have to face the loss of an animal with whom you have formed a special bond. Keeping an open heart and mind and maintaining a good self-care routine will help to keep you strong.

Human clients may call upon your services for many reasons and it may not always be possible to give them the answers that they are seeking. There are so many variables and influences in every situation. Offering Reiki or animal communication can be a catalyst for positive change but it is the people involved in the daily lives of animals who need to implement new ways of behaving, adapt their living situation or change routines. We may receive some useful insights but cannot force change upon animals and their people. It is not our place to do so.

Managing the expectations of human clients and showing them patience, guidance and support is a major part of helping animals. We need to work holistically with all household members, past and present and always remember that honesty and integrity are vital in work of a spiritual and healing nature. Animal communication of a telepathic and intuitive nature can be incredibly insightful but more often than not, a relaxed and trusting atmosphere is required.

Telepathic and Intuitive Communication

Telepathy takes place when there is a sense of calmness and trust has been established between animals or animals-humans. It begins with having an open heart and making a subtle mind to mind connection.

Intuition can be blocked and suppressed in stressful situations. Receiving intuitive information can be difficult when we feel tense or under pressure. There are exceptions to this, such as when Spirit comes through to help us in times of upset or crisis.

I often ask myself why there are so many behavioural problems in our domestic animals, especially when so many of them seem to be fearful or aggressive towards members of their own species. Why don't they simply connect telepathically? Well, this is probably very difficult when experiencing the physical effects of fear.

We expect so much from our domestic animals. Dogs especially have been bred for various purposes over thousands of years and in recent times, their physical features they require for effective communication such as their ears and tail have been distorted to the point that they are almost rendered useless for their intended purpose.

The ancestors of our domestic animals and their current wild family members have not had their lives interfered with by humans so their communication systems remain efficient, fluid and fully functional.

Their domestic dog relatives however, rely on humans to ensure that they breed them wisely with their welfare in mind, raise their pups properly, socialise and habituate them to all aspects of the canine and human world and expose them to the right situations at the right time so that they can learn how to 'speak' dog, human and the language of any other species they may need to learn to safely interact with.

We live in a physical world first and foremost and when we know we are physically safe, we can begin to feel more relaxed to opening up our higher senses and energetic bodies to wider experiences.

I cannot imagine being able to conduct an animal communication session in the wrong part of town surrounded by drunken yobs shouting expletives in the street. Fear, stress and anxiety can all temporarily shut down intuitive abilities and force us to prioritise our physical safety.

This same level of fear may be experienced by a dog who has been poorly socialised as a puppy or has had traumatic experiences in its life. He may be terrified at the sight of other dogs or people. He is hardly going to feel content and relaxed enough to want to engage in a deep telepathic conversation with the stimulus of his deepest, darkest fears. His stress levels will be through the roof and he will either want to attack, mentally shut down or run for the hills!

Two or more animals who live together in perfect harmony are likely to have a lot of 'silent' conversations of which their humans may be unaware. I know quite a few animals like this. I can hear the chatter between them as they walk along or explore the garden. The words are often indistinct but they seem to be filled with humour and light-hearted fun and I've occasionally noticed one dog nudge another as they seem to get to the punchline! It's such a funny sight! Dogs have a highly developed sense of humour, as do most animals. The world of Spirit is also filled with laughter. Laughter raises vibrations and makes it easier for us to experience feelings of wellness and joy and allows Spirit to get closer to us because of the joyful vibrations laughter brings.

I have heard animals laughing during Reiki sessions and they have shown images to me and told me that they are joking! Many animals, especially our domesticated companions retain their youthful qualities which are often lost in their wild counterparts when they reach adulthood. This is a major part of their appeal.

Cats and dogs retain a particularly high desire to play well into old age. Many wild animals are also playful, especially foxes and dolphins, to name but a few.

Domestic animals share many traits and characteristics with wild animals but even those who have had very little contact with humans tend to be aware of which humans are intuitive and spiritually aware because they emit a higher vibrational signature and seem to naturally understand how to interact with wild animals and make themselves appear safe to approach. This may explain why there are many tales of wild animals approaching humans and visiting their properties. Some of it may be food related but injured wild animals tend to know who to approach for help and can be very discerning when it comes to their choice of human helper.

All life is connected to Universal energy but wild animals have a particular awareness and strong connection with the vibrations of our planet and beyond. Those animals who are truly wild and not negatively affected by our urban sprawl are an intrinsic part of the energy of the Earth. Birds and prey animals are lightning fast and many of them negotiate the planet by working with the movement of the sun, moon, stars, jet streams, electromagnetic fields and ocean and river currents. Telepathy and energetic synchronicity may also be at play for flock animals, amongst many other mysterious forms of communication which we can only begin to imagine. Watching flocks of birds in flight and the synchronised movements of shoals of fish are hypnotic and amazing.

When learning to communicate with domestic animals or those in the wild, a calm and relaxed state will allow them to trust and open up to us.

Carrying Out an Animal Communication Session

Animal communication and Reiki are not about following set procedures or protocol. They are about letting go of expectation, remaining calm and open to all possibilities and allowing intuition to lead the way.

Expecting lengthy, wordy conversations with our animal friends is not always realistic. It may happen for some people but animal communication takes place on every level, from the subtle to the obvious and is different for everyone. Sensing and feeling the energy of an animal with a natural, easy flow and remaining open to receiving a wide variety of intuitive impressions is the best place to start.

Animal communication is a unique experience between each communicator and animal and does not have to follow the pattern of what someone else tells you should happen. Our hearts and intuition unlock the potential of animal communication. A teacher, book or manual can only ever serve as a rough guide.

The most important teachers of all are the animals; they are the ones who should be listened to in order to truly learn. Human teachers of animal communication are there to guide and inspire us but they too will always direct you back to the animals as being the ultimate purveyors of wisdom and knowledge.

Sometimes, animal communication takes place within the silence, deep within, just like when we are meditating. It is a place without chaos, thoughts or judgements in which we can just ‘be’ with an animal on a subtle energetic level but this does not happen with every session.

Communication can also take place on a very obvious, physical level. I'm sure that we've all spoken out loud to our animals and are convinced that they respond to what we are saying. This is because animals DO understand what we are saying to them. Not necessarily the exact meaning of every word but they feel and sense the energy and intention behind every word we say. It is not just the words they are receiving; it is our whole demeanour, approach, energy and body language.

Earning an animal's trust is the first step. Animals begin by assessing the physical and energetic approach of a human to see if they are trustworthy. Sometimes, an energetic introduction over a distance using a photograph or offering a distant Reiki session may help to achieve this, especially for nervous animals.

Whether we are working in-person or from a photograph with an animal, we should always begin a session by grounding and protecting ourselves and the animal so that we are both safe and comfortable. This can be done with a simple visualisation and asking for you both to be grounded and protected by pure white light. Of course, animal communication is sometimes spontaneous and there is no time to do this but this is a good way to prepare when you have the opportunity to do so.

Always ask for permission from the animal and invite them to communicate with you, should they wish to. This can be done in your mind so that the peace between you is not disturbed. You do not have to physically touch the animal. Just to do whatever is comfortable for you both. Sitting close to or with them may be the best option. Most animals do not like direct eye contact but this does not mean that you have to keep your eyes closed. Do what comes naturally.

If you are physically present with the animal, they may settle down with you or move around. Animals should not be restrained during a session unless there is a safety issue. The session could be conducted outside of a kennel, enclosure or stable if there are any risks. Stand or sit somewhere safe and relax and the animal will probably relax too. Go with the flow. When you feel the time is right, gently close your eyes and feel peace and calm within your Solar Plexus.

Offer a connection to the animal from your heart and quiet your mind. Be fully present with the animal and allow your thoughts to pass by and float away. Be humble, kind and patient. Remain calm and open to receive impressions and information without judgement or expectations.

You may start to feel a change in your energy field, receive brief images, words, feelings, sensations, a sense of 'knowing' or the animal may telepathically engage in conversation with you. It may sound like a completely different voice to your own or very similar. They will come through in a way that is comfortable for you.

Animal communication is vastly different for all of us and if you're expecting a full-blown, lengthy conversation, you may be waiting for a very long time. You may receive a plethora of images in your mind like a movie screen, feel sensations or aches and pains in parts of your body that do not normally trouble you. This is why it is vital to remain open. Anything can happen and it usually does!

Reading for a former race horse in April 2016:

'As I tuned into his energy, I got nervous shudders and twitches over my upper body, as if my arms were flailing around. This seemed to represent his front legs. I felt as if I was surrounded by so much noise, jostling, bustling activity. There was never any peace; constant noise; nowhere to go. It was a horrible, nervous, buzzing energy. I just wanted to escape and not stop running. I sent him love and peace and asked him to listen to the peace. I grounded and protected him.'

The lady who owned the sanctuary where I carried out the reading told me that the nervous shudders and movements in my arms were exactly the movements that the horse had first done when he arrived at the sanctuary. It took him many months to stop bolting and running from an invisible force. I was sickened to hear that in his racing days, he had his front tendons fused together with hot irons, which was a commonly accepted practice in the racing stables where he was kept. This may have been the terror he was trying to run from. It is an incredibly painful experience that never fully heals.

Don't despair if you do not receive anything at all in some cases. Some animals may not wish to communicate with you at that point in time, especially if they are in a rescue situation and may be afraid of humans. It could also be that you are feeling a bit blocked because you are nervous or not sure if you are capable of such a thing. This is why you should not give up and practice often. Your confidence will grow when you start to receive validation, especially from the animals' guardians and the animals themselves. This will give you a sense of wonder, humility and gratitude. It really is a privilege and honour when animals open up and place their trust in you.

If you are working with someone else's animal, ask them to prepare at least three validation questions in advance. These should be something simple that the animal's guardians will know the answer to, such as a favourite toy, the location of their bed, favourite walking route or the name or description of their animal companion. It shows that you have connected with their animal.

Trust your first impressions, even if they don't make sense. Say what you see, hear, or feel. Don't allow logic to try to second guess it or over-interpret it. You will be surprised at some of the things you receive when communicating with animals! They may even give away their family's secrets. Use your discretion because some information may be sensitive, particularly if an animal is unwell and knows that they may soon pass away. Be kind and explain things in a sensitive way. Some people may not be ready to hear what their animal has to tell them.

Some animal communicators who teach others may suggest that people start learning by imagining what an animal may be thinking or feeling if they seem to be unable to 'communicate' with them. This does not make much sense because this means that we are projecting our own expectations on to the animal and not remaining open to receive anything. It would not be very respectful or polite to impose our own impressions onto an animal and not allow them to speak for themselves.

It can be difficult to remember what you have received during a session so it is important to write things down as soon as possible afterwards or use a voice recorder to dictate into. Some people write things down during the communication session but this can be distracting when you are 'in the zone' with an animal. Guardians love to have something tangible to remember the session by so it is good to write up a report on the session afterwards whilst it is still fresh. A session should finish by giving thanks to the animal and once again grounding and protecting you both so that you energy fields can be independent once again.

Distant Animal Communication

Working from photographs can be very different from working in-person. You may find that you receive immediate energetic impressions, thoughts and feelings and are able to connect with those in Spirit by using this method. Sometimes, intuitive information comes through more clearly when working with a photograph because there are fewer distractions and nobody is watching you in anticipation of what their animal might say. It is easier to write things down when working from a photograph. Grounding and protection should be done in the same way as an in-person session at the beginning and end.

When receiving intuitive information about animals in Spirit, it is not always in the form of them communicating with you directly. Impressions and names seem to be received from a higher source of intuitive consciousness, as well as the sensations of medical symptoms. A sudden flurry of information may spontaneously be received from 'out of nowhere' before you've even had chance to think about grounding and protection. If it's meant to be, it's meant to be. The information may come to you instantaneously or it could trickle through slowly as snippets.

Journal 27.04.16

'I just did a very different reading for a dog who has passed. It's amazing how all of the animals have such a different vibration and stories to tell. I've come so far with all of the practice that I've done but I need to do so much more. It's a vast and amazing world of Spirit, and the living! I've also been picking up on things from photos of people and then checked the comments (on social media) and other people have picked up on similar things. I mainly get a sense for the spirit people who are with them. I can often 'see' them standing behind them or see their face; not in the actual photo but in my mind's eye/third eye.'

Animal Communication Practice

The more that you practice animal communication, the more confident and motivated you will become.

Ask family and friends if you can practice with their animals or if they know of anyone who can help you to gain experience by communicating with their animals. Working with unfamiliar animals gives you greater opportunity to gain validation. Keep things varied to give you wide experience by working both in-person and using photographs.

Ask for three questions for validation purposes that have clearly defined answers that you can check on to make sure that you are connected with the animal.

Private social media groups often allow members to practice their intuitive skills. These could be dedicated animal communication groups, psychic or mediumship groups. It is always best to check with the group administrators first and perhaps be a member for a few weeks to get a feel as to whether or not you are comfortable with the group before offering readings.

Be discerning and make sure you are clear about your intentions. Ask people to post their photos and give three initial validation questions and 3-5 questions for which they would like answers if possible. Set a limit for the number of readings you can manage at the outset or you'll be inundated. Make it clear what you are doing and why so as to avoid disappointment. You may not be drawn to every animal to offer a reading. Be sensitive and kind when giving answers and politely request feedback.

Another option for animal communication practice is to volunteer your services to a local animal charity to help resolve issues in order to get more animals re-homed or for them to feel more comfortable in a rescue environment. Be clear about your intentions here as well though. It can be very easy to over-commit yourself as animal charities are always very busy and need reliable helpers.

Working with your own animals can also be a form of practice. Ask for a response when you communicate with them so that they carry out a particular action so you know they can 'hear' you. Keep the channels of communication open and your bond will become even stronger.

When working as a professional Animal Communicator, it is vital to have the correct insurance and ask the animal's guardian to sign a form confirming that they are happy for you to communicate with their animal and understand the process. You should explain what they could expect from a session and how it works. It is also important for them to prepare any questions they would like answers to beforehand so that you can give them validation. It may not always be possible to answer these so guardians should be asked to keep an open mind and to allow you all to relax during the session. If an animal seems to be unwell or there may potentially be a medical issue, always make sure that you ask for the animal to be checked by a vet to ensure their well-being, using discretion and sensitivity.

Lost Pets

One of the most difficult aspects of animal communication is trying to locate lost pets.

I do not offer this as part of my animal communication service because it is so distressing for the family of the lost animal. It can be hard to know which way to turn or where to begin.

Animal guardians who desperately need to find their companion will pin their hopes on anything that offers a chance of their animal being found. This pressure is absolutely immense on an animal communicator and for me personally, it fills me with self-doubt about my intuitive abilities because it is so important to be accurate. The intense emotions are too much to bear. Managing the expectations of human clients is a big part of working in this way. The likelihood of tension and being accused of failure are very high. It is a skill that needs to be finely honed.

There are many communicators who take on this role as their primary vocation and remain absolutely calm, resolute and focussed on the task in hand, opening their intuitive senses wide to all and any piece of information they may receive as to the animal's whereabouts. I absolutely admire these brave souls. They are a credit to the profession.

In the early stages of my animal communication 'official' training, I was sometimes asked to find lost pets and began to dread any requests because one of my abilities when working with photographs is to immediately be able to tell whether or not an animal or person is alive or deceased upon my first glance at their picture. I had this a few times but had to pass on any offers of help and referred them to someone else specialising in the task of locating lost pets. I could not bear to tell someone that I felt that their pet had died nor would I like to tell them this and risk being wrong.

I would also sometimes see, feel, smell and sense other things from the photographs of lost pets but it was not something I was comfortable with. The results of such things are often inconclusive because smelling grass, sensing an injury, smelling an oily workshop or seeing trees are such vague things to go on. Even when a lead is established, the results may still prove to be inconclusive. I now leave this to the experts with stronger hearts than mine and they do a fantastic job.

There are many practical steps that can be taken when looking for a lost animal, such as putting up posters, asking all of the neighbours to check their outbuildings and putting out a cat's litter tray so that they are drawn home by their own scent but there are also energetic things that may help.

Sending out a loving resonance from the heart and visualising a beacon of light for your pet can help it to find its way home and let you know you have not given up on them. Some animals turn up days, weeks, months or even years after they have gone missing. Animals often form mental maps and follow the electromagnetic field of the Earth to get home if they have accidentally been taken somewhere far away.

There is also a possibility that an animal has moved on because their life's purpose is to stay with one person or family for a while then move on to help others and play a part in their life's lessons. This may sound extreme but it is true in some cases, especially with stray animals who are prone to wander.

Our animal companions are connected to our hearts and when they pass away it is very painful but when they go missing, it can seem even worse because there is no closure and there will always be that hope of them being found. Being an animal communicator assisting in this process is not easy because you may have to tell desperate animal guardians things that they do not wish to hear.

REIKI FOR ANIMALS

What is Reiki?

The word Reiki is Japanese in origin. 'Rei' can be translated as 'Universal' or 'Spirit' and 'ki' relates to the life-force energy that surrounds and penetrates everything. It is pronounced 'Ray-key'.

The healing system of Reiki was founded by Dr Mikao Usui in Japan during the early 1900s. It involves hands-on healing and can also be given over a distance. Reiki promotes healing on a physical, mental, emotional and spiritual level and is passed down from Reiki Master Teacher to student through a process known as an attunement or initiation.

A person giving Reiki is a channel for healing energy which flows through them and out of their hands. It is an intelligent energy and goes to where it is needed for as long as it is needed. The Reiki practitioner does not control the energy, they simply allow it to flow through them for the greatest and highest good.

Human recipients of Reiki remain fully clothed and often fall asleep during Reiki treatments because it is so relaxing. Reiki can do no harm and can be given in any situation but it is not a substitute for orthodox medicine or veterinary treatment. It is a complementary therapy that has many benefits. A Reiki practitioner does not diagnose conditions. Reiki promotes healing and does not promise to cure anything but can sometimes offer healing and relief where medical treatment does not seem to be effective. It is gentle, yet powerful and can often yield amazing results.

If you join a Reiki organisation such as the UK Reiki Federation, you may find that they give contra-indications towards offering Reiki in certain circumstances. This may include people with mental health problems, pregnant women in the first trimester and cancer patients. It is wise to be cautious but use your own intuition and discretion. If something doesn't feel right, then it probably isn't. It's also not recommended to give Reiki directly to a freshly broken bone, as it may set in the wrong position. If someone is under the influence of alcohol or drugs, it is not wise to give them a Reiki treatment for the safety of both of you. Politely ask them to return when they are sober, if you are comfortable with treating them at all. This is common sense and you will know what feels right at the time.

Reiki can be sent to anything, anywhere and even over time and space through distant healing. It is the intention to send Reiki that allows this to work, along with the Reiki II distant healing symbol. Reiki can be sent to people, animals, plants, relationships, situations and inanimate objects. It is a versatile energy that knows no bounds. Reiki has many benefits, including:

- Relief from stress, anxiety and tension;

- Soothing aches and pains;
- Relieving the symptoms of chronic conditions;
- Recovery from injury or surgery;
- Improving sleep patterns;
- Boosting mood and energy levels;
- Deep relaxation;
- Removing emotional blockages;
- Promoting healing in the body, mind and spirit;
- Improving general well-being.

Students of Reiki are offered three levels of learning in the traditional Usui Reiki system. These are Reiki I, Reiki II Practitioner and Reiki Master Teacher. Teaching methods vary and traditionally, Reiki was passed down verbally and was considered to be sacred and not be shared with non-Reiki people.

There are five precepts to learn with Reiki, which help us to remain grounded and lead a more beneficial lifestyle. These should be meditated upon and integrated into the life of the person learning Reiki. These precepts are:

Just for today,
I shall not anger,
I shall not worry,
I shall do my work honestly,
I shall be grateful,
And I shall be kind to all living things.

The wording of these may vary, depending on the Reiki Master Teacher.

Reiki Level I teaches the student how to give themselves a Reiki self-treatment daily and asks them to go through a period of cleansing, meditation and self-treatments for 21 days following their first attunement. They learn the Reiki precepts and how to give Reiki to their friends and family, sitting or lying down. During Reiki I, some Masters give one attunement and others split it into three. Either way, this helps the Reiki to flow into the student and allows them to channel it whenever they wish by the power of intention. Reiki students are encouraged to keep a journal of their progress.

Meditation is also included in Reiki practice. An example of this is the gassho mediation in which the hands are placed into prayer position in front of the heart and soft focus is placed on the middle fingers. At least ten to twenty minutes per day is highly beneficial. If focus is lost in thoughts, it can be more easily brought back when there is something to focus on. Relaxed breathing and sitting upright are also part of the gassho meditation for good energy flow.

Reiki II is more in-depth then Reiki I. Students learn the first three Reiki symbols and how to become a Reiki Practitioner to practice professionally. The Reiki symbols are considered to be sacred and secret but they have been published in some Reiki books and on the internet. They have different meanings and increase the intensity of the Reiki as it flows.

Reiki III, Master Teacher level is sometimes taught as Master Teacher combined or sometimes as Reiki Master with the Teacher element being taught separately as Grand Master level. Both are really the same thing.

A Reiki Master Teacher is given two further symbols to work with and shown how to pass Reiki on to others via attunements. A true Reiki Master Teacher is the embodiment of Reiki and has a responsibility to live a Reiki lifestyle by following the Reiki precepts and being healthy, meditating daily and giving themselves daily Reiki self-treatments, attending Reiki shares and continuing to learn about Reiki.

Traditionally in Japan, the Reiki Master Teacher level could only be reached after many years, sometimes decades spent learning with their Master and accumulating many hours of practice giving Reiki to others. In modern Western society, Reiki is often taught over a few days or a weekend. This is not always recommended as the Reiki energy needs time to settle and students need to gain confidence and experience. It is better to leave a few months between levels whilst learning Reiki to truly embrace it and become accustomed to the energy and new way of life. Sometimes, messages from Spirit can be received during Reiki amongst many other things:

Journal 29.03.15

''Nannan' (Dad's Mum) came to me last night to say 'hello' during Reiki. I was told the name Edward George several times over and Victoria or Vic. Dad's Dad was called Victor so it could have been him.'

Journal 16.09.16

'I had painful hiccups last night. I hardly ever get them. It wasn't easy giving myself Reiki with hiccups but as soon as I placed my hands over my stomach, I could feel it relax from the inside and I saw an ocean slowly calming down, then the hiccups stopped. Reiki is amazing!'

Journal 09.11.16

'When I did my Reiki self-treatment a couple of nights ago, there was what felt like sunlight or pure Universal light streaming down on me from above my head to the left. I had my eyes closed and it was almost pitch dark. It was a wonderful, healing light. Very nice.'

Journal 25.04.16

'I sat quietly for a while but didn't meditate fully. After a while, I felt the need to feel the energy between my hands. As I did so, I could see the energy in my hands! It's like pale, fine waves coming off the tips of my fingers. There's a few tiny sparkles as well, like the orgone in the sky but barely visible; so subtle. I could sit and look at it all night.'

I still do this a lot now. It's grown stronger since then, especially after meditation or self-Reiki. I can also see the outline of my aura when I look at my hands or my reflection in a mirror against a pale background.

Animals and Reiki

Animals readily absorb Reiki and are already tuned in to the Reiki all around them. Most animals find receiving Reiki very relaxing and tend to send healing in return during a session. This is something that is not so noticeable when giving Reiki to humans.

The chakra system and aura of animals are very similar to humans. They have an extra chakra on the front of their chest that flows through to their shoulders. It is called the Key or Brachial chakra and is where they form an energetic connection with humans. It is their healing centre and is similar to our thymus chakra.

Animal communication and intuitive insights often naturally flow during a Reiki session whether it is in-person or via distant healing. Animal communication can also be offered as a separate form of healing, although it is often difficult to separate the two for those who offer any kind of energy healing. If they seem to merge together, it is best to allow this to happen and go with the flow. It will all be for the greatest benefit of the animal. Meditating with our animals can also be very soothing and healing.

We are not here to cure nor diagnose problems but to offer a safe space in which animals can feel comfortable in receiving healing and support, should they so choose. Reiki can also be offered to the animal's guardians to provide them with extra support. It is vital to have a good self-care routine when offering Reiki to animals because it can sometimes be tough as many of the animals that you work with are likely to be poorly or quite elderly. A strong bond is often formed with them during the Reiki space that you share together and when it's time to let them go, it really hurts. Be prepared for this but don't dwell on it. It's not all doom and gloom. Reiki works for the greatest and highest good and it will help you through.

Reiki can bring comfort and relief during end of life transition and make it easier for animals and their guardians to accept that they must let go in order to be at peace.

An Animal Reiki Session

People who are attuned to Reiki I can offer Reiki to their own animals and those with Reiki II and above can practice professionally providing they comply with the law and have the correct insurance. The animal's guardians should be asked to sign and date a consent form if you are working as a professional Animal Reiki Practitioner and veterinary permission may be required. There is more about this in the final chapter.

Begin a session by explaining a little about Reiki and what can be expected from offering Reiki to an animal. Allow the animal's guardians to feel the Reiki energy flowing from your hands, if they so wish. Depending on the animal or if the Reiki session is in-person or over a distance, a safe and comfortable place should be chosen in which everyone can feel at ease. I sometimes sit with the animal on my lap or offer them Reiki whilst they are lying in their bed. Some cats and dogs enjoy lying on a massage table with a comfortable blanket underneath them to receive Reiki. Of course, every care should be taken to make sure that they do not fall off and they should be supervised at all times. Animals should not be restrained. If there is any safety risk, Reiki can be offered just outside of the stable, kennel or enclosure. Horses, ponies and other large animals often like to receive Reiki in their field or paddock so that they can choose to receive the Reiki close up or at a distance. It has to be nice weather for this option of course, or it won't be very relaxing!

The session should begin by grounding and protecting you both, setting the intention for the animal to receive Reiki for their greatest and highest good and visualising the Reiki symbols, depending on your Reiki level. It is good to ask for beings of pure white light, such as angels and the animal's spirit guides and guardians to come forward to help where they feel it is needed. It is also believed that each species has their own angel, particularly cats, dogs and equines. You can ask for help from them, depending on the species of animals you are working with. For example, if you are offering Reiki to a cat, you could ask for the Angel of the Felines to help.

Reiki is offered to an animal by gently beaming it into their aura with your hands about six inches away, usually around their shoulders. This is important because we must ask for the animal's permission to give them Reiki. It is their choice as to whether or not they wish to receive healing. There should be no pressure or force. We should create a safe space for healing with an open heart and quiet mind. Ego has no place in energy healing. If you feel any resistance from their aura, as if the Reiki energy is not flowing freely, the animal may not wish to receive Reiki at that time and their wishes should be respected. If the Reiki seems to flow freely and is being drawn out of your hands, the animal is happy to receive the healing energy.

During a Reiki session, an animal may move around, take a break or choose not to receive any Reiki. It is up to them and they should be loved and respected as a being in their own right. We cannot force healing onto them. Some animals do not like direct physical contact, especially from a stranger, so their personal space must be respected. Most animals recognise Reiki and will come close enough to be touched but if they seem uncomfortable with direct contact, your hands can be placed just above the animal's body when giving Reiki, which is just as effective. Touch has an amazing power but it may be too intense or unfamiliar for some animals. Direct eye contact can also seem intimidating but a few polite glances can help to establish trust.

When giving Reiki to humans, they are usually lying on a massage couch or sitting in a chair and a set of hand positions is most often used in a particular order. Animals do not tend to wish to receive Reiki in this formal manner. They may lie next to you, a few feet away or sit on your lap, if they are small enough. Small animals, fish and birds can all receive Reiki through their tank or cage. If they are tame enough, they may like to sit in your hands.

One of my canine Reiki clients was a very nervous little poodle. Her guardian had asked me to visit to see if Reiki would help her to become more confident, especially when going out for walks and meeting new people. To my surprise, once I sat on the sofa and allowed the Reiki to flow, I eventually felt her warmth next to my leg as she curled up with me, absorbing the energy. After a few sessions, she came to me straight away and lay on my lap, waiting for our session to begin. Her confidence grew and she seemed to a bit less nervous in most situations. She's a sweet girl.

During an animal Reiki session, you may feel sensations in your hands and body, emotions, communication from the animal, clairvoyantly 'see' or sense medical conditions and sore spots etc. Anything can happen during a Reiki session. Simply relax and allow the Reiki to flow. Be present with the animal and clear your mind so that you are in the beautiful healing space together. I have experienced many things when giving Reiki to animals. I have felt their heartbeat when I am not directly touching them, felt their chakras whirling and felt a great sense of calm and healing. Giving Reiki can often make you feel like you are floating in a blissful place.

Sometimes, it may feel as though nothing at all is happening but persevere. Reiki can flow 'silently' and you may not feel it in your hands during some sessions. The Reiki flow may be subtle and gentle yet at other times, you may be unable to move your hands away from an area for a very long time because it feels as though they are stuck there due to the fast flow of energy. In other areas, your hands may be pushed away and drawn to a different part of an animal's body. Reiki and the animal's aura will let you know where it is needed the most. When offering hands-off Reiki, you may find that your hands move independently as they are drawn to the areas that require the most attention. Please do not let this be off-putting, it's all part of working with subtle energy and is nothing to be scared of.

Reiki flows in cycles which can last from a couple of minutes to over an hour or more, depending on the level of healing required. The average is about five to ten minutes for a particular hand position, after which, the Reiki seems to 'switch off' or it feels as if it has stopped flowing. At this point, if you do not move your hands along, you may feel the Reiki flow start up again and last for a few minutes longer before the cycle repeats itself. Once you become accustomed to being a conduit for Reiki, you will get to know when it is time for you to move your hands on to another area.

Sensitivity, tact and kindness may be required if difficult subjects arise during the session through animal communication or if you feel that the animal may have something wrong with them. We are not there to diagnose or promise a cure so you should word things appropriately so as not to cause any distress or upset. It is best to phrase it so as to gently suggest that they visit the vet for reassurance that there are no underlying medical conditions or ask for a second opinion if they have already been to the vets beforehand.

You may feel the need to start the Reiki session around the animal's head or chest, which is often best done in a hands-off position, then work your way along down the to the base of their spine or tail. Sometimes, you may feel drawn to start elsewhere and the animal may sometimes guide you by placing part of their body into your hands. Remain open to all possibilities. Reiki is an intelligent energy and will go to where it is needed.

Animals know Reiki, usually respond well to it and seem to find it very soothing. During a Reiki session, the animal may go to sleep and snore loudly, walk about, keep taking breaks, lick their lips, chatter their jaw, yawn, sneeze, sniff, lick or nibble your hands, especially the palms. If they have had enough or are uncomfortable, they will be sure to tell you and you must respect their decision by finishing the session or moving your hands elsewhere.

Journal 16.02.15

'Monty wanted to come in and watch Mum have her Reiki treatment today. He then followed her into the lounge and sat on her lap. I think he wanted to offer her some healing too!'

This is very unusual. Monty is very friendly but not a 'lap cat'. He loves Reiki.

It isn't always easy to remember what has happened during a Reiki session because most practitioners go into the 'Reiki zone' which is a meditative and relaxing state. In this state, intuitive impressions often become free-flowing. You may receive images, words, tastes, sensations, colours or a sense of knowing about potential sore areas or places of discomfort, emotional releases or tension. Your hands may vibrate, start to tingle or become hot or cool.

Try to remember as much as you can and write it down as soon as you can after the session. Write things exactly as you received them and try not to place too much interpretation upon them. Even if some of the things seem random or strange, keep a note of it. This will reassure you and the animal's guardians and is helpful to monitor progress. You may soon find answers to things that did not make sense at the time they were received.

When you feel that the Reiki session is coming to an end, sweep the animal's aura slowly and gently with your hands to see if any further Reiki is needed anywhere and if there are any energy blockages remaining. These may feel sticky, tingly or sludgy and your hands may be drawn to certain areas to offer more Reiki. After this, gently sweep them away from the animal and flick them off your hands for the Universe to transmute the energy. This process is known as Byosen scanning.

Balance up the animal's energy by giving Reiki with one hand on their shoulders and the other at the base of their spine. Visualise energy flowing healthily and efficiently through their body and aura for a couple of minutes or as long as you feel is required.

To finish a session, ground and protect both of you and give thanks for the Reiki. Ask for it to go where it is needed for as long as it is needed and for any spare Reiki to be released into the Universe as loving, healing energy to be used again. The length of a session can range from a few minutes to a couple of hours. On average, it is around 45-60 minutes.

Ask the animal's guardians to let you know if they see any improvement in the animal after the Reiki session. It is reassuring and important to receive feedback because it builds confidence and knowledge. Three or more sessions are recommended but some animals may only seem to need one.

Occasionally, a healing crisis may occur in which an animal's symptoms worsen slightly after a Reiki session. This is the body releasing toxins and healing itself. Animals may also be more sleepy, hungry, thirsty or need the toilet more often after Reiki. This is nothing to worry about and will soon pass. Guardians should be reassured about this.

Reiki for Larger Animals

When offering in-person Reiki to larger animals such as horses, ponies and donkeys, the same principles apply as above but it can feel a little intimidating if you are not used to it. They sometimes seem very big and it can be difficult to know where to start! I begin by beaming Reiki into their aura to ask permission. It is best if they are unrestrained in field or stable. Sometimes, my hands are drawn to a certain area and other times, I begin with the chest, head and shoulders then work my way along the horse and down its legs. Horses like you to stand to one side of them rather than directly in front so that they know where you are.

Equine species are very spiritual animals and seem to have a deep connection with Reiki. One of the first horses I ever offered Reiki to was 17hh and it seemed as though he towered above me. I love horses but I must admit I was a bit scared. I quietly slipped into his stable and was assured that he was a gentle soul. He was unrestrained and as soon as I started to offer Reiki into his aura, his head began to droop and I could feel him absorbing the energy. I got a little closer and beamed Reiki into this head and chest. As our peaceful session continued, I was able to place my hands on him without any fear at all. He gladly welcomed me into his personal space and was very relaxed. He wanted Reiki over this head and shoulders and would nudge me if I got too far away from this area. He was a fabulous teacher and I shall never forget him.

There will always be safety concerns when working with any animal but larger animals can be dangerous, even if it is unintentional. Work with the animal's guardian to find out about the animal's temperament and give yourself the option to get out of the stable or field, should you need to. It is highly unlikely that a horse or pony who is usually calm and friendly will take a dislike to you but more caution may be required when working with unfamiliar rescue animals. Give them plenty of space and allow them to come to you if they so choose. Animals can still receive the benefit of Reiki from a distance but most horses like to get close to feel the energy in your hands.

Show them love and respect and try to avoid standing directly behind them or making them jump. When changing hand position, move one hand first, then the other in a fluid motion. This maintains contact and energy flow. Once you are in the energetic Reiki zone with a horse, your energies merge and they will often become sleepy. Allow them to be your guide but still keep an eye on the position of their head, feet and rear end. They may lean into you or place a body part in your hands to receive Reiki. This is a great privilege but not so great if it means you are pinned against the stable wall by a horse's bottom! Use your common sense when working with larger animals and everything should be fine. Giving Reiki to our equine friends is a wonderful thing.

Distant Reiki for Animals

Offering Reiki to animals over a distance is the same process as sending distant healing to people and can be done by Reiki II practitioners and above. An energetic connection can be formed with a photograph of the animal, using a surrogate cuddly toy, your upper leg or by writing their name on a piece of paper and holding it in your hands.

Sit quietly in a place where you are comfortable and will not be disturbed. Set your intention in the same way you do for Reiki in-person but ask for the Reiki to be sent over a distance and received in a time and place when it will be for the animal's greatest and highest good. Be sure to use the distant healing symbol during your intention. Ground and protect both of you.

Offer Reiki to the animal and feel their energetic response. If it feels as though they wish to receive Reiki, go through the hand positions or to where you feel drawn on a surrogate toy, your leg or imagine the animal is in front of you. If you are using a surrogate toy, it should be cleansed with Reiki before and after each session by giving it a short burst of Reiki for a few minutes with the intention of cleansing it of any negative energy and to make it a clear vessel for Reiki to flow. It is the power of intention that enables the Reiki to flow over a distance. Carry out the session as normal and try to remember what you experienced so that you can make notes afterwards.

Finish the session as normal and ground and protect you both. Once the session is over, do not continue to focus on it so that the Reiki can be released to heal the animal. Write up your notes and send them to the animal's guardians and wait for feedback. A distant healing session is often shorter than giving Reiki in-person, usually around 20-30 minutes. Of course, this isn't set in stone and could be longer.

Journal 23.11.16

'Oh wow, I did distant Reiki for a lady and her Old English Sheepdog this morning. It was so powerful, I was crying big tears and there was a huge release. It'll be interesting to see if it makes a difference. It has to me!! Wow! The top of my head feels lovely, like my brain has just thawed out.' And her feedback on 27.11.16:

'The lady says that the distant Reiki really helped her and her dog. What I sensed and felt was uncannily accurate! Her dog has seemed a lot brighter since then and she has taken steps to move forward in life after her emotional trauma. I'm so glad that the Reiki helped. It was a very emotional session but in a positive way.'

Animal Reiki Practice

Practising animal Reiki will build your confidence and enhance your awareness of what to expect when giving Reiki to animals. There are so many things that can happen and animals teach us a great deal by giving us healing in return and guiding us to the parts of them that need the most healing.

Veterinary permission is required where possible, even when practising with animals belonging to friends and family. The only time it is not required by law is when offering Reiki to your own animals but obviously they should be taken to the vet's if they seem unwell. Insurance is also required to work on other people's animals, which is available for people attuned to Reiki II and above.

Giving Reiki in-person is good to gain experience but giving Reiki over a distance can be just as powerful and has a different feel to being in the physical presence of an animal or person. Taking time to practice both options is important. You may find that you also practice animal communication at the same time because this often naturally flows when giving Reiki to animals.

Offering to give Reiki on social media groups is not always a good idea because getting veterinary permission may be difficult. There are lots of other options though and if you are working voluntarily to gain experience, quite a few people are likely to come forward asking for their animals to receive Reiki.

Ask local vet's, grooming parlours, hydro centres, pet sitters, dog walkers and day care centres etc. if they could recommend your services for free Reiki practice sessions but don't get taken advantage of! Limit the number available so you are not offering free Reiki forever.

Voluntary work for animal rescue centres and sanctuaries is another option. They often have a dedicated vet who serves the whole centre who can give permission for all animals to receive Reiki, providing there are no obvious medical issues that need urgent attention.

Practising with your own animals is also excellent because not only does it provide you with experience, it also deepens your bond and gives you both lots of healing.

Feedback and validation help to build confidence and encourage you to continue in your Reiki development.

ANIMALS IN SPIRIT

How Animal Communication and Reiki Can Help

Reiki and animal communication have their origins in subtle energy and can be a tremendous help with end of life transition and preparing to allow an animal to pass peacefully. Looking after a poorly animal who will soon be ready to make their transition into Spirit can be a harrowing time but animal communication and Reiki can bring comfort to the animal and their human and animal companions.

Giving Reiki to an animal who may soon pass can support their spirit because the energy of Reiki is spiritual energy and has a high vibration to ease the transition from the physical body into the higher realms of Spirit. It can also reduce pain, suffering and distress on a physical, mental, emotional and spiritual level, helping to make something that can be traumatic into a more peaceful sensation, as it should be.

Communicating with an animal during this time to allow them to share how they are feeling and pass on any reassuring messages to their human guardians and they can also receive words of comfort to reassure them that they are free to let go whenever they wish to and no longer have to suffer any pain or discomfort they may be experiencing in their physical bodies.

Reiki and communication can also help to ease the intense pain of grief for those who are left behind at the moment of transition. Simply having someone there who understands can be a great comfort in itself.

Grieving the Loss of an Animal Companion

The pain of grief over losing an animal can be just as profound, if not more so, than losing a human companion. The connection we form with an animal companion whilst here on Earth is of a different frequency to a human-human connection.

Animals are often sent to us for a purpose and can fill a deep void for people who may otherwise be very lonely without animals in their lives. They give us unconditional love and healing; something which is rare in human relationships. It upsets me deeply when people are mocked for grieving over the loss of a beloved pet. Pet loss is excruciatingly painful and should not be laughed at. I still find it hard to talk about the loss of Millie, our beautiful tabby cat. She passed away a few years ago and I cried over her loss several times a day for weeks, especially whenever I arrived home and she was no longer there to greet me.

Guilt is another factor that can wreak havoc during the grieving process. This may be especially prevalent when we have had to make the awful decision to have our pet 'put to sleep'. This can make our pain even more harrowing because we feel the guilt of choosing to end their life, even though this was done from a place of love because we wanted to end their suffering.

Communicating with animals in Spirit can help someone who is grieving the loss of their pet to unburden themselves of this guilt. Animals understand life and death so well and usually show us very clearly when it is time to let them go. We should allow ourselves to go through the grieving process with a pet, just as when we have lost a human loved one. If other people do not understand, that is a reflection on their character and we should focus on looking after ourselves at such a time and avoid spending precious energy on worrying about what others may think.

Animal spirits live on after physical death in the same way the human spirits do. The concept of the Rainbow Bridge brings a lot of comfort to grieving animal guardians but the way that animals transition into the afterlife is the same as for all spirits. It is a beautiful, peaceful place and, whatever we choose to call it, we can take comfort from the fact that our animal companion is no longer suffering. Their spiritual energy is at peace and they never really leave us.

Adopting Another Animal After Loss

Losing an animal can leave a huge hole in our lives. The emptiness can seem unbearable. Listen to your heart and you will know when you are ready to love again. You are not replacing your animal, you are pouring out your never-ending well of love onto another animal who needs a home. There is no need to feel guilty. You will know when the time is right and your animal in Spirit will be glad that your love knows no bounds.

Animals often find us or seem to stand out amongst all of the others in a rescue centre, as if there is a mutual energetic attraction. People often find that they go to a rescue centre or sanctuary to adopt a dog and come home with two cats or another unexpected animal. Adopting an animal comes from the heart and our hearts are very wise, as are the animals.

Animals Grieve Too

Animals can form incredibly strong bonds with members of their own species and those of others. Humans grieve the loss of their animal companions but so too do other animals in the household. Losing a member of the family, whether they have fur, feathers, scales or human skin can be painful for everyone. Time is a healer and everyone should be patient and kind to help each other through such a difficult time.

It is sometimes difficult for an animal to understand where its companion has gone after they have passed away. In the wild, animals seem to be better able to comprehend that their companion has died when they see their body. This may sound morbid but animals understand that death is part of life and this may help them to get through the grieving process by having some closure. Elephants are particularly well known for displays of intense grief but they have to go through it, just as we do, as a natural process after losing someone close to us. Holding it all in would be even worse.

If possible, a domestic animal may find it easier to accept that their friend has passed on if they are able to see the body. It depends on the feelings of the animal's guardian and what they are able to cope with themselves. Having something around that smells of their companion may also help and keeping to the usual routine to help them feel secure will make things a little less daunting for them. Pheromone diffusers can also be a comfort.

Losing a loved one is difficult for the whole family but animals have incredible powers of healing and they can be a huge support during the grieving process.

ANIMAL SPIRIT GUIDES AND MEDITATIONS

Animal Spirit Guides

Spirit guides can seem very elusive when you first start to become aware of them. For many years I expected my spirit guides to appear before me and fill the room with their magnificence. I had been told many tales about tigers walking around the room or wolves appearing through doorways. I have since discovered that they step forward in much more subtle ways. Sometimes I hear a whisper in my ear, receive an impression in my mind, a touch on my cheek or feel invisible fingers playing with my hair. When I hear a voice in my head that isn't my own, it is often my spirit guide or guides communicating with me.

At other times, I have noticed an unusual bird or other animal on my travels, heard distant music, animal sounds in my bedroom at night or had visits from them in my meditations or dreams. Spirit guides come in many guises and are masters of stealth and subtlety. They do not wish to make us jump or scare us but they will always try to find a way through. The ideal time is when we are quiet, relaxed and peaceful. If you wish to meet your spirit guides or recognise when they are with you, the more calm and patient you are, the better. Animal spirit guides seem to be frequent visitors for me.

We all have spirit guides in the form of animals, whether or not we are aware of them. Some animals come to us to help with a momentary decision and others stay with us for a lifetime. These are called Totem animals in Native American culture or Power animals in Shamanism. Both of them relate to animals who come along as our spirit guides and may crop up as a chance meeting with a real animal in our physical life or they may visit us in dreams or meditations. I have suggested a meditation below that may help you to meet one or more of your animal spirit guides. Sometimes they visit spontaneously but you can also call upon them if you need some guidance at any time. There are many books and websites on the subject if you do some research which give explanations as to the meaning and qualities of each animal.

I often dream about animals, which is no great surprise, given my love of them. One of my most recent dreams was about a snake which seemed to be friendly and purred when I stroked it under the chin. I looked up the meaning of a snake and was pleasantly surprised to discover that a snake represents healing, life changes, transformation, primal energy and spiritual guidance. I had been led to believe that dreaming about a snake wasn't a good thing but this seems to be untrue. The dream was positive and uplifting and I would like to see the snake again sometime!

Animal Meditations

Meditation really helps to enhance animal communication, as well as having many benefits in daily life. As mentioned in the 'Meditation' section in the 'Intuitive Development' chapter, it quiets our mind and helps us to connect with Universal energy on a deeper level. I had a wonderful experience during one of my recent meditations:

Journal 08.04.17

'My outdoor meditation was blissful and serene tonight. It was mild and balmy. I could feel myself relaxing into the energy of nature all around me for miles, connecting me to the distant Mediterranean air. At one point, I rested my forehead against that of a big cat. He was luminescent turquoise and green. It was so beautiful. I could feel myself deeply seated in the mesh of my spiritual network including lots of animals.'

I often sense spirit animals around me whilst meditating. Some of these are guides and others are animals who have passed. They also feature in my dreams nearly every night.

Animals often meditate. They simply switch off for a while and allow themselves to drift off into a different state of consciousness. Not sleeping, but being as one with the Universe. You may wish to meditate with your animals as part of your daily practice.

I have suggested two meditations below but there are many you can try which should be available on the internet or you can create your own. There are also books available that give guidance as to the meaning of spirit animals. If you wish to, please try these meditations which you may enjoy. You may wish to record yourself reading out the meditations and play them back with or without soothing music. They are intended to last for ten to fifteen minutes or however long you wish. Reading them out slowly and softly with pauses in the places where you would like to linger would be of the greatest benefit:

'Meet Your Spirit Animal' Meditation

Sit in a comfortable position with your back straight and feet flat on the floor with your eyes closed. Focus on your breathing for a little while; inhaling through your nose and breathing out through your mouth until you feel yourself relaxing. Return to breathing normally and feel your mind start to drift into a peaceful state.

As you are gently breathing, you feel yourself walking along a path. You are surrounded by a beautiful, lush meadow on either side. It is warm and sunny. Feel the gentle sunlight on your face. As you continue along this path, you see a gate up ahead. When you reach the gate, you know that you are safe to go through. On the other side of the gate, you find yourself in a peaceful place. Look around and see what is there. What are your surroundings? How does it smell? As you explore, you see more and more things that bring you comfort and help you to relax.

The path continues in front of you and leads you to a comfortable bench. You sit down on the bench and take in the fresh air around you and feel completely safe and happy here.

Take a while to relax on this bench. As you sit, you realise that someone has come to join you. This someone is an animal. When you are ready, look over to see the animal. It is safe to be with this animal, no matter what it is. They are filled with love and respect for you.

If you do not see an animal at first, be patient and simply sit and relax, enjoying the peace in this place. After a while, an animal may appear.

If and when they do, you can speak to them if you wish, stroke them or simply sit in silence, enjoying their company. Feel their energy. What is it like to be with this animal? Have you seen them before? What do they have to tell you? Spend some time getting to know them.

When you feel ready to leave, thank your spirit animal for their time and effort in coming to see you. They will always be there when you wish to visit them again.

Slowly get up from the bench and make your way back to towards the gate. Open the gate and walk back along the path. Begin to bring yourself back into the room when you are ready. Wiggle your fingers and toes and open your eyes when you wish to. Sit and relax for a while until you are ready to get up from your chair.

'Being an Animal' Meditation

Sit in a comfortable position with your back straight and feet flat on the floor with your eyes closed. Focus on your breathing for a little while; inhaling through your nose and breathing out through your mouth until you feel yourself relaxing. Return to breathing normally and feel your mind start to drift into a peaceful state.

As you relax, imagine that you are any animal you wish to be. See the animal in your mind's eye. Feel the energy of your body and imagine how it feels to be that animal and how it would feel to be in the animal's body. Sense how your facial features would change. Feel that your face now looks like that animal's face. Do you have a soft furry muzzle? A beak? Whiskers? Large eyes?

Take a few more relaxing, deep breaths. Feel that you are the animal and have taken on all of its characteristics. What is it like to be the animal? Allow the energy and sensations of being this animal to fill your entire being and rest there in this blissful experience, breathing softly, sensing the instincts and qualities this animal embodies. Stay in this peaceful place as long as you wish.

Allow yourself to be in the place where this animal would live. Is it warm or cold? Are you on the plains of Africa? In the rainforest? Resting beside a beautiful river or diving in and out of the ocean? Immerse yourself in the sensations. Flow with the magical energy. Stay here for a while.

When you are ready, slowly begin to remember what it is like to be human. Gradually prepare to leave the place where your animal lives. Feel yourself sitting in the chair. Remember what it is like to be in your own skin. Give thanks for the experience of being your chosen animal and know that you can return there any time you wish. Slowly move your hands and feet and open your eyes when you are ready. Sit and rest for a while until you have fully returned from your meditative state. Sit quietly until you are ready to get up and continue with your day.

I hope that you enjoyed these meditations. You could create some of your own to add to them.

Spending time with animals is a wonderful thing. In the final chapter of 'Weird Is Wonderful', I offer guidance and pointers for those who wish to set up their own animal healing, communication and Reiki practice.

Working with animals is life-changing and deeply enriching. It is more of a calling than a job and doesn't really seem like work because you are doing what you truly love. It becomes a way of life.

SETTING UP YOUR OWN ANIMAL COMMUNICATION AND HEALING BUSINESS

Insurance and the Law

Professional indemnity and public liability insurance are required to practice as an Animal Reiki Practitioner or Animal Communicator with other people's animals. If you are a member of a Reiki organisation, they may offer discounts on an insurance scheme.

UK law states that veterinary permission is required for hands-on healing so you may wish to take a look at the Veterinary Surgeons Act 1966, which can be found through an internet search, for clarification or check the relevant statues in your country if you reside elsewhere. Veterinary permission can be obtained over the phone if the Reiki is for a non-medical related reason but discretion is advised.

When working professionally, you should also set up a consent form for the animal's guardians to sign and date which states that they have permission from the vet; gives them space to state any medical conditions or other treatments the animal is receiving and explains what they may expect from the session. Reiki organisations should be able to provide a template for this.

Other legalities will also need to be taken care of when you become self-employed. You will need to register as a self-employed sole trader with the tax office and file annual tax returns. This will vary depending on which country you live in so you will need to do some research to make sure you do everything properly. An accountant, bookkeeper or your local tax office should be able to help.

Choosing a Business Name

Choosing a name for your business can be tricky because coming up with something that is original and catchy but not tacky isn't always easy. If in doubt, go for something simple or use your own name. My business has had a few names over the years but I eventually settled on 'Karma Paws' because it covers pet sitting and animal healing. I also use the name of this book and sometimes my own name for advertising purposes, depending on what it relates to.

When trying out different business names, choose something that resonates with you and ask your guides and intuition for some help. Let a name come to you. There's no need to rush. Once you have decided on a name, make sure you are not treading on anybody else's toes, especially in your local area.

Carry out internet searches to make sure that the name isn't already in use and also search for trademarks and do a WebCheck at Companies House. If it isn't being used then you can go for it and get started.

Websites

When it comes to setting up a website, check that similar domain names are not in use. Keep it short and sweet but relevant enough to get your business found online. I'm not an expert on setting up websites but I pay monthly for mine although you can get free websites but I've found them lacking in choice and quality. It depends on your budget and how much information you wish to feature on there.

Advertising and promotion can be done on a low budget. When I first started out, I thought that throwing money at pay-per-click advertising, paid directory listings and glossy magazine adverts would bring me a flurry of prospective clients – wrong! All they did was cost me an arm and a leg for very little return.

Search engine optimisation is a big part of getting things right with your website. Most of your work will be local so it is important to use key words correctly and be clear on the description for your business and areas that you cover. A good website designer can help with this or you can do some research online or buy a book.

Your website will organically climb up to the top of the first page of the internet search engines if you get this right but it can take a few weeks. Use search terms that will make you show up as a local business. You should also get an email address as part of the package or a little extra.

Low Cost and Free Advertising

Leaflets, business cards, posters, car door magnets and other promotional materials can be obtained at a fairly low cost and will all help to get you noticed locally.

On the first day I left my office job way back in 2011, I was pounding the streets that same afternoon delivering leaflets that I printed at home. I immediately got my first client and it built up from there. Creating local awareness is key. Be positive and the work will start to come in; you just have to keep on top of it every day. I must have delivered over 5,000 leaflets in my first 12-18 months of setting up my business. After that, I became too busy to do it!

There is a vast array of free directories on the internet that help to boost your online presence and get you noticed by search engines. I have a long list on my computer of my directory listings, usernames and passwords. This helps me to update my adverts whenever I need to.

The first step is to do an internet search as if you are a potential customer looking for a business such as yours. Make a note of all of the directories that pop up and place as many free adverts as you can. It takes a week or two to get them all set up but it is well worth it. The only issue is that you may receive a lot of marketing calls but these will die down after a while. I have blocked their numbers on my phone! Some of the directories try to sell you paid advertising but this is a ruse to grab your cash. Paying for adverts is unnecessary because they rarely show up more frequently than the free ones. You will also need to write some really good advertising 'blurb' and put as much detail as you can into the fields for your ads. You'll be surprised how these improve your online presence.

Social Media

It is vital to have a good social media presence these days. Set up pages on the main social media sites and keep them up to date and share them with your friends and family. Lots of 'likes' will help you to get noticed. Always remember to make sure that you have your clients' permission to post any photos of their animals or before you mention them on your pages.

Blogging is another way to get noticed online but I have never mastered the art myself. I may get to grips with it one day but it just doesn't seem to be my 'thing'.

Local Businesses and Events

Asking local businesses for support can be very helpful and most of them are usually more than happy to oblige, especially when you can help to promote their business in return. Do some research into the animal and spiritual business in your area and ask if you can place some leaflets, business cards or posters with them. Even local salons and cafes may allow you to do this as well. It's worth spending an hour or two going around your local area to create awareness and make business contacts.

Promotional events and gatherings are good places for promotion, such as mind, body and spirit events or psychic evenings. There may be psychic or spiritual groups in your area that have regular meetings.

Word of Mouth and Voluntary Work

Word of mouth and building up a good reputation are wonderful ways to get new clients. It is a big compliment when you are recommended to others by your clients. Reward them for their loyalty to show your gratitude. It's so heart-warming to know that people place their trust and faith in you on a personal and professional level.

Working for free is also an excellent way to promote your business but this should always be done from the heart, such as offering your services to local charities and to friends and family. 'Taster' sessions could also be offered at local events but don't give too much away for free or you won't earn enough money to grow and sustain your business! Work voluntarily when it feels right to do so.

Be creative with your business promotion but beware of con artists and marketing scams! You don't have to spend much when running a local niche business. All of the right clients will find you at the right time. Good luck!

CONCLUSION

This may be the conclusion of this book but it is not the end; it is only the beginning. I hope that a great many wonderful things will flourish in your life from reading this book, even if it was just a few words that touched your heart and inspired you to try something new.

Intuitive development is a life-long process and learning about the intricacies of being an Empath and HSiP can be absolutely fascinating yet exhausting at the same time.

Each book that I have ever read has touched a part of me that was previously unexplored. Even the ones that weren't so well written still had an energy all their own that resonated within my soul. Words have unique power that can be the catalyst for change, especially when it comes to spiritual matters and intuitive development.

'Weird Is Wonderful' was written to appeal to everyone, from beginners to accomplished Intuitives as a reassuring guide and source of information. Intuition lies dormant in some people yet rages fiercely in others. Some people may find that they are naturally able to communicate with animals yet others may desperately want to be able to do this but didn't know where to start until they read this book. There may have been Reiki Masters or Reiki beginners with a desire to offer healing to animals but felt unsure how to go about it until they delved into 'Weird Is Wonderful'. Perhaps people who were terrified by their psychic abilities now feel more relaxed after realising they can embrace who they truly are without fear of ridicule; at least these are my hopes for what my book is aiming to achieve. Maybe you were one of those people?

'Weird Is Wonderful' is much more than words on paper, it comes from a place of honesty, integrity and love; not just from inside of me but from the spiritual energy all around us. The words were sent to me as a gift, which I managed to catch hold of just long enough to share them with the world. If you have read this whole book and are now reading this conclusion, I must express my deepest gratitude to you for taking the time and energy to do so. You should now be left in no doubt that there are people out there with genuinely extraordinary abilities who simply want to share what they have experienced with others to help them on their way.

As you spend more time exploring your intuition and continue to flourish, you will become more aware of your own true nature and what is going on around you in the world and the Universe beyond. Being intuitive can be great fun but it also comes with a big responsibility towards ourselves and others. Working with intuition naturally makes us wiser and more inclined to feel our way with our hearts for the greatest and highest good. It is a life-long process.

Life is what you make it and when we share our positive energy, we don't feel so alone. It gives us a nourishing sense of connection. 'Weird Is Wonderful' is just the beginning and much more will grow from this. Writing this book has been a healing and cathartic experience for me and I have many more words to impart upon the world to make it an easier place for those who share in my highly sensitive and intuitive ways. Please get in touch if you wish to know more or to share your own experiences. Keep up the good vibrations!

ABOUT THE AUTHOR

Sally Emma Chamberlain was born in Solihull, England in the late 1970s. She is a caring and honest person with a real passion for animals and all things spiritual but doesn't follow a religious path.

After spending many years working in an office, Sally took the plunge to set up her own pet sitting and dog walking business in 2011. This was one of the best decisions she ever made. It inspired her to study animal behaviour, animal communication and become a Reiki Master Teacher in 2015.

As an Empath and Highly Sensitive and Intuitive Person, Sally discovered that her abilities flourished once she was attuned to Reiki and further increased in strength when she became a Reiki Master Teacher.

It was around this time that she began to feel the need to share her experiences with others and she started writing down ideas to create a guide for people with psychic and healing abilities. Her journey as an author gathered pace in 2016 as she began to create the structure for her book. Sadly, her father suddenly passed away a few months later. During this incredibly painful time, Sally found herself going through a powerful spiritual awakening as her dreams and intuition became much more vibrant and intense.

A few weeks after losing her Dad, Sally found that the words of her book were coming to her each and every day in great rushes. She captured the words as quickly as she could, making notes on her phone, scraps of paper, envelopes and napkins if there was nothing else to get hold of!

'Weird Is Wonderful' was soon born and kept growing until it became the published book that it is today. Sally has many more ideas for books and resources that will help those on a similar journey to her own. Her purpose in life is to empower others to feel confident in expressing their true, authentic self and to show them how to deepen their bond with animals through animal communication and Reiki with an open heart and mind.

She continues her work as a pet sitter, Animal Communicator and Reiki Master Teacher alongside her writing. She has lived in South Derbyshire, England since 1996 with her husband, two children and Monty the cat. Animals are a big part of her family's life and always will be.

To find out more about Sally's work, please visit her website at www.karmapaws.co.uk.

Printed in Great Britain
by Amazon